abel
10.26

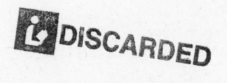
DISCARDED

# REVOLUTION AND COUNTER-REVOLUTION
## IN HUNGARY

# REVOLUTION AND COUNTER-REVOLUTION IN HUNGARY

BY

## OSCAR JÁSZI

WITH AN INTRODUCTION BY

## R. W. SETON-WATSON

NEW YORK

Howard Fertig

1969

First published in English in 1924
by P. S. King & Son, Ltd.


HOWARD FERTIG, INC. EDITION 1969

Library of Congress Catalog Card Number: 68-9595

PRINTED IN THE UNITED STATES OF AMERICA
BY NOBLE OFFSET PRINTERS, INC.

TO THE MANES OF

## LOUIS KOSSUTH

THE MOST FAR-SEEING OF HUNGARIANS,

WHO PREDICTED HIS COUNTRY'S DISASTER

AND CLEARLY DISCERNED

THE PATH TO HER RECOVERY

# PREFACE

## TO THE ENGLISH EDITION

In coming before the English public I feel acutely the faults and shortcomings of this book, even more than in the German edition, because it is much harder for an Englishman to understand the chaotic and semi-Balkan conditions in Hungary than for a German struggling with analogous difficulties in consequence of an analogous national tragedy.

In the isolation of exile, deprived of access to most of my documents, notes, and authorities, I have not attempted either to give my personal reminiscences or to write a pragmatic history of these stormy years. I know, too, that the state of mind of an exiled and shamefully maligned émigré is hardly adapted to the determination of historic truth. My purpose was more modest, but more exacting and of wider scope. My aim was to show to all who really care for a democratic and peaceful evolution in Europe, the main forces which led Hungary into the two revolutions and the counter-revolution of the past five years, in order to show in the light of the past the future possibilities of this country, in connection with the general situation in the Danube basin and the Balkans.

For us Hungarian democrats, both Liberals and Socialists, Great Britain is at present the only Power in Europe to which we look with any hope of real help in the reconstruction of our shattered country. But we have often found British opinion curiously uninformed as to Central European problems. Unfortunately International Democracy is entirely without organisation, either for action or even for the collection and dissemination of information in regard to foreign affairs. Foreign Policy is its weakest point. This immensely important sphere of political activity is left almost exclusively to the intrigues of the *ancien régime*, based on the information service of old-style diplomatists.

This unfortunate fact has been specially manifested in Great Britain's recent dealings with Hungary. With the best of intentions, Great Britain has gone completely astray in her efforts to solve the Hungarian problem. It will be a humiliating and well-nigh inexplicable fact for the future historian that the diplomacy of Great Britain—of this most advanced Commonwealth of the world—played the principal part in rendering possible in Hungary the bloodstained and reactionary rule of Admiral Horthy.

This ill-informed state of International Democracy was furthered by the success of the " Whites " of Hungary in depriving the Liberal and Socialist Hungarian émigrés for some years of access to Western public opinion. This was done by means of a systematic campaign of vilification, a very effective foreign press service and a large staff of political emissaries being maintained at enormous expense out of the public resources of their bankrupt country. We were all painted as quasi-Bolshevists.

Under these circumstances I am anxious to show not only the true genesis of the Hungarian catastrophe, but also the preponderant importance of the Hungarian question in the solution of the Danube problem as a whole, and therefore in the re-establishment of equilibrium in Central Europe. Quite apart from the Russian problem, Europe has at present two " Sick Men "—Germany and Hungary. There can be no hope of a durable peace until the wounds of these two countries are healed. At present their fever is infecting the entire Continent.

I should have preferred to rewrite this book entirely on lines specially suited to enlightened public opinion in Great Britain. Unfortunately I have at present neither the time nor the physical strength for such a task, I must therefore submit this book to the British public as it stands, with all its faults and sketchiness. My only consolation is that in spite of these defects and the rather subjective tone which runs through it, I have consistently endeavoured to be objective in my presentation of facts, and to be just towards my political opponents. I endeavoured to remain the sociologist rather than the politician, even in the most

controversial parts of this little book.    I can say with a
clear conscience that I am completely free from the influence
of race or class hatred.    Throughout treating the Hungarian
problem as a *European* problem, both in the past and the
future, I cannot accept any scheme of reconstructïon,
however advantageous for Hungary it may appear, which
would be detrimental to the just claims of the adjacent
countries.    And I am convinced that a new war would not
only solve nothing, but would be the final catastrophe for
all the peoples of Central Europe.

This deep faith in ethical and scientific principles
encourages me to hope that in spite of the weaknesses of this
book in construction and presentation, enlightened British
opinion will still understand it and will agree with the main
point of my argument, which is this : *Only a thorough-going
democratisation of Hungary, and loyal and intimate relations
between this democratised Hungary and the new States, can
create such an atmosphere in Central Europe as can cure the
gravest evils of the present situation and clear the way for a
democratic Confederation of all the small nations which are
now tormented by the rigid dogma of national sovereignty.*
Only a democratic Confederation could really solve the
question of the national minorities in these States and
achieve any real economic reconstruction.

Unless this path is followed, no diplomatic wizardry, no
international loan can help unhappy and martyred Hungary.

OSCAR JÁSZI.

New York City.
    *September*, 1923.

# CONTENTS

# INTRODUCTION

To no country in Europe did the Great War bring such a reversal of fortune as to Hungary, which purchased complete independence only at the price of its territorial integrity. The dissolution of the Dual Monarchy and its armed forces brought with it as a natural consequence the partition of Hungary between her four neighbours—Czechoslovakia, Jugoslavia, Roumania, and even her partner in defeat, Austria ; and as it proved physically impossible to establish new frontiers on a strictly ethnographic basis, a very considerable number of Magyars found themselves transferred to the rule of those whom they regarded as inferior, and whose forcible assimilation had been a foremost aim of Hungarian policy since the forties of last century. The monopoly of political power hitherto enjoyed by the Magyars was at one blow restricted to something like one-third of the area of the old Hungary. The economic dislocation which these changes brought in their train, spelt ruin for thousands of families ; and the situation was further complicated by the presence of numerous refugees from the lost territories—officials and other exponents of the old régime who had lost their jobs and whose interest it was to fan the spirit of *revanche* and irredentism. Thus defeat was followed by violent oscillations of public feeling, and in the short space of one year Hungary went through three dangerous convulsions—the Radical Revolution of October, 1918, the Communist Revolution of March, 1919, and the White Counter-revolution of August, 1919—events associated with the very different names of Károlyi, Béla Kun and Horthy.

The present volume is devoted to an analysis of these three revolutions, and deserves the close attention of all who are interested in the future of Central Europe. Its author speaks with an intimate knowledge of the facts, and though belonging very definitely to the progressive camp, never allows his critical faculty to be silenced. The present reactionary régime has expended much effort upon propaganda in the West, and in particular has attempted to discredit the leaders of the October Revolution, Károlyi, Jászi and the rest, by identifying them with Bolshevism. This book provides the best commentary upon such a charge ; for, while doing full justice to the idealism which prompted a certain section of the Hungarian Communists, it is, by reason of its very moderation, far the most damaging criticism that has yet appeared, both of the theory and practice of Communism under Béla Kun. This is followed by a no less detailed analysis of the White Régime—the so-called " Christian Course " of Admiral Horthy—and its methods of reaction, illegality and outrage, which the Western press, with but rare exceptions, has treated with a strange leniency, and indeed too often passed over in silence. That the present rulers of Hungary, possessing such a record as is revealed here, should be anxious to depreciate their exiled Liberal opponents before foreign public opinion, need cause no surprise. For while Béla Kun's corrupt and incompetent rule may be said to have rendered Hungary virtually immune from any further attack of Bolshevism, the ideas for which the October Revolution stood, are not merely not dead, but exercise a growing attraction upon the disillusioned masses. The task which confronted Count Michael Károlyi and his colleagues in October, 1918, was obviously beyond their powers, and it may be that for many of them there is no political future. As this book shows, they themselves were never under any illusion on the subject. But failure on the part of individuals at a moment of supreme crisis does not mean a permanent eclipse of the principles which they proclaimed. The Horthy régime represents a desperate attempt to reimpose upon Hungary the narrow oligarchy which involved her in disaster, and to arrest by terrorism and proscription the movement for social and political reforms. But four years of power have brought this régime to the verge of moral and material bankruptcy, and it is increasingly difficult to resist the conclusion that the democratisation of Hungary, on the lines advocated during the October Revolution, is in the long run the only sound alternative. Such is the main thesis of Dr. Jászi's book, and it is one which, I believe, the reader will only be able to resist, if he rejects as false and unreliable the facts which it contains. It is a perfectly straight issue between the Old Hungary and the New.

\*      \*      \*      \*      \*

A few words as to the personality and qualifications of the author. Born in 1875 at Nagy Károly as the son of a provincial doctor, of partially Jewish extraction, Oskar Jászi studied philosophy and political science at Budapest University, and became an official in the Ministry of Agriculture. But finding himself out of sympathy with the reactionary agrarian policy of that department, he resigned his post and became one of the founders and most active leaders of the Hungarian Sociological Society, which may fairly be described as the Fabian Society of Hungary. He edited its organ, *Huszadik Század* (The Twentieth Century), a monthly review of advanced opinions, which soon acquired a high reputation for its thorough analysis of social and economic problems and its courageous advocacy of political reform. Not content with demanding Universal Suffrage—the point round which Hungarian internal politics revolved from the year 1905 onwards—and such democratic guarantees as Land Reform and freedom of association and assembly, Jászi and his group pled for justice for the non-Magyar nationalities of Hungary, and the fullest possible linguistic and cultural liberty in local administration, education and justice. He drew upon himself especial obloquy by the publication in 1912—at a time when Magyar Chauvinist feeling had reached its height—of a volume entitled *The Development of National States and the Question of Nationalities* (Á Nemzeti Államok Kialakulás és a Nemzetiségi Kérdés). Unhappily this very important book fell between two stools : it was denounced with unmeasured violence by the exponents of the old régime in Hungary, and being published in Magyar only, was still inaccessible to the

Western public when the outbreak of war destroyed the last
hope of a peaceful solution of the racial problem.

On the very eve of war Dr. Jászi and his friends had
founded the so-called Radical Party, whose daily organ,
*Világ* (The World) acquired increasing prominence as a focus
of Hungarian pacifism. At first it appeared to advocate those
ideas of " Mittel-Europa," which attained such vogue in
1915 among the Germans. But Jászi was not in any real
sympathy with the imperialistic and Pan-German dreams
of which Friedrich Naumann made himself the mouthpiece.
He looked rather to the growth of a peaceful confederation of
races on the Danube, united by close economic ties to its
more powerful neighbour to the North ; and his book, *The
Collapse of Dualism and the Future of the Danubian States*,
published in the autumn of 1918, when catastrophe was
already imminent, reveals him as moving still more rapidly
away from Naumann and back to the ideas which Louis
Kossuth upheld in exile (though not while power was in his
hands).

At the October Revolution of 1918, Jászi entered the
Károlyi Cabinet as Minister of Nationalities, in a last
despairing effort to win the non-Magyars to a policy of
genuine racial and linguistic equality. It was, of course,
too late ; for full unity with their free kinsmen beyond the
frontiers was now within their grasp. The policy of a
" Hungarian Switzerland," resting on federation, free trade,
democracy and plebiscites, was brushed aside by the march
of events ; and he had already resigned office sometime
before the collapse of the Károlyi experiment. He had been
for some years Lecturer at the Transylvanian University of
Kolozsvár, and was now appointed Professor of Sociology
at Budapest. But with the advent of Bolshevism he was
obliged to leave Hungary, and when the Whites displaced
the Reds, he, like most of Károlyi's friends, was subjected to
even fiercer proscription and calumny. Since 1919, then,
he has lived in exile in Vienna and collaborated in the
Hungarian daily newspaper *Bécsi Magyar Ujság*, which the
*émigrés* maintained as their organ till the close of 1923, when
lack of funds forced them to cease publication. In August,

1923, he went to America, in the hope of spreading Liberal views among the Magyar colony there, and of counteracting the very active reactionary propaganda in the American press.

It was high time that the full facts regarding the three Hungarian Revolutions should be published by a man whose whole career has been marked by fearless honesty and critical acumen, and who has won the right to speak with authority. For in this country calumny has been especially busy with the persons of the leading Hungarian Democrats, and Count Károlyi in particular, has been the object of more than one particularly gross libel. The legend propagated by his enemies even found its way into standard works of reference. Until his own memoirs can be published in English, Dr. Jászi's book may serve as the first step towards rehabilitation.

Two charges in particular have been levelled against the Károlyi Government ; it has been held responsible on the one hand for the disintegration of the Austro-Hungarian Front, and again for the final partition of Hungary by the Little Entente. Dr. Jászi does not in any way exaggerate when he describes the statement that the Austrian Front was proud and unbroken till Károlyi's War Minister recalled the Hungarian regiments, as " a deliberate lie, invented to save the artificial Habsburg legend "—and, he might have added, to exalt the present régime at the expense of its Liberal rivals. Before ever Károlyi came into power or Colonel Linder gave the order for surrender, the whole Austro-Hungarian army was riddled with disaffection, and entire regiments had thrown off all discipline and actually left the front. It was Dr. Wekerle, the Premier of the old régime, who ordered the surrender of Fiume to the Jugoslavs ; it was no less a person than Admiral Horthy who handed over the fleet at Pola to the revolutionary Jugoslav Committee ; and Linder, in recalling the Hungarian regiments, merely followed the precedent of the Zagreb National Council and the Prague revolutionary government. The plain fact is that it was the army itself, as it hurried homeward, that really made the Revolution and carried Károlyi into power.

In the same way it was military anarchy quite as much as the attitude of the Entente which undermined the new régime. No possible effort on the part of Károlyi or anyone else could have prevented the dissolution of the old army, and there was no Republican Guard or similar organisation to take its place, with the result that the Government had literally no force behind it, and was at the mercy of subversive elements.

Again, Dr. Jászi brings out very clearly the efforts made by Károlyi and his colleagues to save Hungarian integrity, and their utter powerlessness in the face of Entente commitments to the Czechoslovaks, Jugoslavs and Roumanians, and of General Franchet D'Esperay's brutal attitude during the Armistice negotiations in Belgrade. Some of these facts appear for the first time in English, save, I believe, for brief summaries in *The New Europe* at the time. The Belgrade Armistice was fatally bungled in both directions—both as regards Hungary and as regards the Czechs and Roumanians. What finally brought down Károlyi was his refusal to comply with the Vyx Note of March, 1919, demanding the final evacuation by Hungary of territories which had till then been regarded as a subject of negotiation. Whether Károlyi would have been able to maintain himself, if the full extent of the sacrifices demanded of Hungary had been made clear to government and nation at the very outset, is quite another question ; but it is simply preposterous to hold him responsible for a partition, over the terms of which he was entirely unable to exercise the faintest control. At the time, it was fancied by many that Károlyi, who had always favoured an understanding with the Western Powers, who opposed the war and even advocated a separate peace, would now be able to obtain more favourable terms from the Entente than representatives of the fallen Tisza régime. They forgot that Prague, Belgrade and Bucarest had established prior claims in Paris, and that Paris was absorbed in a score of other problems, and therefore in the matter of Austria-Hungary was content to ratify accomplished facts.

While, however, it is easy to understand the bitterness with which Dr. Jászi writes of the Entente, it is necessary to

enter a certain caveat against what he says of Sir George
Clerk's mission to Budapest, as delegate of the Supreme
Council, in the winter of 1919. To blame him for not
bringing about a settlement of the acute party discords from
which Hungary was then suffering, is really not quite reasonable ; and it should be remembered that it was he who
compelled the Government to uphold universal suffrage, as
one of those achievements of the October Revolution which
it would not be justifiable to reverse. He thereby provided
for the first time a basis for popular representation in Hungary.
The arbitrary curtailment of this franchise by something
like a million votes in 1922—involving, as it does, a real
perversion of the popular verdict—is one of the greatest
scandals of the Bethlen régime. Where Dr. Jászi is fully
within his rights, is when he complains that neither this nor
the many still cruder scandals associated with the
" Awakening Magyars " and other terrorist bands, have
ever prevented the permanent representatives of the
Entente in Budapest from according their hearty support
to the Horthy-Bethlen régime, and from consistently watering
down or denying the most patent facts which told
against it.

Even in the short time that has elapsed since Dr. Jászi
wrote his preface, the untenable nature of the present régime
in Hungary has gradually become more appareut to the
outside world. The steady decline of Hungarian finances,
the solidarity of the Little Entente, and latterly the advent
of Labour to power in England, have weakened the reactionaries, and have therefore made it possible for the Liberal
elements to raise their heads. The latest act of terror—the
bomb outrage at Csongrád on December 26—stung them
into action, and the régime has been criticised in the
Hungarian Parliament with an openness hitherto unheard
of. On January 4, 1924, Mr. Paul Sándor—not a member
of the Extreme Left, but a veteran parliamentarian,
industrialist and financial expert—made a long speech, from
which the following extract may be quoted, as showing that
Dr. Jászi by no means exaggerates. " Not the Premier or
Government, nor the majority party either," he declared,

" represent the real power in the country. I dare to maintain
that one per cent. of the authorities, as a tiny minority,
rule the whole land by their terror. I maintain that this
whole system of government is only a formality. The Red
Bolshevism was replaced by a White Bolshevism, which
used the same means, but for far more dreadful deeds. It is
an unpardonable sin of the majority, that it has not deprived
this minority of the power, but far rather has tolerated
every crime committed by bomb, ecrasite and printing ink.
. . . This minority falls into three groups—one to
which an amnesty has been granted, one to which passports
have been given, and one which goes about unpunished for
its crimes."

On January 22 the Deputy Victor Drodzy made
sensational revelations regarding the massacres of Orgovány
and Izsák in the winter of 1919, and amid a deathly silence
in the House, read out a long list of those accused of the
murders, but never brought to justice—beginning with the
names of Ivan Hejjás and four other members of his family.
The Bethlen Government is at last allowing public discussion
of the White Terror ; but even to-day Hejjás enjoys such
high protection that he is merely interrogated by the police,
and not arrested. To such lengths has " Bolshevism from
Above " struck root under the so-called " Christian
Course."

The Great War has led to a tremendous political, and
above all social, upheaval and transformation throughout
all the wide territories lying between Germany, Russia and
the Mediterranean. There is only one point at which those
who were predominant before the war and helped to frame
the policy that plunged Europe into disaster, are still all-
powerful, and still inspired by the same outlook and ambitions.
That is the Hungary of Admiral Horthy ; and so long as
his régime survives, it is useless to expect really consolidated
and normal conditions among the Succession States of the
former Dual Monarchy. Hence the desperate attempts of
certain financial circles to bolster up a crumbling régime, are
foredoomed to failure, and are not conducted in the true
interests of either Hungary or her four neighbours. The

democratisation of Hungary is an essential preliminary to the restoration of cordial relations between the rival races of the Danubian area, the removal of economic inter-state restrictions, the reduction of armaments and the establishment of permanent peace.

R. W. SETON-WATSON.

1st *February*, 1924.

CHAPTER I

BEFORE THE COLLAPSE

FROM the middle of 1917 onwards it was plain to everyone
who could see at all below the surface that we had lost the
war, and that there remained only one conceivable line of
policy which the Monarchy could reasonably follow : to
compel Germany to make peace, even at the cost of great
sacrifices, or if she would not, to make a separate peace
without her. I was already completely convinced of this
at the time of the Berne pacifist congress, when I had the
opportunity of getting into touch with several Entente
politicians and diplomats. One of the British diplomatic
agents in Geneva, Mr. Edwards,[1] a man of great intelligence
and broad views and a sincere upholder of radical principles,
made a strong and lasting impression on me. Apart from
general considerations he was able to bring concrete evidence
and statistics to show that America's intervention in the
war was not the mere bluff which the press bureaux of the
Central Powers called it, but a terrible reality of which it
was hardly possible for continental eyes to perceive the
full dimensions and import. Mr. Edwards' statements so
impressed me as quite unanswerable that I arranged a
meeting between him and Michael Károlyi, as I was anxious
that Károlyi too should have an opportunity of considering
the facts and data communicated by Mr. Edwards.
Károlyi fully shared my feeling. I remember vividly our
return in the early hours of the morning from a long
discussion with the Englishman. We continued our talk
in the empty hall of the " Beau Rivage," and we were agreed

[1] Mr. Middleton Edwards was acting as British Consul in Geneva
during the latter part of the war, and as such had to watch the activities
of the numerous emissaries of enemy Powers who made that city their
headquarters.—Trans.

that the hour of final disaster was close at hand unless, through an intelligent and resolute peace policy, the Dual Monarchy and, above all, our Hungary, could break away from the fatally wounded militarism of Central Europe before its last mad plunge.

From that time onwards my views as to Hungary's external policy were completely at one with those of Michael Károlyi. My opponents are making use of this fact to charge me with inconsistency. After my active work as a publicist in the interest of the conception of " Mitteleuropa " during the first period of the war, they condemn my later adherence to a pro-Entente policy as inspired by opportunism. But the inconsistency was only apparent. My support had never been given to Naumann's militarist " Mitteleuropa," but to the idea of a democratic and pacifist alliance of all the peoples which are thrown by their geographical and economic situation into dependence upon one another, and, whether they like it or not, are bound up irrevocably with one another. In the second place, I have never regarded this other " Mitteleuropa " as more than a transient formation, a stage on the road to the United States of Europe. I was convinced that a democratic Central Europe must rapidly develop complete freedom of trade with Western Europe, so that there would no longer be any obstacle in the way of the economic forces making for a larger union. Finally, I clung to the symbol of " Mitteleuropa " only so long as the Russia of Tsarist autocracy was the ally of the Entente Powers. I saw clearly that the victory of the Entente in association with that Ally would place the economic, cultural and political life of Central Europe under the heel of the Russian reaction, however liberal, democratic and pacifist might be the ideas of the Entente. But the moment Russian absolutism was broken, the moment the Russian revolution had at one stroke brought the age-long home of serfdom to the forefront of radical and progressive countries, I at once recognised and declared in my published writings that the conception of " Mitteleuropa " had become a reactionary one, and that we ought now to work for the democratisation and economic unification of the whole of

Europe, under the control and sovereignty of a genuine League of Nations. Naturally it was impossible for me then to imagine that the apocalyptic whirl of events would give the idea of " Mitteleuropa " a fresh lease of life ; not this time as a counter-movement against Tsarist autocracy, but against the plutocratic and militarist reaction of the West. Nor was I blind at any time to the Janus-headed policy of the Entente, and from the first I asked in perplexity, " When will it be turning its imperialist face towards us in place of the democratic, pacifist face which is smiling at us at present ? "

I have still a lively memory of one moment in our conversations with Mr. Edwards. He asked what was our conception of the future of the Danubian and Balkan States, and to my astonishment Michael Károlyi drew a bold and broadly-conceived sketch, essentially in agreement with Louis Kossuth's well-known programme of confederation. In this plan, worked out in exile, Kossuth had urged alliance and co-operation between Hungarians, Roumanians and Serbs against the imperialism of the Habsburgs. It is important to note that this statement was made by Károlyi at a time when no one had yet come forward with plans of this sort, either in the press or in public life. This occasion threw quite a new light for me on Károlyi's personality. I realised, as I had many occasions to realise afterwards, that Károlyi is not the impressionist and amateur of politics for which he has often been taken by the public. On the contrary, the basic element in his character is a measure of dogmatic stubbornness, rooted in deep intuitions, an element which, notwithstanding his decided leanings to rationalism, I cannot help describing as religious.

After our return from Switzerland, Károlyi and I did our utmost to convince Hungarian leaders of the extreme seriousness of the American intervention and the urgent necessity for a deliberate re-orientation in foreign policy ere it was too late. Unfortunately not one of the responsible statesmen realised the unexampled gravity of the situation. Czernin oscillated between pro-Germanism and pro-Ententeism with every momentary change in the

situation ; Tisza, like a doomed hero of tragedy, pressed on
blindly with his traditional policy of the maintenance of
Dualism and of German-Magyar supremacy.  It is hard now
to judge Tisza harshly ;  the tragic memory of his great
qualities towers over the condottieri and panamists who now
control Hungary.  But it has to be said that this strong
man proved completely unable either to lift himself above
narrow class interests or to look beyond the immediate
future.  Only a few months before the collapse he was still
completely blind to the fact that the day of the class-
domination of junkers and plutocrats, and of the artificially
sustained supremacy of the Magyar element, was over.
During his last months of power his first concern was still
how to rob the common people and the nationalities of their
rights, despite the King's command to introduce a franchise
reform.  Towards the end of September, 1918, when the
outlines of the Jugoslav State, already clearly defined, could
not but be almost a physical, palpable reality to him, this
deluded Don Quixote hurried to Sarajevo and poured brutal
insults upon every Jugoslav aspiration.  At dinner with
Sarkotić[1] he cried, as immovable by argument as an
automaton, " The Monarchy lives and will endure ! "

It will be realised that if the two principal statesmen in
the Dual Monarchy were so helpless and purblind in the face
of events, the others could count only as soulless marionettes
on the stage of history.  The Transylvanian politicians,[2]
especially, were indescribably narrow in their outlook.  At
the very moment when universal collapse was imminent,
when every intelligent Hungarian was trembling for his
country, this company of pashas, blinded by class pride
and apprehensive of limitations of their absolute rule in the
counties, were still dreaming of peace with annexations.
And what a pitiful figure was cut even by the heroes of the
so-called Hungarian democracy !  The Minister for Franchise

[1] Major-General Baron Sarkotić, a Croat by birth and an advocate of
the Trialist solution of the Jugoslav problem, was military governor of
Bosnia-Herzegovina during the war (having succeeded General Potiorek),
and held that office until the collapse.—Trans.

[2] Their leader was Count Stephen Bethlen, the present Prime Minister
of Hungary.

Reform, for instance, prostrated himself before the forces of nationalist reaction, and exercised his ingenuity in devising means to defraud a few hundred thousand electors among the nationalities of their votes.

In face of this reactionary movement the democratic forces proved very weak, the more so as the leading socialists turned a blind eye to the vacillating and opportunist policy of the Franchise Minister. Erwin Szabô, the distinguished Marxist, was driven to expose the opportunist tactics of the Socialist party organ in the columns of a so-called " bourgeois " paper, " Vilàg."

It may be said that there were only three groups in Hungary which at all realised the situation : Michael Károlyi and his intimate associates, the radical minority of the Socialist party who regarded Sigismund Kunfi as their leader, and the small group of Radical intellectuals. The views of these groups were expressed, so far as the censorship permitted, in numerous articles and speeches, but I know of only one document containing a fairly complete synthesis of the general attitude of the educated classes in Hungary ; even this with the moderated tone and dynastic bias which the circumstances imposed. This document is the memorial laid before the King[1] and some of the leading Austrian politicians in October, 1918, by a few high officials and professors. This memorial, in the drafting of which I took an active part, took the form of a pamphlet, with the title " The situation in Hungary : a warning from a group of anxious patriots who stand apart from the politics of the day." It actually reached the King, and in my view it throws so clear a light on the antecedents and causes of the October revolution that a reproduction of its essential passages seems the best introduction that can be offered to my readers to enable them to understand subsequent events.

The text of the memorial began as follows :—

" Hungary is faced with a grave crisis. Unless a serious and energetic beginning is made at a very early date with far-reaching social reforms, the country will witness disaster not only to the State but to the dynasty.

[1] i.e. the Emperor Charles.—Trans.

" We are well aware that this diagnosis differs fundamentally
from that of the Government and of the older political parties.
This is, however, no criterion of the accuracy of the opinion we
have expressed, but only of the aloofness of the Governments
and the older parties in Hungary for decades past from the ideals
and aspirations of the people.  All who have been brought by
their work as active business men or as scientific investigators into
close contact with the people, and who are consequently familiar
with the needs and moods of the people, their efforts and
passionate aspirations, in a word, all of Hungary's true intellectual
workers, are convinced that she is passing through the most
critical period of her existence, and must face the danger of changes
which it is a sacred duty in the interests of the country and the
dynasty to forestall and prevent.  This unalterable conviction
has impelled us to draw up this memorial, and must be our
excuse for its harsh tone.

" In the past months and the last few weeks events have
been ripening, unfortunately, into confirmation and fulfilment
of our fears.  The danger arises obviously not only from the ill-
success of the operations in the war zone but to a still greater
extent from conditions within the country.  Even more dangerous
than their shells are the ideas which the Entente Powers have
proclaimed ! The conviction is now widespread among the public
that the Monarchy is not only unwilling to satisfy the just
demands of its subject peoples but is incapable of doing so ;
that it is unprepared either to grant democratic liberties or the
right of peoples to self-determination ; that it is a feudal and
militarist organisation, forcing itself upon many millions of
unwilling subjects.

" In face of this very formidable current of popular opinion
rapid and energetic measures of reform should have been taken.
But every plan and every attempt is deliberately blocked by
the dominant oligarchy in Hungary.

" The present situation is only intelligible in the light of
the political and social conditions of pre-war Hungary.

" The Hungarian people is one of the most forlorn and
neglected in Europe.  In this country, with all its wealth of
natural resources, and with a population of admirable racial
qualities, the common people are in poverty, having hardly
any opportunity at all to work for themselves and in their own
interest.

" There is hardly any other country with so lamentable a
system of land distribution as Hungary, where a comparatively
diminutive proportion of the land is in the possession of the
peasant farmers and a relatively enormous proportion in the
hands of the large landowners.  Frequently a single owner holds
domains of immense size.  Apart from pasture and forest lands,
which are naturally the predominant type among the large
estates, the cultivable area in Hungary is roughly 24,000,000

hectares[1], divided into about 2,800,000 agricultural holdings. Of these, 2,400,000 small estates (up to 20 yokes[1]) account for barely 7,600,000 hectares, while 3,977 large estates of over 1,000 yokes account for 7,452,640 hectares. The contrast is still more striking if we include pasturage and forest lands, which are mainly in private hands, and if we remember that in Hungary estates of 20,000 yokes are nothing unusual, and in many cases belong to a single owner.

"The situation is rendered still worse by the large extent of entailed property : including meadows and forest lands, the area of entailed property totals 15,680,000 yokes (without Croatia and Slavonia). This largely accounts for the inability of the people to buy land. And as industry is far too little developed to be able to absorb the landless masses, this system of land distribution may be regarded as the cause of the enormous emigration from Hungary, unparalleled elsewhere in Europe."

Conditions, the memorial added, are growing worse, since in Hungary, unlike other countries, the tendency is in the direction of the extension not of small but of large ownership.

The memorial proceeded to refer to the inadequate harvest yield, attributable, in view of the richness of the soil, purely to feudal mismanagement and the backwardness of the peasants resulting from the feudal conditions. The following statistics were given in evidence : Out of every 100 inhabitants over six years of age in Hungary, 33 can neither read nor write, a proportion comparing with 0.2 per cent. of illiterates in Denmark, 0.4 per cent. in Germany, 6.8 per cent. in Sweden, and even in Austria no more than 16 per cent. Nor was this accidental : it was the consequence of the foolish policy which imagines that a people kept in the darkness of ignorance will not realise its degraded condition.

A further result of these conditions is the high cost of living, which hampers production, handicaps it in competition with other countries, and depresses the standard of living. In Budapest, the capital of the country, the meat consumption per head is less than the consumption per head for the whole of Germany. From the yield of their rich soil the Hungarian peasants receive less than the German and Russian agriculturists from theirs. The sugar

[1] A hectare is 2.47 acres. The Austrian *joch* (" yoke ") is 0.575 hectares, or about 1.42 acres.

consumption in Hungary is less than two-thirds of the mean consumption in Europe. It is easy to understand that the output of a people so fed fails to attain the level reached by its better nourished competitors.

The situation of the poorer classes is best exemplified by the backwardness, almost unexampled in Europe, of the Hungarian labour legislation.

" If by any chance some social reform passes into law, no one dreams of extending it but only of how to defeat its application. In Hungary, where the labour of women and young people predominates, there is no obstacle whatever in the way of the exploitation of labour by the employer. Exploitation is favoured by almost mediæval and ruthlessly enforced conditions of labour, heedless of the worker's family life or educational needs or human dignity."

For lack of all legislative protection, the Hungarian workers are thrown entirely upon their own resources for self-defence. The ethical sense and the clearer vision of other countries, justified even from a conservative standpoint, has granted to the workers by legislation conditions which the Hungarian workers can only secure through hard contests injurious to themselves and to the whole community. If the worker makes a fight, he is condemned as unruly and unreliable. If he does not, he remains in brutish servitude.

" Poverty, ignorance, social isolation are the causes of the high mortality in Hungary, exceeded only in Russia and Roumania. Public health legislation has remained, like other social legislation, a scrap of paper. Infectious diseases, especially tuberculosis, sap the vitality of our people to a degree unknown in other civilised countries : every sixth person in Hungary dies of tuberculosis. Yet there is nothing in which the government and the administration show so little interest as the saving of these millions of lives. Their one object in life is to assure the care-free existence and unhindered enrichment of the upper ten thousand, and the continuance of these privileges to their descendants, shutting out from these privileges all who do not belong to their class.

" Until now there has been only one means of escape from this situation : Emigration. In this way Hungary suffered greater losses than any other European countries. In the decade before the war she lost more than a million and a half of her people by emigration. Only Ireland and Italy show higher absolute figures, and relatively to density of population even these countries are out-distanced by Hungarian emigration.

" It might seem a mystery how the conscientious and hard-working people of a country so richly endowed by nature can go on living under such wretched conditions. The explanation is to be sought in the spirit of our legislation and administration. There is no other country, except Roumania and pre-revolutionary Russia, with so reactionary a franchise as Hungary. In Denmark and Serbia, in England even before the war, two-thirds of the adult male population had the vote, in Belgium 79 per cent., in Spain 81 per cent., in Bulgaria and Greece 83 per cent., in Germany and Switzerland 84 per cent., in France 87 per cent. Norway and Finland had women's suffrage before the war, and here there are 135 and 168 voters respectively to every 100 male adults. Under the Hungarian franchise law of 1913, thirty-three men out of every 100 have votes, and these only in theory.

"Not the slightest improvement was made in this vicious situation by Tisza's second franchise law. All who are familiar with educational conditions in Hungary are aware that a franchise dependent on the passing of the sixth elementary standard is simply provocatory. It is an open challenge to the working classes, for under the educational policy of the Hungarian oligarchy this qualification is accessible to very few. Moreover, this disgraceful law has given sanction to the corrupt electoral practices of the country. In short, it has not only failed to allay the surging passions of the public, but robbed the great majority of the people of all hope that any future effort would be made to ameliorate their unhappy lot.

" The economic and social conditions which we have described, and this feudal electoral legislation, have determined the course of political life. The public opinion of the working classes has been excluded from all influence over legislation and administration. There has been nothing to counterbalance the grip of feudalism and finance on the Government. The over-whelming economic power of the great landowners and Capitalists has been used to crush out all possibility of bringing any serious democratic influence to bear upon politics. The peasants and the middle and working classes of the towns were and are hardly represented at all in Parliament. The opposition between the ideas of 1867 and 1848,[1] the party cries of Dualism

---

[1] The Hungarian Revolution of 1848 was directed against Austria and the Austrian dynasty. It was suppressed by armed force, by Austrian troops assisted by contingents of Russian troops lent by the Czar ; the latter decided the issue of the conflict. At the armistice of Világos, the rebels submitted unconditionally to Austria. The period is for Magyars one of memories of heroism and martyrdom. The year 1867 is that in which the " compromise " (Ausgleich) was arrived at between Austria and Hungary through the efforts of the Hungarian statesman, Deák. The Ausgleich was the keystone of the Austro-Hungarian Dual Monarchy. The issue between " 1848 " and " 1867 " was thus that between Hungarian separatism and loyalty to the Dual Monarchy.—Trans.

and Personal Union, have long ceased to be realities, merely serving to divert public attention from burning economic and social problems by endless wrangling over constitutional and racial questions. This antiquated electoral system, in which, as we have already said, Tisza's so-called reform has made no substantial change, has prevented the popular will from finding expression, and the democratic currents of opinion from uniting against feudalism and plutocracy, all the more effectually as even this wretched law has not been loyally administered, but has given place to terrorism. Drinking bouts and banquets and bribery, falsified voting registers, the heavy hand of the county administrations and the shameless application of armed force have been used on every occasion to suppress popular opposition. This system of fraud and force, purchased votes and administrative Terror, has grown so open and unashamed that the great majority of the serious and reputable elements in the country have almost entirely withdrawn from the political arena, which has become the almost exclusive hunting ground of the territorial magnates, the short-sighted local potentates and the highwaymen of industry and finance.

"It is only too easy to understand how this system has crippled the development of the rich economic and cultural resources of the country. The ruling oligarchy would not hear of a modern land policy or of educational and taxation reform, changes which would have been against the interests of their own circle. And they block all constructive work by keeping public opinion in continual turmoil with constitutional controversy and chauvinist bickerings against the nationalities.

"This morbid social and political order was driven further on the road to its doom by the world war. The extremes of wealth and poverty drifted into more violent contrast, the best and most enlightened elements among the people bled to death on the battlefield, the cynical misuse of class domination awakened infinite bitterness and hatred among the hungry and ill-clad masses. The revolutionary feeling has been further increased as the greater part of the brainworking middle class has fallen to a proletarian level, abandoned its class attitude and passed over to the social democratic camp.

"With the social problems of the country its racial difficulties have become acuter. The world war has inflamed the racial discord. The ruling classes have done their utmost to ferment this discord, as it is all to their good if the masses, instead of trying to heal or relieve their sufferings and to expose war-time abuses, lay the blame for their ruin at the door of their non-Magyar fellow-citizens. The chauvinist press is taking care that the fires of this unlucky hatred are kept up. Public opinion in Hungary is being poisoned by unbridled nationalist demagogy, directed now not only against Austria but also against the nationalities in our own country, of which nearly all have made enormous sacrifices of their life-blood in the defence of the fatherland. Unfortunately there have been frequent cases of treason, mostly in the ranks of the intellectuals, among the nationalities inhabiting the periphery of the country. This has surprised no-one familiar with the atmosphere of ignorance and hate, unworthy of any civilised country, amid which these nationalities had to live, even before the war. But the chauvinists have held the whole working and middle class of the national minorities responsible, and have visited the sins of a few individuals on the whole public by draconic punishments, internments, confiscations of property, emergency decrees and the closing of schools, although these nationalities were just as patriotic and as loyal to the dynasty as the Hungarian people.

" This unfortunate policy has rendered social and national differences insupportably acute. The mass of the people have the feeling that the country belongs not to the people but to a few tens of thousands who hold the power and misuse it, and that all the institutions of the state are at the service only of the short-sighted policy and the selfishness of these few, while the suffering millions pay. No wonder if under such circumstances the lower classes also fall beneath the spell of egoism and they become the enemies of the State, the State which allows them no say in its affairs, which takes no thought for their fate, which is only concerned to demand their lives and all they possess. No wonder if, while in other countries national ideals are taking precedence over class interests, in Hungary the belief in a national mission is lost and there remains nothing but class war and class hatred, two furies always standing ready to hurl the state to destruction ! This is frightful in a period in which the influence of the Russian revolution is all-pervading ! The masses of the people are penetrated with emotional rather than deliberate Bolshevism, and it is impossible to speak a few words to poor people without hearing the most violent imprecations against the State, the officials and the propertied classes.

" For these deserted common people the burdens and pains of the war have grown beyond endurance. The spirit of the people has got to be strengthened and encouraged if we are not to experience upheavals which, in the existing world situation, might lead to a catastrophe. It is essential to satisfy the masses through effectual, carefully thought-out, humane measures, that the State is fully alive to its duty to them, and is prepared to reward their labours, which are in the truest sense of the word the salvation of their homeland, by far-reaching extensions of their privileges and beneficent social reforms.

" It is plain that this was the purpose which inspired the publication of the historic autograph letter from the Crown on April 17th, 1917, authorising Count Tisza to introduce a far-reaching extension of the franchise and institutions for social amelioration. This resolve of His Majesty matured in the succession to power of the Esterházy cabinet under a pledge to introduce universal suffrage and to set up the Ministry of Social Welfare. The signs have rarely been more propitious. It looked as if the young King were showing his face to his people, in the midst of a world ablaze, to promise them refuge and protection against the abuses of feudalism and plutocracy ; as if the policy was returning of our great national kings, who sought and found the strength of their country and throne in the union of the people and their sovereign. All who are in touch with popular opinion can bear witness that the King's resolve was acclaimed with joy in the country, and that the soul of the suffering people turned trustfully and hopefully towards the Crown. And the new day of democratic change and broadly conceived social reforms would in truth have dawned, if the King's government and counsellors had been adequate to their task or had sought its solution in the spirit of the Crown and with love for their people.

"Unhappily what happened was the very opposite. The new government was formed partly from weak elements and partly from elements belonging to the feudal and plutocratic order. The convinced and clear-sighted representatives of the democracy of the middle and working classes and peasants were still excluded from power. Day after day, the new government committed the gravest errors, till in the end it sank into the moral and intellectual slough of the old régime, while the forces of reaction, gravely wounded by the King's democratic resolve, slowly recovered strength and reconquered their old position. The plan of an honest franchise and a ministry of social welfare was brought to nought, and the Tisza régime awoke to new life.

"Public life in Hungary has thus reached a critical stage. The unbiassed observer almost has the impression that the reawakened feudal and plutocratic forces wish to provoke the people and drive them to revolution, in order to discredit them ; subtly calculating that their own schemes would then be easily put through. They think it is easier to quell a revolution in war-time ; a post-war revolution demanding justice and land and bread would explode with elemental force. Naturally we are well aware that most politicians are innocent of any such gamble; the majority of them simply pass their days in inactivity, and have no inkling of their position as they feast and bargain above the crater of popular fury.

"But this situation is pregnant with incalculable dangers, both present and future.

"At the present time it is a forcing ground for Bolshevist ideals. It definitely turns the unpropertied classes into enemies of the State ; they will regard Russian anarchism as the only dependable and effectual method, since the only reward for their unexampled heroism and sacrifice is to be beaten for their pains. And the harried and oppressed national minorities look more and more for salvation to the Entente, with its promise to extend to them the right of self-determination of peoples."

This, the memorial urged, is a movement of opinion which at the present moment must be prevented from spreading.

But, it added, the maintenance of the old régime is also exceedingly dangerous as regards the future. The old electoral system which Tisza and his followers desire at all costs to preserve, will make it impossible for the country to recover and consolidate itself after its terrible sacrifices in blood and in economic loss. It will make that impossible because we can only cope with the intolerable burdens of the war by a greatly increased productivity, a just taxation policy, an honest administration, and a broadly planned policy of re-population and social reform ; in a word, by a policy to which the present oligarchical union of vested interests will not dream of agreeing.

"This revolutionary atmosphere will become yet more threatening as the homecoming men from the trenches will no longer be the blind, submissive, humble peasant mass of old. No ! The front has taught our people to think, has awakened them, and they will no longer endure the domination of county pashas and city profiteers.

"Only the democratisation of the country can heal the present poisoned relations between the nationalities. The Hungarian people has lived for centuries in perfect harmony with the national minorities. But these naturally good relations are disturbed by the gentry living on their sinecures, by the army of professional politicians, Magyar or nationalist, who fish in troubled waters, and by the partiality of the administration. If only the Law of Nationalities brought forward half-a-century ago had been carried into effect, it would have sufficed to dissolve in an atmosphere of reconciliation the unhappy incompatibilities which remain to this day . . . And if universal suffrage is not introduced now in Hungary, the peripheral Hungarian territory inhabited by other nationalities will be in a condition of chronic unrest which will defeat every constructive effort."

This is equally true, continued the memorial, of the relations between Austria and Hungary. The feudal conditions in Hungary stand in the way of every corresponding effort of the other nations in the Monarchy—Czechs,

Jugoslavs, Poles—to secure amendments of the constitution to bring it more into line with their interests.

"Nothing but the democratisation of Hungary can create an atmosphere in which the Monarchy could fulfil its historic mission : the creation of a free league of nations, avoiding both the Scylla of Pan-slavism and the Charybdis of Pan-germanism, and based on the free co-operation of the peoples living here. Failing the introduction of universal suffrage and the ending of of the present régime, both the Czech and the Jugoslav questions threaten to produce revolutionary outbreaks.   Even if revolution does not actually break out, it is clear that when the peace congress assembles it will not recognise a Monarchy whose very existence is hated by the majority of its peoples.   Thus the continued existence of the Monarchy depends on its success in replacing the obsolete Dualist constitution by a free league of nations, which even our enemies will have to recognise as a good and equitable solution."

We give here only the most important of the concluding passages in the memorial :

"The last hour has struck !  And if it is not yet too late, Parliament must be dissolved as soon as possible, in order that the will of the people may find expression.   If the new elections are allowed to proceed without bribery or terrorism, if the citizens are not intimidated by armed force, if, in a word, the old corrupt system is cast aside, the supporters of an honest franchise and an honest policy with regard to racial and social problems will have so compact a majority in Parliament that the path will be clear for the remodelling of Austria-Hungary, the only possible way to avert ruin."

There are good grounds for believing that the King read through this memorial.   Needless to say, nothing whatever was done in the direction of our proposals.   Not that the King was lacking in goodwill ; but his advisers were adamant against any movement which threatened the interests of the old Dualist clique.   At first there were great hopes of Charles of Habsburg even in radical circles.   A university professor, a socialist, who had the opportunity of several hours' conversation with him shortly after the death of Francis Joseph, gave the following account of the conversation to friends ; and his account squared with the general feeling at the time.   " I was able to talk to him as unaffectedly as to my brother," he said. He told the sovereign that he was "no adherent of the dynastic principle," but the King passed by this confession in perfect good nature. The impression left on this Austrian professor after the exchange of views was that he "had found in the King a radical Intellectual, whose warm sympathy for the oppressed and ardent love of peace were beyond all doubt." This view unfortunately proved to be premature ; Charles of Habsburg showed himself weak and resourceless against the pressure of the Austro-Hungarian camarilla. Afterwards, when he turned to Lammasch[1] and his circle, it was already too late. Events pursued one another with appalling rapidity. Klofač[2] declared in the first days of September that "the Bohemian question has already passed beyond the stage at which it can be dealt with by negotiation with the Vienna Government."

In October the revolutionary movement of the national minorities was in full swing, and the revolutionary "National Councils" made no secret of the fact that they were out to set up new sovereign States. On October 7 the Czech and Jugoslav deputies published a joint manifesto declaring that the Vienna Government was not competent to make peace proposals in the name of the Slavs. Towards the middle of the month the Deutsche Volksbund (German People's League) had commenced activities in Vienna with a gigantic popular demonstration demanding a German Austria. On October 16 the Emperor's manifesto on a federal Austria was published, but the National Committee in Prague declared that it refused to negotiate with Vienna, and the National Council at Zagreb expressed dissatisfaction with the manifesto. The middle of October saw the appointment of "Czechoslovak" Ministers to Paris and London. On the 24th the news reached the Hungarian Parliament that the Hungarian honvéds (militia) in Fiume

[1] Professor Heinrich Lammasch, the well-known Austrian pacifist. It was proposed to entrust him with the formation of a government, in the hope of influencing Entente opinion, and he did actually form a Government late in October, 1918 ; when it was already too late.—Trans.

[2] One of the most uncompromising of the Czech leaders, who had been imprisoned early in the war.—Trans.

had been disarmed by a Croat regiment. The same regiment had also set aside the police and arrested the public prosecutor ; the Governor reported that the military and a mob were moving on Fiume from the neighbouring Sušak with machine guns, and so on.

An equally furious storm was raging over the international scene. In mid-September the Bulgarian front was broken through by the Entente, and from then onwards it became a more and more open secret that on the German and Austro-Hungarian front the resistance was steadily weakening. The situation was reflected in the American notes, which rejected the peace proposals of Germany and the Dual Monarchy in terms which were almost an open call to revolution. Thus Lansing's reply to the German note stated clearly that peace negotiations must be subject not only to the acceptance of President Wilson's fourteen points, but to " the destruction of every arbitrary power anywhere that can . . . disturb the peace of the world. . . . The power which has hitherto controlled the German nation is of the sort here described."

In these weeks of supreme national excitement only children or fools could fail to realise that the Dual Monarchy was at an end, and that an independent and thoroughly democratic Hungary had become an urgent and inexorable necessity. In this condition of childish folly the Hungarian parliament and the dominant political groups remained up to the last. On October 22 they insensately voted down Michael Károlyi's motion for a declaration of independence. There was only one way in which the old régime could have done anything to calm down the menacing waves of popular fury : by appointing a popular government and announcing without further delay a series of real and substantial national reforms. Instead of this, its one concern was to keep the King from appointing the Károlyi government, which was being demanded with remarkable unanimity by every progressive element in public opinion. These frantic efforts of the reaction had the most fatal results. Had the Károlyi government been appointed six or even four weeks earlier, events in Hungary would have taken a very different course.

The worst convulsions could have been avoided, and without either Bolshevism or White Terror we might have secured all that was reasonable and attainable in the aims of the two revolutions. But the blind obduracy of the ill-counselled King and the leaders of the old régime, destroyed the bonds of tradition and custom which might have secured organic continuity between past and future. We were precipitated into a whirlpool of hatred and exasperation. The resistance of the *ancien régime* was due mainly to three politicians : Windischgrätz, Vázsonyi and Szterényi. The intrigues of Windischgrätz are easily accounted for by his social position and his narrow outlook. Vázsonyi's course was inspired by a thoroughly low type of vanity and jealousy. Szterényi was merely continuing the deals of a business politician. These were the men who made the King believe that the returning masses from the broken front and the civil population crushed by four years of war wanted nothing better than a government formed out of the discredited heroes of the old régime, and the concession of a few modest reforms. Next to the unscrupulous instigators of the policy which brought about the war, the main responsibility for the catastrophe which was upon us belonged to the self-seeking clique which misled the King up to the last as to the true nature and significance of the events in Hungary.

## CHAPTER II

## THE OCTOBER REVOLUTION

REVOLUTIONS are born, not made. In these fevered October days I realised as never before the irresistible force of mass movements towards social change, the impotence in the face of them of all who seek deliberately to guide and control them. What happened was almost always the opposite of what the intellectual general staff of the revolution had planned or proposed ; everything was carried through at a different point or by other persons than was intended. At such times even the primitive, subconscious promptings of ingrained tradition lose their power, while all normal means of influencing public opinion prove equally ineffectual. Argument and persuasion, the careful weighing of data, the logical design and strict execution of plans, the considered distribution of functions and other rational accompaniments of political action in normal times, stop short as though under an enchanter's wand ; in their place there form in society mysterious magnetic fields, attracting masses to themselves with merciless violence, and subjecting to their influence the vast bulk of so-called independent opinion. It was to these magnetic currents that Stephen Tisza fell a victim in October, 1918, and Béla Kun would certainly not have escaped a similar fate in August, 1919, had he remained in Budapest, even if the White government had not officially sent out its bandits to assassinate him. That is the meaning of revolution. Events prove incapable of proceeding through the normal path of discussion and compromise to the end which irresistibly beckons them. The bridge of reason collapses, and the fresh indispensable equilibrium is attainable only through the wild, animal collision of opposing wills, the clash of the extremes. The government of the October revolution was a last effort to maintain the rule of reason amid the whirl of social disorder, and as we shall see, the moral and intellectual structure of Hungarian society was too weak to be able to dispense with catastrophic methods of social transformation. But let us look more closely into events.

Since August every discerning spirit among my acquaintance had been impressed by the irresistible growth of the influence of these " magnetic fields " over the masses in Budapest. I may fairly say that we felt as a physical, biological fact the more and more intolerable pressure of approaching events. We got through our day's work feverishly, distractedly ; at every meeting the first question would be, " What is going to happen now ? " Whither would this awful avalanche carry us, this avalanche set in motion on the French front, with an ominous roar that we could hear continuously in the silence of our studies ? The feeling was much more than a mere state of tension. We sought to picture the coming events in detail. We were almost all agreed that the crisis in the Dual Monarchy, and still more in Hungary, would be much more severe and more dangerous than in Germany. The disharmony between the nationalities, the great poverty, the enormous lack of education, would plunge us into inevitable anarchy, unless we could succeed at the last moment in organising, directing and moderating the elemental mass movements.

Erwin Szabó had from the first warmly supported my plan of uniting all the progressive forces in a single organisation adapted to the situation. We knew that the Hungary which until then had been shut out of all share in legislation, administration and jurisdiction, was now coming *nolens volens* into power. Szabó was almost a fanatical worshipper of the " class war " theory, a hater of parliamentary compromises, a pioneer of the idea of " direct action." But he was now incessantly urging the union of Socialists, Radicals and Károlyists without delay in a common organisation, and influencing his socialist colleagues in this direction ; from such a union, he contended, a government programme would emerge, the moment the moribund militarist and oligarchical régime received its deathblow. We were also in agreement in seeing the greatest weakness of the revolutionary movement in its lack of men with practical experience in public life. The Hungarian democracy had had no schooling. Opportunities of public service in the legislature and in the county and municipal administrations had alike been rigidly closed to it to the last. We had a number of speakers, publicists and trade union officials, but we had very few men who had been in actual contact with the everyday tasks of public life. And knowing the abyss of crudity and corruption in the old Hungarian administration, we were thoroughly aware that the revolution could only succeed and do creative work if we could set up a fresh administration at a moment's notice, out of human material adequate both in spirit and brain to its great task. We felt that one of the principal tasks of the coming National Council would be the immediate compilation of a list of all the experienced officials, intellectual workers, and officers of the reserve, who could be relied on as administrators in the work of reorganisation. The covetous army of opportunists naturally ridiculed this proposal of ours as the plan of unpractical doctrinaires and theoreticians! Not until the day came when they were eating the bitter bread of exile, did they see that the revolution came to grief for the precise reason that we had not this panel. In its absence the task of finding two or three thousand educated Hungarians who could be entrusted with posts of authority under the revolutionary government, had been beyond us, for the good reason that serious and dependable persons are generally modest and stand aside, while the pushing and unprincipled rush for jobs at the first moment.

This desperate lack of organisation in the Hungarian democratic forces weighed upon us like a millstone through every phase of the revolution, and as we shall see it was nothing but this that brought Bolshevism upon us. It was this same defect which for weeks made it impossible to call the National Council into being; the Council was, indeed, only formed at the very last moment, when soldiers and students were already throwing up barricades. These weeks'

delay cost us untold loss : had the National Council been
constituted four weeks earlier, we should not only have
been better prepared for the work of government, but the
unmistakable expression in the Council of the trend of
public opinion would certainly have exerted a decisive
moral influence on the vacillating King.

The responsibility for this ruinous delay in the constitution of the National Council rests chiefly upon the right-wing
Socialists, who thought fit to block, for petty tactical reasons,
the formation of this all-important organ.

To enable our situation at the time and the subsequent
course of events to be fully appreciated, it is necessary to
pass briefly in review the various organisations of the
Hungarian democracy upon which it might have been possible
to count in varying degrees for support in the constructive
work of the revolution.   (For it must not be forgotten that
the true revolution consists ultimately not in blood and
violence but in a new spirit and a new organisation !)

1. *The Social Democratic party* was certainly the best
organised group in the Hungarian democracy.   In the part
it had played in the organisation of the workers and the
dissolution of the old Hungary it had undeniably great
achievements to its credit.   But in these critical days of
revolution the party showed only too plainly the great
defects which had long marred it, its combination of a
doctrinaire spirit with bureaucratic tendencies, its readiness
to throw about at all times the commonplaces of the
revolutionary Die-Hard, combined with a tendency when
it came to action to engage in petty opportunist deals.
Great harm was done by the moral indifference evidenced
in its lack of fastidiousness in the choice of political
expedients, and occasionally in a tendency to place the
personal interests of the political leaders before the welfare
of the labour movement as a whole.   It is no mere coincidence
that a substantial proportion of the leaders of the Communist
Party, when that came to be formed, consisted either of
men who had been unable to endure the atmosphere of the
older party, or who had quarrelled with its leaders (in most

cases purely on personal grounds) and dropped out of the movement, or of men who had not been in it at all because the party leaders had always shown such hatred of the intellectuals that sensitive and self-respecting persons hardly had the courage to join. Erwin Szabó had often bitterly denounced the intolerance and the centralising and bureaucratic attitude of the party leaders, their pseudo-revolutionary spirit, saturated in reality with opportunism, their moral Nihilism. The great bulk of them would probably never have moved a finger for revolution if the unexpected initiative of a section of the soldiers, students and workers had not suddenly brought matters to a head.

2. Still less could the *Károlyi party* serve as a firm foundation for a democratic régime. Apart from its leader and his few close associates, it was neither a true middle-class party nor a peasant party; the bulk of its members were still under the hypnotic influence of the nationalist Kurucz ("crusaders.")[1] There was little of the spirit of Justh[2] and Károlyi in the leaders of the party, and it included all sorts of political malcontents and adventurers. It was quite unable to contribute to the revolution a serious and well-organised popular force, united on a clearly defined economic programme.

3. The third of the parties associated in the October revolution, the *Radical (bourgeois) party*, was not only weak but, in consequence of the great divergence of views between its component sections, incapable of energetic initiative and thorough-going organising work. Up to the end it included the most heterogeneous elements, elements which but for the amorphous condition of Hungarian politics could never have combined in a single party.

The right wing of the party consisted of those representatives of trade and industry who could be found to favour an anti-feudal policy. They were mainly advocates

[1] The Kurucz were opponents of the Habsburg dynasty (in the early XVIII Century) and advocates of a secession of Hungary from Austria.—Trans.

[2] At one time " President " (Speaker) of the Hungarian Chamber of Deputies, and leader of the more radical wing of the Party of Independence. He died during the war.—Trans.

of radical land reform, but were up in arms the moment there was any danger of injury to the interests of industrial capital.

An important part was played in the party by the group of *Marxist Socialists* who were unable to join the Social Democratic party either for the tactical or moral reasons already mentioned, or on account of their social position, or because they regarded the revolutionising of the middle-class as a necessary preliminary to socialism, and took this task upon themselves in the absence of bourgeois elements (in the political sense) prepared to undertake it. In their ranks there were many serious men of high attainments and pure character. The leader of this section was Paul Szende, who became Minister of Finance in the October revolution.

The most recent group of adherents to this party was formed by elements who could be described as *free Socialists.* I count in this group my own immediate circle, and all those who agreed with us in adhering to Socialism but were increasingly alive to the errors and inadequacies of Marxist orthodoxy. We disagreed with the Social Democrats in our belief in the primary importance of brainwork to society, in our view of the land system as the prime factor in the capitalist order, in our advocacy of free co-operation and decentralisation in opposition to the State Socialism of the Marxists, and in our disapproval of their doctrine of the class war. I should place this group as nearest to the programme and ideals of the Labour party in England, but more radical than that party.

There are some who use these very differences of view to charge the Socialist leaders of the Radical party with betrayal of the middle classes. But there can be no question of betrayal in the efforts of a party whose task in normal circumstances would have been to prepare the ground for a just and reasonable compromise between the working class and the working middle class. On the other hand, I must admit that in consequence of these internal differences the party was ineffective in propaganda, and that as the stage in the revolution was approached at which the middle-class interests were in full collision with Socialist aims, these differences reduced the party to impotence.

4. In reality middle-class interests were entirely unorganised. The *Democratic Party* of Vázsonyi was expressly concerned with Jewish denominational interests, and very little interested in economic and social questions ; it virtually limited its activities to a so-called liberal policy in local government.

5. Not only the middle-classes but the smaller peasants were almost entirely unorganised. The *Peasant Farmers' Party* of Szabó of Nagyatád had hardly arrived at a clear realisation of its opposition to the big estate system, and the great majority of its leaders was in any case composed of completely unreliable elements, men who time after time betrayed the peasant masses to the State and to the great landowners.

6. Equally impotent was the *Christian Socialist Party*, which was never able to free itself from the influence of the higher clergy, the Court and the clerical landowners. This small group, led by the distinguished prelate, Alexander Giesswein, fought to the end in complete isolation.

In a word, nowhere, nowhere was there the slightest sign of organising capacity outside the Social Democrats ! Normal political life is the contest between well organised parties, united on clear programmes and fighting with carefully considered tactics for definite political views and ideals. Of any such system there was in Hungarian public life not a trace. On one side stood the feudal reaction, in alliance with the plutocracy, on the other side, Socialism ; and this was the only true issue, the only dynamic reality in Hungarian public life.

This review of the progressive forces would, however, be incomplete without a mention of certain organisations which stood outside party politics, and were unconcerned with the advocacy of class interests, but exercised great influence over the change in popular feeling which nurtured the two revolutions. Among these organisations was the *Sociological Society*, which had a very great influence, though only over a limited circle ; it played much the same part in intellectual life in Hungary as the Fabian Society in England. The Sociological Society with its organ, "Huszadik Század" ("The Twentieth Century"), which for two decades had a very wide circulation and provided the only rostrum open to every sincerely progressive thinker without distinction of class or party, was for a generation the bridge of communication with Western progress. In addition to a wide range of theoretical studies, its members did a great deal of practical work in the most varied fields in public life. We find them working as propagandists within all sorts of groups and organisations for universal suffrage, for agrarian reform, for the taxation of unearned increment, and for equal rights for all nationalities.

From among the younger disciples of the Sociological Society there was formed the *Galileo Club*, which grew to importance as an educative influence among the University students, and campaigned against the various associations of young men belonging to the religious orders, and the students' drinking clubs. The Galileo Club gradually grew into a distinctly Socialistic undergraduates' organisation, in which the Jewish members tended increasingly to play the leading part. Amid the privations and passions of the war it fell more and more under the influence of anti-militarist and syndicalist propaganda, so that the police suppressed it a few weeks before the outbreak of the revolution, and arrested several of its members. Among the intellectuals in the camp of the Communist revolution, the youths in their twenties were almost exclusively drawn from the membership of the Galileo Club ; and amid a great deal of crudity and conceit and unmannerliness there was plenty of true worth, self-sacrificing idealism and intelligence to be found among them.

There was one other factor in the progressive movement in Hungary, to which the "Whites" of to-day, with their Asiatic mentality, attach quite exaggerated importance : *Freemasonry*. It would not be easy to say why, of all the progressive elements, this primarily religious, retiring, philanthropic body should figure as the special *bête noire* of the reaction of to-day. It is no doubt true that the great majority of the Freemasons are in sympathy with the efforts of modern democracy, but they have never ventured to make any serious sacrifice for it.   There was a very small minority of really distinguished men among them, cultured, courageous, and unselfish ; but the type of Free-mason who played a prominent part in public life remained to the end the mediocre, phrase-making diner who was ready enough to protest against the " powers of darkness " in the dim seclusion of his lodge, but when the situation grew serious, stepped subserviently aside at the slightest nod from a *föispán*[1] or a Secretary of State.   Indeed, a very important part of the electoral apparatus under the Tisza régime was directed by Freemasons.   The society also included among its adepts great numbers of the industrialists and business men who made a point of keeping on good terms with the government at all times, and whose radicalism would necessarily be of the frailest.   It is naturally an unwelcome task to have to pass this judgment on Free-masonry, at a time when illiterate hooligans have been expelling from their lodges masons who remained behind in Hungary, and when so many blameless masons worthy of a better fortune are being viciously persecuted.   But alike in the interest of truth and of future guidance, we are bound to point out that Freemasonry has attained martyrdom through the same defect which gave the Galileo Club its excessive influence—through Hungarian wrongheadedness and indolence ; through the total lack of rival organisation, of criticism and of serious work.

Finally, in this survey of the revolutionary forces, I must give some account of the continually increasing *Bolshevist* group.   During the last year of the war the doctrines of Russian Communism steadily penetrated by way of the Press or pamphlets and through émigrés and wounded soldiers, and they exerted an especially powerful influence on the starving and war-tortured intellectual classes.   Still more effective than any indirect propaganda were the actions and speeches and wireless messages of the Russian Bolshevist leaders.   Some of the young journalists of the bourgeois

[1] Lord Lieutenant (and actual administrator) of a county.—Trans.

Press were soon adherents of the Bolshevist doctrine. But they were scattered and entirely unorganised, and only began to be a force that counted when Béla Kun and his comrades arrived from Russia with a store of Russian money and their well-learnt propaganda clichés.

The last name in this review is that of one man, who in himself counts for more than the work of whole organisations— the poet Andrew Ady, whom the proud Napoleonic dictum fits well : *L'empereur = cent mille hommes.* He lived only through the first months of the revolution, a doomed body and a broken soul. But his deathless spirit shone always on the horizon of the revolutionist aims. He was the conscience and the living symbol of the whole period which culminated in the explosion of the revolution, and at his bier all who had had any serious thought for spiritual values through the past twenty years stood overwhelmed with grief. His sublime visions, his flaming pictures, the lash of his prophecies and warnings, were among the most powerful driving forces of the revolution, as they are now our chief consolation amid the ruins of our fallen country. If there is ever a future for Hungary it can only proceed from the soul of Andrew Ady, the truest of Hungarians and the truest of internationalists.

The final act of the revolution was, however, carried through by quite other forces. The activities of the politicians and publicists and trade union leaders might never have culminated in revolution, but for the entirely unanticipated violence with which the soldiers streaming home from the disintegrating front threw themselves into affairs. This was the Birnam Wood in which hesitating theories and cautious plans shot up in a night into the act of revolution. The White counter-revolutionists have naturally spread a tale that the Hungarian front stood boldly and unflinchingly and was perfectly reliable, until the October revolution and the capitulation ordered by the Károlyi government destroyed it. That is the Habsburg legend. It is a deliberate lie, invented and carefully kept up in order to save the prestige of the dynasty and to discredit the October revolution. It is easy enough to see through it. The old régime has every interest in so representing the situation, and in picturing a Budapest *mafia* of Jewish scribblers and political adventurers disorganising an unspent army which would later have made easy work of the defence of Hungary's territorial integrity.

This malicious invention is belied by a whole array of indisputable evidence as to the uncontrollable demoralisation of the Austro-Hungarian front. I have not space here, nor is there any necessity, to refer in detail to the literature of the military collapse. The advanced decay of the Austro-Hungarian army and the complete bankruptcy of the " home front," months before the revolution, have been attested by every impartial observer of the political and military situation.

Suffice it to point out that every demonstrable fact points to an uncontrollable state of disintegration and insubordination in the army. On October 30, Jekelfalussy surrendered Fiume to the Croats on orders from Wekerle.[1] The National Council at Zagreb telegraphed to General Metzger instructions that " the Slav troops are to cease hostilities and to be transported at once to their homes." On October 31, under orders from the Imperial naval command, Admiral Horthy, the national hero of to-day, surrendered the entire fleet to the Jugoslav National Council. At the same moment General Kestranek was being imprisoned in Prague after attempting to suppress the revolution by means of Hungarian soldiery ; the soldiers had refused obedience.

It is unnecessary, however, to go so far afield. In the last months of the war it was a matter of general knowledge in Budapest that the desertions had reached an appalling figure, and that even the notorious courtmartial of Lukachich, the Military Governor of Budapest, was failing to arrest the disintegration. In some parts of the country the rougher elements had broken loose. Armed bands of deserters, supported by the villagers, were wandering in the forests.

It would be easy to continue indefinitely to accumulate this evidence, but for any thinking person this simple

[1] The Hungarian Premier.—Trans.

consideration should be still more convincing : How could the dilapidated, hungry and embittered Austrian or Hungarian front, bleeding from a thousand wounds, divided by national differences, and faced with a contrary order from the victorious new National States, continue to offer opposition to the world league, vastly superior in economic and military resources, which with its legions of tanks was smashing the German Western front, where there was a hundred times greater strength and confidence and unity, and far better supplies of food and munitions !

The immediate cause of the October revolution was the gradually returning tide from the disintegrating fronts and the accumulation of great masses of people in Budapest. The soldiers and students and munition workers were the true leaven of the revolution. It was in the first instance a military and national revolution ; not until much later did it become a social revolution, then Socialist, finally Communist.

The spirit of revolution had penetrated into every sphere of human relations in the course of September and October. Men lost all interest in everyday affairs and were looking fixedly into the future. Quiet pupils of philosophy and metaphysics came to me with eyes aflame, and passionately denounced the pusillanimity of the revolutionary parties. An electrician's apprentice, come to repair the wires, prophesied that we were on the threshold of revolution and of appalling events. The maid bringing in the soup told us that she had it from her relatives in the country that the old world would last very little longer now. The young men of the Galileo Club pursued their anti-militarist propaganda almost openly, and the imprisonment of a few of them only increased their revolutionary enthusiasm. Soldiers and even officers spoke aloud in public of the collapse of the front. In the tram one heard passionate outbursts against the war, the authorities and the propertied classes.

This diffused revolutionary excitement was first precipitated into united action at the funeral of Erwin Szabó.[1] In token of their grief the workers went on strike for five

[1] A prominent exponent of Hungarian Socialist theory.—Trans.

minutes. The most various groups were assembled at the
graveside : workers, soldiers, students, artists. It was
evident that the great crowd had assembled not only to bid
farewell to the dead man they had loved, but to find strength
and inspiration for the trials to come. The appearance of
Károlyi affected them as a declaration of war on the old
world. " Károlyi is here, too ! "—the words were whispered
through the crowd. During the addresses at the graveside
this feeling grew tenser. Kunfi invoked the revolutionary
spirit of the dead man as their judge in the heavy duties
before them. As he spoke he strove with his suppressed
emotions, and his words affected all as those of a man praying
for help and guidance under the heavy burden of duty
imposed by irrevocable destiny. I seemed to see in a vision
around the grave of my friend the embodiment of all the
suffering and striving and yearning of our generation, and
forgetting my weakness and isolation I was able in faith
and completely without rhetoric to make this vow :

" This country shall no longer remain the country of robber
barons. This country shall no longer be the country of heartless
speculators. . . . This country shall no longer be the
country of atheistic parsons. . ."

Naturally no one spoke at first of revolution by violence ;
the demand was for the constitution of a National Council
and its direct association with the Hungarian army. The
universal desire was for a free and independent Hungary,
democratic and socially progressive. Everyone was eager
for the formation of a Károlyi government, and no one
doubted that sooner or later the popular will would carry
the day. It was generally believed at first that the King
would soon give way before the insistency and unanimity
of the popular demand.

But the nobles and the Vázsonyi clique intrigued against
the plan of a popular ministry. Poor and rich were
summoned to Gödöllö to discredit Károlyi with the King
and to prove that he had no popular following. Continual
pressure was brought for the formation of the impossible
Hadik coalition.[1] Blood flowed at the Suspension Bridge ;

[1] Which was to have included all parties.—Trans.

the Palace was stormed by students. Peaceful demonstrations, as imposing as Budapest had ever seen, were of no avail. Károlyi was perfidiously lured to Vienna, simply in order to keep him away from the people of Budapest on a critical day. Only then, and when the Hadik ministry was already appointed, did popular opinion grow so exasperated and inflamed that officers and common soldiers were constantly to be heard declaring that the farce was no longer to be endured, and that the time had come for military intervention.

By this time the National Council had been formed, in imitation of the adjoining countries. It was the joint executive organ of the Social Democratic party, the Károlyists and the Radicals. Even now it had no immediate thought of effecting a violent revolution, particularly as the situation was regarded as not yet ripe for it. We knew that the garrisons were full of discontented elements, but we believed that Lukachich was still master of the situation. The Council preferred, therefore, to wait for the new government to find itself completely paralysed ; it could afford to wait, as the principal organs of the State, police, post, telephones, etc., were one after another coming over to its side.

We regarded it as certain that the Hadik government would be a mere shadow, unable to exist for more than a few days, and that in any case it would not venture to use force against a people passionately united and ready for anything. For the time the National Council contented itself with issuing its proclamation of October 26, 1918, in all the papers, in defiance of the censorship. The proclamation ended with the following words, in which the Council openly declared itself a counter-government :

" Finally we ask all foreign peoples and governments to deal, in all matters concerning Hungary, directly with the Hungarian National Council, instead of the existing arbitrary government, which has now completely lost all touch with the workers of Hungary. Only the Hungarian National Council can speak or is authorised to deal in the name of that Hungarian nation on whose blood and labour Hungary depends."

From now onwards, however, there developed various groups and coteries, independently of the National Council, which elaborated a definite scheme of propaganda among the garrison of Budapest, and discussed various plans of offensive with a view to the military enforcement of the will of the National Council.  Up to the last moment the attitude maintained by the leaders in the National Council towards these groups was one of restraint and moderating counsel. Even those among us who regarded direct revolutionary action as an unavoidable necessity, still felt that the situation on the fateful night of October 30 was not yet ripe for action.  We considered that several days' propaganda and organisation were still needed, and should have preferred to see the feeble forces of the government take the offensive against us.  When, then, we found that the explosion had come, that a few hot-headed and impatient officers had commenced action on their own responsibility and occupied the Budapest Headquarters and various other public buildings, we were dismayed at the news.  We knew that the revolutionary movement had no organised troops at its disposal, that there were at most only a few companies on which we could rely.  We therefore spent the whole night in expectation of the arrival of Lukachich and the loyalist troops to arrest us.  It was an anxious night that the actual leaders of the revolutionary movement passed in the Hotel Astoria.  Virtually the only members of the National Council who remained at their posts were the Social Democrats, the Radicals and Károlyi himself.  The others had vanished completely on this critical night.

"We shall probably all hang at dawn," I said to Sigismund Kunfi, the leader of the left-wing Socialists, who was lying sleepless beside me on the floor.

"I expect so," he answered.  "These young officers have gone too fast.  We needed another two or three days, for the propaganda to sink in, and to enable us to arm the workers."

There was a violent crackling of machine guns before the windows of the hotel.  Then the thunder of guns. (So the arrested General Várkonyi diagnosed the sound.  It proved later to have been the banging of doors in the restaurant, but we could not dispute his judgment : he was the expert.)

Some officers shouted hoarsely at the telephone. Demands for reinforcements came to us from every quarter. But where were they to be got ? All we had was a few hundred men.

There was a continuous stream of alarming news. A Bosnian regiment was on the march against us. Lukachich himself was at its head. That settled it. So these callow youngsters had spoilt everything !

The better-known leaders of the revolutionary officers were nowhere to be found. They, too, had had no idea that in this very night some over-hasty elements were to let loose the revolution.

The loud mouthed Stephen Friedrich (who later became premier in the White government) had been talking days before of sending to fire on the palace of the Archduke Joseph. He was nowhere to be found : not a trace of him.

Still no sign of the approach of Lukachich. Evidently he had over-estimated our forces and was preparing to attack us with several regiments simultaneously ! If only he would waste a little more time ! If he waited till dawn we were saved, for the whole of the workers of the Csepel[1] factories and the neighbouring works would be marching up and we should be able to hold out. After all Hadik was a serious and conscientious man, and would have no desire to let loose a purposeless massacre in Budapest.

Broad daylight had come. The incredible had happened. Lukachich had not come : he had even fewer troops than we ! The Budapest garrison had wasted away to nothing, like the army at the front. Enormous crowds were filling Louis Kossuth Street, Rákôczy Street, and the boulevards. Groups of armed soldiers were continually arriving in motors. Company after company marched up. Eyes were sparkling, and every buttonhole showed a white hollyhock flower. The crowd was seized with indescribable intoxication. Everywhere waved the national flag and the red flag. Everywhere there was shouting of " Long live Károlyi ! Hurrah for the revolution ! " and often a cry which had not been heard before : " Hurrah for the republic ! " All

[1] An island in the Danube, below Budapest.—Trans.

Budapest was beside itself with joy. Never had there been such unity between nationalities and between classes !

Yes! We had won. Early in the morning came a telephone message. The Archduke Joseph[1] desired Károlyi's presence. Károlyi proceeded at once, with Kunfi and myself, to Buda. The goodnatured giant, Count Hadik, was awaiting us, pale and drawn, in his black court dress, and took us to the Archduke, who in his usual cordial manner, but moved now to tears, told Károlyi that the King had appointed him to be Prime Minister and desired him to proceed at once with the formation of his cabinet. Károlyi tried to ring up Vienna, and asked Kunfi and myself to inform the National Council and the Budapest population of what had happened. As our motor flew round the streets of the town we shouted wildly to the moving crowds, " Károlyi is premier ! The King has appointed the Károlyi government ! "

We thought that this news would kindle great enthusiasm and quickly restore the popularity of the King. Just the opposite happened. After the night of revolution the masses had regarded the Károlyi government as a matter of course. There was loud cheering for Károlyi, but from the Palace to Louis Kossuth Street there was not a single cheer for the King. On the contrary, when I came to the balcony of the Hotel Astoria to communicate the King's decision to the crowd, I heard many such cries as these :

" The King ! Who is King now ? "

" The King did not appoint Károlyi—the revolution appoints him ! "

" Long live the republic ! "

---

[1] The Archduke Joseph had always taken up the position of a national, specifically Hungarian Archduke. Until the end of the war he was in command of Austro-Hungarian troops in Tirol. In the last week of October, when the army was in dissolution, he sent a report to headquarters calling attention to the spread of Bolshevism in the army and urgently advising the earliest possible conclusion of an armistice.—Trans.

# CHAPTER III

## THE MEANING AND AIMS OF THE OCTOBER REVOLUTION

BEFORE we pursue further the rapid course of events, we must devote a moment to clearly defining the task before the Károlyi government. It was as difficult a task as is conceivable. These were its principal elements :

1. A treaty of peace had to be concluded, taking account of the new international situation ; the Dualist system had finally to be liquidated, and the best attainable economic and political relations set up with the new National States.

2. The nationalities question had to be settled on the basis of the Wilson principles.

3. Legislature and administration had to be democratised.

4. Popular liberties had to be set on a firm foundation all along the line.

5. The population, exasperated by the monstrous suffering and injustice of the war, had to be appeased and contented by radical social reforms, the great masses assisted to the ownership of land, industries of the nature of monopolies socialised, and " excessive accumulations of capital checked and as far as possible appropriated for public purposes by means of a stringent system of taxation."

6. Production, which had fallen exceedingly low, had to be restored after the lifting of the blockade.

7. An immediate end had to be made to the shedding of blood and to all existing alliances.

These were the main problems facing Hungary in her new freedom and independence. They were clearly realised by the leaders of the revolution, as is evidenced by the first proclamation of the National Council, issued on October 26, in Sigismund Kunfi's revision of my draft. I do not think we need fear the judgment of future historians on this document. It will be clear to them that every line of it is impregnated with a sincerely democratic and socially progressive spirit, and that in the reforms demanded we went to the utmost limit attainable in the existing stage of the country's economic and cultural development. The state independence of Hungary, universal suffrage for legislature and administration, a democratic peoples' alliance with the neighbouring States, the partition of the *latifundia*, and a social policy following the example of the most highly developed industrial States—in a word, the sovereignty of the industrious masses of peasants and town workers in the State, under the guidance of the genuinely creative intelligenzia—these were the fundamental principles of the October revolution; and in them were agreed originally not only the three parties but, as I can affirm with a clear conscience, the whole of the workers in the country.

True revolutions are to be distinguished from revolutionary *putsche* by the fact that the minority which makes the revolution voices the supreme common interest, proclaims the true contemporary forward movement, and thus represents an ideal which conduces to the well-being and the advancement of every really productive element in society. The true revolution hurts the interests only of a tiny minority which lives on the abuse of monopoly and privilege ; the great majority, the whole of the productive classes, feel their chains falling away, and see the dawn of an era of further advance in justice and freedom. This great revolutionary liberation profoundly influenced every section of Hungarian society at the time, and the emotion aroused was so strong and so general that some of the finer spirits even among the old privileged classes were unable entirely to resist its attraction. Peace, justice, land, labour : everyone hoped for something new and better. No doubt our adherents included others besides sincere and selfless enthusiasts : when the revolution had succeeded, there streamed into its camp those elements who support whatever government comes to the surface, and others who had past sins to cover up by the loud profession of new loyalties

These elements are now pretending that their adherence was wrung from them. Who compelled them ? Who in these days of enthusiasm and victory and work troubled about the fallen great ones of the old régime, or needed to lure in the place-hunting nobodies ? The truth was that there was an uninterrupted stream of truckling deputations, crowding forward to swear allegiance at any price to the National Council. It taxed the powers of its eloquent president, John Hock, to reply to the multiplicity of enthusiastic offers of revolutionary service. One after another they presented themselves, the bankers, Leon Lánczy and Beck von Madarasz, the president of the Academy of Sciences, Albert Berzeviczy, the Archduke Joseph and the Democrats of the sect of Vázsonyi ; everyone was eager to swear allegiance, to ecstasise over the revolution and to have a hand in the realisation of its high aims.

Many of us felt from the first that we who were leading the revolution were not masters of the situation, that we were confronted with the boundless imperialism of the new States, and from another quarter with the challenge of the great masses of men returning from the front, who were in sentiment, if not by conviction, Bolshevist. But at all events at first, and in hours of optimism, we did not regard our task as insoluble. We had confidence in the democratic and pacifist quality of public opinion in the Entente States, and especially in the policy of President Wilson, a policy which stood higher than any mere nationalism. We did not deceive ourselves for a moment with thoughts of preserving the territorial integrity of Hungary, in the geographical sense ; but we were convinced that the conquering Allies would show the utmost goodwill to her pacifist and anti-militarist government, and especially to Károlyi, who had so often stood with unexampled courage for the policy of the Entente ; we were sure that they would apply the plebiscitary principle on which they had so often laid stress, and that if we had to suffer losses of territory it would still be possible, with the aid of just and liberal commercial treaties, to assure the undisturbed continuance of communication with the lost areas.

During the revolution, and also later, a good deal of censure was directed against the Károlyi government, and especially against me, for our insistence on territorial integrity, as making our position much worse both in regard to the Entente and the new States. I regarded this charge as entirely groundless, and do so still. Károlyi frequently made it clear that he was concerned with territorial integrity in an economic sense, and I stated repeatedly that we loyally accepted the principle of the plebiscite, as enunciated by President Wilson, without reservation or thought of revanche. To have conceded more than this would have been neither opportune nor in accord with my principles. I believed and still believe that a Hungary reorganised on the model of Switzerland, closely united in federal bonds with the neighbour States, would have been a better guarantee of democracy, of economic progress and of peace, than a mutilated Hungary, robbed of the means of existence, embittered and pursued by dreams of revanche, and hardening her heart against the surrounding States.[1] In any case, what were we called upon to renounce ? We had then no information as to the terms of the peace treaties, and the Entente continually declared that the lines of demarcation fixed had no relation to the ultimate political boundaries. To have abandoned all claim to territorial integrity would at that time only have meant delivering over the country to the mercy of imperialist megalomania and capitalist greed.

Unhappily we were soon to see clearly that we were in a situation in which every element necessary for the achievement of our heavy task was lacking. There was no longer any possibility of preventing the complete conversion of the masses to Bolshevism.

---

[1] I had already stated my position in these terms before the Revolution in my book, " The Collapse of Dualism and the United States of the Danube." This work passed through three editions in a few weeks and was received with lively sympathy by progressive opinion in Hungary.

CHAPTER IV

## THE KÁROLYI GOVERNMENT

I THINK that in any case the unbiassed future historian will bear witness to the good faith and good intentions of the government set up by the October revolution, and to its full consciousness of the heavy moral responsibility which lay on its shoulders. He will be able to add that Hungary can scarcely have had at any period a ministry whose hands were cleaner. This, indeed, was one of the main sources of the weakness of our government, both in home and foreign policy. The army of business politicians, financiers and company-promoters and speculators, who swarm round every government and win it support and prestige and useful connexions in return for the provision of opportunities for profitable transactions, were sent empty away by the Károlyi government, without even the customary polite phrases. No wonder if big finance, at home and abroad, and the influential "rastaquouères" from all quarters grew constantly colder and more hostile to the Károlyi government, and journals of the type of " Az Est " and " Pesti Hirlap " were soon venting their wrath upon it. The following bequeathed to us by the capitalist governments of the past soon scented a new quality in the revolutionary government, and hated its inconvenient puritanism, not only for solid reasons of interest, but with the bitter hatred of the corrupt for the clean and honest.

The feeling against our government grew still more bitter as it became clear to all who had profited from the old régime that we were in earnest, that we intended to carry out the full programme of the October revolution ; that there was definitely to be an end of the old type of parliament and of the old county government ; that we really intended to

partition the *latifundia* after a definite date; and that Paul
Szende was elaborating a taxation reform of a severity
" unexampled in history."

Our rigid puritanism also greatly damaged our position
abroad. We were, indeed, naïve politicians, and did not
realise how to manage foreign military and diplomatic
missions. If we behaved towards them with courtesy and
sincerity, and carefully kept to our engagements, we
imagined we had done enough. We failed to realise that
many of the members of these missions expected something
else from us : fine dwellings, profitable business deals,
champagne dinners, and more than that : attractive,
patriotic ladies, ready for any sacrifice for their country.
In a word, the full programme which the Horthy government has staged with such a wealth of inventiveness and
gentlemanly delicacy and oriental prodigality. It is true,
we failed to understand this. Our tastes did not lie in this
direction, and even if they had done, we were too weighed
down day and night with work and responsibility (a twenty-
hour working day was nothing unusual for us) and
frequently utter despondency, to have either time or
inclination or elasticity for such functions. We should have
made a failure of them even if we had made the attempt
*contra naturam*.

For we were already doomed, and by the very internationalism which was the basis of our whole policy. Here
too, we were all too naïve, and it was only later that we
realised that this internationalism of ours, the internationalism of work and pacifism and the serious things of
the spirit, has no place in this world, or at most an occasional
flicker of life in the solitary room of the student or in a
Labour congress ; that there is only one internationalism
which has any strength, any virtue in world-relations in our
day—namely, that of the old world, the " Internationale "
of the aristocrats and soldiers and bankers. With this
Internationale we very quickly came into collision.

Quite apart from these tactical difficulties, the
revolutionary government had to contend with menacing
physical obstacles, which proved too much for it ; difficulties

in the social and military spheres and in that of foreign politics, and also difficulties produced by the errors of the Károlyi government.

Social conditions were already beyond mending when the democratic government came into power. There was no possibility of stopping the avalanche of social dissolution and revolution, still less of guiding it. I had no illusions as to this. I said frequently to my intimate friends that I regarded our effort to govern as hopeless, and only joined in it from a sense of duty. A reckoning was coming for the insane bloodshed and brutality of the four years of war, for the cynical luxury at home, the systematic squandering of our economic resources, the incredible corruption of the wartime State Socialism, the appalling abuses of the pasha-ridden county governments, and for half-a-century of a grasping and unprincipled class policy which had made all serious democratic organisation and all reform in Hungary impossible. It was perfectly plain to me that when the soldiers came back from the front, tortured and bleeding, verminous and half-dead with hunger, when they came home to find their children ailing and stunted, martyred by the greed and obstinacy that had prolonged the war, or to find their wives the mistresses of profiteers,—then, there would be a day of savage judgment. Whenever I had come back from my work as a war correspondent in some part of the front, I had warned the men who idled in luxury at home : " I have only been a spectator from a comfortable distance, I have hardly seen anything of the real horrors out there, but the little that I have seen is enough for me to prophesy to you that when the dehumanised men from the trenches come home they will drive us out of our houses, instal themselves in our place, devour the last crust in our cupboards and put our last coat on their backs—and I shall not venture for a moment to say they are not in the right." This war has been the meanest and the most horrible of wars, but in no community was the class-war between the men who were driven to the front and the men who fraudulently evaded military service so bitter or marked by such ruthless tyranny as in Hungary, where the over-whelming majority of the aristocracy, the rich gentry, the Jewish plutocrats, the influential journalists, even the socialist and trade union leaders, had made good their escape from liability to service at the front.

*Post equitem sedet atra cura :* from the first the spectre of Bolshevism hung over the Károlyi government.  It was at first an inchoate, diffuse Bolshevism, Bolshevism without doctrine, a Bolshevism of simple robbery and anarchy, but it was so much the more dangerous.  The home-coming soldiers and the wounded men besieged the government with an uninterrupted stream of impossible demands. There was a widespread disinclination to get back to work, although there was plenty of work waiting to be done in the fields.  Barna Buza, the Minister of Agriculture, reported time after time that many million crowns' worth of agricultural land was going to ruin for want of labour.  This again was a natural result of the strain and over-excitement of the life at the front :  no one was inclined to face the monotony of peaceful work, all were looking for adventure and distraction, politics and *putsche*.  All Budapest was turned into a gigantic debating society, wrangling all day and all night over constitutional and social problems and problems of foreign relations.  There was no limit to the number of lectures and addresses ; every ignoramus discovered in his primitive brain a stock of theories and ideas and a call to expound them.  Besides this theorising the excited passions of the masses found vent, especially during the first weeks of the revolution, in frequent explosions of violence and looting. It was this dangerous state of public opinion which called forth Sigismund Kunfi's despairing appeal in his speech of November 2 :

" We must have peace in our country ! And if we are to have peace there must be an end of looting.  I will not be the leader of robbers and looters.  We must burn into everyone's brain that whoever says a word to suggest the predatory and subversive ideas which would reduce our heavy labours to futility, is a traitor, an abettor of war, an enemy to the rule of the people, an ally of the system we have destroyed and an *agent provocateur* in its interest."

Thus unmistakably, on the very first day of the revolution, did the avalanche which five months later swept away the October régime, start on its course. A much more immediate threat to the Károlyi government than the anarchy among the people, was the anarchy among the soldiery. We must not forget that the October revolution was primarily a military one, and that the night of October 30 was virtually the private venture of a few groups. It is also clear that in these bands of soldiers it was not always the serious and responsible elements, but frequently the desperadoes of the front who had taken the lead, and who now hastened to present their accounts to the revolutionary government, under various heads—organising expenses, printing, hire of motors, arms and munitions, and so on. Each one would come with a great tale of his services and initiative, and hint that he had behind him a large number of discontented soldiers for whom he could not be responsible if the government failed suitably to reward their valour. The first task of the Károlyi government was to shake itself free from this military rabble, and there were large numbers to be "appeased"—and disarmed. Often enough, when we retired to rest, we found ourselves wondering which of the dissatisfied condottieri would put the whole government under arrest in the course of the night.

But only ignorance and malevolence combined could concoct any charge against the quality and the honour of the leaders of the October revolution on the basis of these melancholy episodes. There never was a revolution in history but had its unwelcome rabble of hangers-on. It is clear that the ordinary restraints of society cannot be broken down without the emergence of the lower passions of humanity as well as pure heroism and noble self-sacrifice, and as in the social order of to-day the evil is stronger than the good, it is obvious that in every social revolution the darker instincts of the masses will predominate.

Still more disreputable is the attempt of the supporters of the Horthy government to connect the sums handed out to the bands of soldiers—insignificant amounts in comparison with the naked robberies of the Horthy detachments—with the assassination of Tisza. I have already said that the assassination was a veritable tragedy of destiny. It was hardly conceivable that a people embittered by five years of horror and oppression, would allow the man who had been the outstanding symbol of it all to remain alive through these fevered days of upheaval. Not only the capital but the whole country was filled with rumours of the murder before it actually occurred. Most of these rumours were believed, the catastrophe was so in tune with the public itching for lynch law. Some weeks later a conservative journalist published the following account of it :

" The crowd grows continually denser, and then suddenly some hundreds of men band together. . . . Now a sheet of paper is put up ; on it, in blood-red letters, ' Count Stephen Tisza has been shot ! ' Before one has entirely made out the letters the crowd has delivered judgment on the deed. There are shouts of exultation and thunderous clapping ; it is as if a play actor were being applauded. A soldier shouts facetiously, ' Long live Tisza now he's dead ! ' . . . Men and women run back in the rain and pass on the news, happy and laughing, saying again and again to themselves, ' Splendid ! Stephen Tisza dead ! ' As they go on their way they shout the good news to everyone who passes. A motor decorated with flowers and flags swishes past me ; a salute is fired, reverberating away into the gathering twilight ; young girls are smiling at the news— ' Tisza has been assassinated ! ' "[1]

The general feeling is shown even more unmistakably by the fact that the newspapers belonging to the Tisza party merely reported the news of the assassination, without a word of comment or a word in praise or appreciation of the dead leader. They now, of course, plead in excuse, the terror then reigning. It is a lying excuse ; at that time the Press had complete freedom, and the Radical daily " Világ " devoted an obituary notice to its great opponent. The truth is that in those days of revolution the public accepted the tragedy of Tisza's end as an act of historic justice.

The hated Lukachich would have suffered the same fate,

[1] Arpád Pásztor, in "The Book of the Victorious Revolution," published by the arch-reactionary Brothers Légrády ; p. 103.

if some of the members of the National Council had not succeeded at the last minute, at the risk of their own lives, in concealing him from the murderous frenzy of the soldiers, who would have torn him to pieces. But Tisza was a figure of far greater and more representative importance, the very symbol of the broken *ancien régime*, and for a man of his defiant pride and manly resolution, escape was hardly possible. Stürgkh[1] was a far lesser offender than Tisza, but he had to suffer the penalty, and it was not a drunken sailor who killed him, but an idealist philosopher.

The malevolent absurdity of the charges against the government of the October revolution is clear enough. One thing is certain : the military question was our Achilles' heel, and we all realised it. We knew that our situation would sooner or later become untenable without a reliable, well organised military force, in sympathy with democratic aims. There has probably never been a government so entirely dependent on moral force as the Károlyi government, which for months was absolutely without a military arm. It was impossible to prevent the dissolution of the old army ; the men streamed away from all military units like wine from a burst cask. The few who remained were not the sort of human material on which the democratic and revolutionary government could have relied. The danger of counter-revolution from the special officers' formations, was clear to us from the outset. But the elements which had remained in the army were just those which continually jeopardised the existence of the Károlyi government with their blackmail and threats of *putsche*. When Béla Linder, the War Minister in the October government, broke out into those strange words for a War Minister, " I don't want to see any more soldiers ! " it was not from mere pacifist sentimentality, but from the fear that if he allowed this demoralised army, bent only on adventure and looting, to continue in existence, the situation of the government would definitely become untenable. I am not competent

[1] Austrian Premier from 1913 to 1916, when he was assassinated by Friedrich Adler.—Trans.

to say whether a man of greater military gifts would have been able to sift the desirable elements out of this disintegrating army, and to organise them into reliable republican guards. But in any case the task was made impossible by the attitude of the Social Democratic party, the predominant partner in the government coalition. The Social Democrats would not hear of the preservation of the old army, and led by Joseph Pogány, they pursued from the outset a systematic propaganda at the railway stations to win over the returning military formations to the revolution, to disarm them and to dismiss them to their homes. Their success was so complete that when we visited Belgrade on November 6, the Ministry of War was no longer in a position to provide a couple of dozen soldiers for the protection of Károlyi's special train, despite a whole day's search ; this difficult problem in mobilisation was finally solved by the Soldiers' Council !

The scattering of the old army was nothing peculiar to Hungary ; it happened in greater or less degree in all the conquered States. It was a natural accompaniment of disaster. Linder's policy and the Socialist agitation may have furthered it, but even without them I doubt if the result would have been very different. What was much more serious and fatal was that we were not in a position to replace the army by any substantial military formation. It may fairly be said that until, under the dictatorship of the proletariat, the organised workers were served out with arms as a last despairing measure of protection from the hooligan rabble, neither of the two revolutionary governments had any serious armed force for defence against an attack from outside or a *putsch* from within. No army is dependable in the absence of discipline, and the whole psychology of the first months of revolution was incompatible with any possibility of the restoration of discipline. The revolutionary defence force was little but a Praetorian troop, with very strong political currents of its own, living in comparative comfort and ease under a group of military leaders who admitted allegiance to no one. We could only have removed the evil if we had organised a small reliable defence force by voluntary enlistment, chiefly from among the peasants and the industrial workers, under officers of republican convictions. This was the solution urged from the first by the bourgeois members of the cabinet and by Károlyi himself; but it was unrealisable owing to the strong opposition of the Socialists, who were convinced that a peasant soldiery would be unreliable and would easily be seduced by any counter-revolutionary movement. I frequently urged that it depended entirely on ourselves whether the peasantry were revolutionary or counter-revolutionary. If we gave them land at once it was an absolute certainty that we should retain their support. I made a proposal that the government should guarantee 10 yokes (14 acres) of land to all who voluntarily joined the revolutionary army, the land to be handed over to them free of all payment after two years' service. Unhappily this proposal was not adopted, and as we shall see, the military question and the land question were the primary causes of the fall of the Károlyi government.

Under these circumstances, and under the steadily increasing pressure of the Social Democrats, we had no alternative (short of breaking up the coalition and so destroying all that had been won by the revolution) but to submit to a course to prevent which three War Ministers had resigned, the creation of an exclusively socialist army. Károlyi was as fully alive as others amongst us to the danger of this. A class army of this sort was hardly likely to stop at a reasonable, generally agreed stage. Under the influence of the extravagant and unbridled Communist agitation it would easily get beyond the control even of its Socialist leaders, as in fact it did in a few months. Nevertheless, in view of the effect which the growing revolutionary movements were producing, we had no choice but to continue on this course, which seemed free from danger so long as the Socialist leaders retained control of their following. As to this point, William Böhm, then Secretary of State for Army Affairs, and the other Socialist ministers in the government, repeatedly reassured us, contending that the Bolshevist movement was nothing serious, that the organised workers held fast to a reasonable socialism, and that the army would never be the tool of ill-advised *putsche*.

These, we felt, were none too reliable assurances, but it was neither from naiveté nor folly that we permitted the Socialist remanning of the army, but simply from the compulsion of circumstances. We were left no choice between breaking with the Socialists to work with the old army officers (which would have turned the army into an irresistible organ of counter-revolution) and the course we actually took of permitting the Socialisation of the army, despite the risk of complete Bolshevisation.

It is very easy, after the event, to blame the Károlyi government. Germany adopted the opposite method—and it led to the Kapp *putsch*. A Kapp is, of course, an impossible anachronism in Germany, but in Hungary the first Kapp was bound to become a Horthy. Consider, on the other hand, Austria, with her powerfully organised and thoroughly class-conscious peasantry and her strong Christian Socialist party, with her people still saturated with dynastic traditions : it is an open secret that despite this, and despite all paper guarantees, she still has an essentially Socialist army, controlled by the Social Democratic party.

In addition to the social and military questions, there appeared a third and totally unexpected constitutional question, that of the Republic, to undermine still further the position of our government. Little mention of the idea of a republic had been made up to the time of the appointment of the government. During the revolution we came across a few officers of republican views, but we attached so little importance to this question that on November 1st the whole of the cabinet proceeded to the palace without the slightest scruple, to take the oath before the King's representative, the Archduke Joseph. The first proclamation of the National Council does not devote a single word to the form of the State. And this was from no consideration of mere tactics, but because even at that date the leaders had been exercised very little indeed over this problem. In the cabinet there was probably no one who was attached in principle to the monarchical system, but on the other hand there was no one who thought it served any useful purpose then to discuss it.  Several of us attached little importance to the question of the head of the State, and were extremely sceptical of any superior virtue in, for instance, a Poincaresque republic as compared with the British monarchy.  Those, like Sigismund Kunfi, who were definitely republican in feeling, still regarded the question of the monarchy as a secondary one beside the enormously difficult problems which were calling for a solution at our hands. All of us considered that King Charles would in any case be no serious obstacle to the programme of the October revolution : in the existing international situation he would be fortunate if he could save his throne at this price.

That was our theory.  The facts turned out very differently.  We had forgotten that the course of a revolution is not guided by reason and reflection, but by the irresistible attraction of the " magnetic fields " to which I have referred. On the evening of the swearing-in we had not the faintest notion that Budapest and the whole country had turned in a single night to a fanatical republicanism.   I must admit at once that the masses, and not we, were in the right.   For all our aims the republic was the only logical and adequate form.

The next day, November 2, when I went in the morning to convey some information from the government to the National Council, I found to my astonishment that this by no means extreme body had made a confession of republican faith.  If I am not mistaken, it was Eugene Landler, later People's Commissary for Home Affairs, who asked me what was the view of the government with regard to setting up a republic.  I replied that the government had not concerned itself with this question up to now, and we should regard it as a great mistake to burden ourselves, amid our existing difficulties and responsibilities, with a fresh problem which might be a source of incalculable complications.  I added that I doubted whether there could be any serious republican feeling in the country.  Landler replied, amid loud applause, that the government was completely misreading the situation, that the capital and the country were loudly demanding a republic, and that the government could not last forty-eight hours as the King's government. I was astonished at Landler's reply, and startled to find one bourgeois member after another rise to repeat his declaration in still more emphatic terms. I looked questioningly at Francis Harrer, the Burgomaster of Budapest, whose sound political intuition and independent spirit I always respected, and who was not in the habit of trembling at every breath of public opinion. Harrer evidently understood my difficulty, and associated himself unhesitatingly with the rest : " Yes," he said, " there is no question that the movement is irresistible. Not only the working class and the lower middle-class, but the rich bourgeoisie are demanding the proclamation of a republic. I have been talking to-day with a large number of leading industrialists, *Hofräte* of the Leopold quarter, and financiers ; and all were condemning the government for taking the oath of allegiance to the King after the October revolution and the arrest of the generals, especially as the Czechs and Germans will certainly declare for a republic. . . . There is no time to lose ; the existence of the government is at stake."

After a short discussion, it was to the best of my memory the President of the Council, John Hock himself, who summed up the general opinion by saying that the National Council unanimously demanded that the government should make preparations for setting up a republican form of State, and requested me to lay its views at once before the Council of Ministers.

I was back in the palace in a few minutes, and asked the Premier to suspend business in order that I might convey this far-reaching decision of the National Council. My communication was received with great concern by all present. There was general depression and anxiety. Everyone felt that this serious complication was unneeded and premature. Sigismund Kunfi gave expression to the general feeling when he said with impatience that he was a keen and convinced republican, but was not inclined to be at the beck of every attack of hysteria which the National Council might indulge in. He had heard nothing of this " loud demand " for a decision as to the constitution of the State. And so long as such pressure did not exist, it would be the greatest of political blunders to add a fresh difficulty to the almost insuperable ones which already faced us. After a very lively and excited debate we finally agreed to postpone our decision till the afternoon ; in the meantime each of the Ministers would try to test the true feeling of the public.

At the afternoon meeting there remained no differences between us ; Kunfi himself was the first to declare that there was an immense public desire for a republic, which must at once be satisfied. The first thing to be done, in his view, was for the King to release us from our oaths, as it was impossible to persuade him at once to abdicate. Even here there were difficulties, but the Archduke Joseph did every-thing possible to secure the carrying out of the government's desire. In the course of the afternoon, Count Theodore Batthyány, Minister of the Interior, and I left the Council of Ministers and visited the Archduke, in order to hasten the King's decision. I had to go again to him later. On these two occasions I was present at several telephone conversations between the Archduke and the King or leading persons at Court. The Archduke again spoke in his earlier emotional, sobbing voice, beseeching the King not to stand out against the elementary desire of the people. He stood sponsor for the sincerity and loyalty of the Károlyi government, he even repeated emphatically that his own personal conviction was that the monarchy was irredeemably lost in Hungary, and that the King's resistance would only make the situation worse, and might endanger him personally.

Judging from the excited telephone conversations, the resistance of the King and the Court must have been obstinate. I was not surprised at it then (the Archduke mentioned that Count Julius Andrássy took the lead in influencing the King in the wrong direction), but now it seems to me a little strange, as we have authentic evidence that on October 30, with the King's knowledge, the supreme army command had instructed the commanding officers on the

Piave front to take a plebiscite of the troops to determine their choice between monarchy and republic, and that those who were asked shouted for a republic.[1]

While I was waiting, the Archduke asked me whether the government wished to proclaim a republic on that very day. " No," I answered, " the view of the majority of the government is that the National Council, as at present composed, is not competent to make a final decision in a matter of such great importance. This evening we propose merely to inform it that we have been released from our oath by the King, and that the National Assembly, to be convoked as soon as possible, will decide the form of the State." The Archduke was visibly surprised at this answer, and my impression is that he was not agreeably surprised ; his reply was : " Indeed ! But will it not be too late ? Will not this delay irritate public opinion and lead to fresh complications ? "

It is a remarkable fact that the leader of the republican current in these fevered days was no other than this Joseph Habsburg, who had hastened unasked to tender his oath of allegiance to the National Council, and had earnestly considered assuming the name of Alcsuti, in place of the hated name of Habsburg. Some of us had opposed this idea, contending that the name of Habsburg had by no means lost all claim to honour, while that of Alcsuti had already been adopted by a number of middle-class Magyars, and this would put Joseph Habsburg in a rather ridiculous light.

The best evidence of the strength of the republican movement is the fact that in the evening several members of the National Council were dissatisfied with the solution proposed by the government, and stood out for the immediate proclamation of the republic, contending that the government's procrastination (that is, its decision that a future National Assembly should decide) would be taken as evidence of weakness, and would destroy its prestige and throw open the gates to every rebel movement of monarchists and counter-revolutionaries. This point of view found many

---

[1] See the excellent book by Karl Friedrich Nowak, " Der Weg zur Katastrophe " (" Towards the Catastrophe "), p. 292. Marshal Conrad von Hötzendorf has testified to the accuracy of the account there given.

powerful supporters, so that some members of the government began to hesitate. Then John Hock made a characteristically courageous speech, pointing out that an immediate decision would be denounced by our enemies as a falsification of the will of the nation. His arguments were so weighty and so unanswerable that in the end the original plan of the government carried the day.

But the public were unprepared to wait for the election of the National Assembly. The demand for a republic continually grew in intensity, and the country districts joined in it with surprising unanimity. Accordingly we convoked for November 16 the so-called " extended National Council," which, amid unexampled enthusiasm, proclaimed the republic. (Before this Julius Wlassits, President of the House of Magnates, the Primate and several of the Magnates had voluntarily undertaken to endeavour to break down the King's resistance, which in the end they did.) On the very next day the Archduke Joseph presented himself again to take the oath. The National Council conducted him through an extraordinarily solemn ceremony, a touching, highly emotional swearing-in.

Graver than any of the difficulties of the revolutionary government yet mentioned, or at all events more immediately threatening, were the sinister developments in foreign affairs, on which we had not counted before the revolution. The conviction was universal among the public that the Entente would recognise the splendid and self-sacrificing campaign which Michael Károlyi had carried on during the war against the imperialistic policy of the Central Powers, and that the national minorities would recognise the loyal character of my peace policy. It soon proved that both anticipations were pure illusions. The armistice negotiations at Belgrade on November 8, the rough, sabre-rattling behaviour of General Franchet d'Espérey, the merciless armistice treaty imposed on us, deeply embittered public opinion all over Hungary. The little general put on the airs of a Napoleon, and showed an ignorance and a narrowness which would have disgraced a Breton village dominie. We had in very truth to summon up all our self-control in view of his Prussian manners. I remember how, as he stood by the stove in the feeble light of the oil lamp and offensively " told us off," the phrase came to my lips, " Les vainqueurs sont toujours boches," and to this day I do not know if it was wise or unwise of me to suppress this outburst. Our opponents, of course, in the wisdom which they have been able to bring to bear after the event, have discovered that our mistake lay in negotiating with this officer while General Diaz was also responsible for affairs on the Hungarian front ; from him we should have received " amazingly good " terms, with the old Hungarian frontier as the line of demarcation ! In reply to this legend there are only two remarks which I need make. The first is that Károlyi opened the conversations with the question whether it was true that we should have to deal with General Diaz himself ; we had gathered that he, too, was concerned with the matter of the Hungarian armistice. Franchet d'Espérey replied with the most categorical " No ! " HE was exclusively empowered to treat with us. The other point is that our main trouble was not that we obtained hard armistice conditions, but that even these hard conditions were not kept to. This agreement brought relief on the most important point : it recognised that the line of demarcation had nothing to do with the future political frontiers, and that on the farther side of the line of demarcation the administration and the maintenance of order would remain in the hands of the Hungarian State.

If only these fundamental points had been honourably observed, and if the question of the frontiers had really been left to the peace negotiations, what a magnificent agreement this armistice pact would have been ! Hungary's economic system would have remained unharmed ; the streams of Hungarians fleeing before foreign invaders would not have flooded Budapest ; all those thousands of Hungarian officials and workmen would not have lost their daily bread ; endless local skirmishes and collisions would have been spared us ; the fires of social misery and national humiliation would not have flamed up so frightfully ! The main causes of hunger, anarchy and demoralisation would have been stopped at the source. But the most perfect treaty with Diaz would have been no protection to us, for the Entente had not the slightest intention of respecting any agreement whatever ; the adjoining States had been given full liberty of armed occupation up to the frontiers already promised them, under the pretext of advancing up to the line of demarcation ; they were left free to set up any system they chose, and to expel the Hungarian officials from their posts.

After the armistice the work of the Károlyi government in foreign affairs was reduced to the single task of continually protesting against the constantly repeated and increasingly brutal infringements of the armistice agreement, until the last note of Colonel Vyx produced the culminating disaster in an impossible situation.

As the poison in a system spreads and attacks fresh tissues, so the senseless and inhuman policy of the Entente daily ripened the spirit of Bolshevism ; and no part of this policy was more effectual than the wholly uncalled-for economic blockade. All of us recognised the mortal danger of this process, which filled the soul of the people with universal exasperation. We warned every foreign journalist, every foreign mission of the danger. It would have been impossible for us to talk of anything else ; every reasonably clear-sighted visitor recognised the *facies Hippocratica* of the unfortunate country, and the approaching spectre of Bolshevism. I may quote Kunfi's words to the correspondent of a Dutch paper who visited us on December 7 :

" Yes, the men returning from Russia are carrying on propaganda for Bolshevism. It is as yet quite ineffective. But if the Entente does not change its policy the position may alter, and the Entente will then be driven itself to take in hand the maintenance of order."

When Colonel Vyx demanded the withdrawal of the Hungarian troops from the Slovak counties, the anti-nationalist " Világ " cried :

" Fourteen million Hungarians will take to passive resist-ance. Let the Entente take over the government ! "

*" Let the Entente take over the government ! "* This cry
grew apace in Hungarian public life. At every stage the
government found itself face to face with irresponsibility,
ill-will, ruthlessness. Finally, on December 31, the
Armistice Commission sent a note to Colonel Vyx showing
the impossibility of carrying out the conditions of armistice
owing to the occupation of Hungary.

The feeling of the hopelessness of the situation grew daily
more universal. I had frequent opportunities of analysing
this feeling in the presence of English and American visitors.
I replied to their stereotyped question, whether there was
really any serious danger of Bolshevism in Hungary, with
this simile :

" Suppose that London and its immediate surroundings
were cut off from the rest of England. That Scotland, Ireland
and Wales were occupied overnight by foreign troops. That
every economic and cultural bond and all means of communication with these parts of the country were severed. That the
beleaguered area were completely isolated from the British
Colonies and the outside world. That English workmen were
expelled from the mines, and English officials from their posts.
And that this process of torture had been preceded by a four
years' war, with millions of deaths, millions reduced to beggary,
many hundreds of thousands thrown into unemployment. Under
such circumstances would not England have every reason to
anticipate Bolshevism ? "

The general exasperation was still further inflamed by
a note from the Entente revealing an amazing cynicism.
The Armistice Commission had approached Colonel Vyx
on the subject of the steady encroachments of the
Roumanians. On December 18 Colonel Vyx replied that
in accordance with instructions received from the Allied
High Command, " the Entente regarded Roumania as an
Allied Power, whose army had the same right as those of
the other Allied Powers to take part in the occupation of
the areas defined in the Armistice agreement." The bright
promise of Wilson's League of Nations, the just peace and
the right of self-determination and the plebiscite, in which
the Hungarian people had placed their trust, burst like soap-
bubbles. We saw ourselves not only defeated, broken and

plundered, but, a much crueller wound to public feeling, bluffed and swindled.[1]

Another disillusionment which quickly overtook Hungary and further undermined the moral prestige of our government, was provided by the national minorities. A considerable section of Hungarian public opinion hoped that my policy would provide a solution for the nationalities problem, which had become acutely inflamed in the war.[2] I myself never shared this illusion. The moment we had lost the war I realised that the political integrity of Hungary was beyond saving. I knew that the war, or rather the infinite baseness of the home administration during the war, had heaped up such a fatal store of embitterment among our national minorities, that the idea of reconciliation and mutual accommodation could win no support for the time being. Even apart from this they did not hold the key to their own destiny ; that was in the " liberating " hands of their kinsmen over the frontier, the young national States with whose swollen nationalism and frenzied imperialism I was only too familiar. Finally, I had more or less reliable information which went to show that the territorial claims of the Czechoslovaks and Roumanians had already obtained treaty recognition from the Entente during the war.

Under such circumstances there were only three aims for which I could reasonably work : to save the principle of the plebiscite and so secure the best attainable settlement of Hungary's future frontiers ; to preserve the old economic and transport connexions between the motherland and the territories to be detached from it ; and to prepare the way for a future reconciliation and federation, assuring complete autonomy to each of the nations living within the Danube

[1] The internment of Field-Marshal Mackensen was one of the events which did most to excite Hungarian public opinion. Bitter complaints have been made against the Hungarian government in this regard. I will not deal with them here, as Michael Károlyi, who is more competent to do so than I am, will undertake this task in his forthcoming Memoirs.

[2] This policy in regard to the national minorities, for which I had fought hard for twenty years, rested on the immediate recognition of the equal rights of all nationalities and the development of national autonomy on the Swiss model.

basin, where possible on a territorial basis, and where that
was not possible, on the basis of the registration of
inhabitants. Thus my policy was directed to the future
rather than the present. I aimed at defeating the Entente
with their own weapons (even though I could not hope for
much more than moral success for the time being) by means
of argument based on the principles they had enounced
and supported by the plainest exposition of economic,
geographical and cultural considerations ; and on the other
hand I worked to preserve for the future the conception of
a free Hungary living at peace in a confederation of Danubian
peoples.

This was the only conceivable course for a politician
whose internationalism and pacifism was a matter of conviction, and not a mere husk concealing the old nationalist
and imperialist aims. I was not prepared to stand for the
other possible policy, which would perhaps have been
preferred even by some members of the Károlyi cabinet :
the policy of submission to the orders of the Entente,
combined with the organisation at home of leagues for the
defence of national integrity and the despatch of secret
agitators into the occupied territories to stir up insurrection
—the policy which is now being so unscrupulously pushed
forward by Horthyists in the Succession States, in
combination with extreme pseudo-Bolshevist propaganda.
I was not the man for this, since in my view the principal
problem was not to save the old Hungary but to create a
new, commonsense and morally defensible international
order; and I should have regarded it as an act of sheer
insanity to push the Hungarian nation, brought already by
the world war to economic and biological bankruptcy, into
new and unprincipled military adventures.

In the interest of the future, therefore, I was compelled
to assume responsibility for the consequences of a policy
which promised very little in the immediate present. I
was not the naïve and unpractical professor at whom the
Roumanians and other national minorities laughed in their
sleeve. I regarded it as my first duty to prove to all the
world that the imperialistic proposals for the partition of

Hungary were incapable of solving the problem of the nationalities, and could only replace the old irredenta by a new one ; and that the guarantees of a better and more stable order could only be found in the genuine autonomy of each nation, and in a union of these self-governing entities on a basis of equal rights for all.

It proves very little to point to the temporary failure of my policy in that environment of overwhelming force and of wildly insurgent national ambitions, amid events of which the culmination is yet to come. Even my " victorious " opponents felt this. I had not the impression that my Roumanian opponents in Arad[1] had won either a juristic or moral victory over me. I warned them, " You will do well not to go too far ; if the Entente continues its present policy of selfish and merciless imperialism, the final outcome of the world peace will not be determined by generals or diplomats, but by Europe's Soldiers' and Workers' Councils " ; and my impression is that this warning (which has generally been misquoted and has aroused virulent comment) was not regarded as merely doctrinaire or naïve and unpractical. And Julius Maniu, the wisest and most cultured man among the Roumanians of Hungary, knew very well that the solution I had proposed, the independence and autonomy of Transylvania in a democratic alliance of the " three nations " on a basis of equal rights, and the complete economic and cultural freedom of this alliance from control either by Hungary or Roumania, might conceivably appear naïve or doctrinaire in the light of the conditions of the moment, but was neither the one thing nor the other on a long view. Even in those desperate days the system of free autonomies kindled the enthusiasm of all the peoples of Hungary. My proposals were received with open joy by the Germans and the Ruthenes, and I should have been able to come to an agreement upon them with the Slovak leaders, at all events until the peace negotiations, if Milan Hodža had not been so definitely disavowed at the last moment by Prague.

[1] Professor Jászi had arranged a conference at Arad with the representatives of Hungarian nationalities and the Roumanians.—Trans.

In any case, sooner or later, it must have become obvious to every impartial student that the momentary bankruptcy of my policy for the nationalities was due to no fault of mine I have never pretended that this policy could be successfully applied immediately after an unsuccessful war and between nationalities in a state of extreme antagonism to one another. I was as fully aware of this, as that the insane policy of nationalist braggadocio represented by the " twenty million Hungarians " cry could only lead to world war and disaster. And in the second place, even after the collapse we might very possibly have had a better result with this nationalities policy if it had been preceded or at least accompanied, as I had always urged, by the partition of the Hungarian *latifundia* among the peasants of the national minorities.

On all these grounds I am still unprepared to disavow any essential point in my policy for the nationalities, and I appeal with confidence to the judgment of a coming generation, freed from the paroxysms of imperialism, nationalism, and Bolshevism. It even seems as if already we may detect a few pale rays of this coming day on the horizon. It is surely significant that at the Peace Congress, Count Albert Apponyi and his colleagues, these former apostles of compulsory Magyarisation and of the " national war,"[1] were compelled to take up and repeat the leading ideas of my nationalities policy—for all that they mangled and butchered them with insincere exposition and unconfessed reservations. An English observer wrote as follows in the " New Europe " of November 20, 1919 :

" Oskar Jászi was one of the very few men in pre-war Hungary who had the courage to denounce the corrupt and brutal policy of the old régime alike towards the non-Magyar races and the Magyar peasantry and proletariat. In the October Revolution he became Minister of Nationalities, but his opportunity of carrying out a programme of equal justice to all the races of Hungary only came at the twelfth hour, when all without exception preferred the full independence which was by then within their reach. Mr. Jászi failed, as he was bound to fail. If Jászi had been listened to by the statesmen of

[1] i.e. the " war " for a Magyar Hungary.—Trans.

Hungary ten or even six years ago, one of the main factors which made for war in 1914 might have been eliminated ; yet to-day he is still not listened to."

These were the main physical obstacles and difficulties with which the government of the October Revolution had daily to do battle. There were also, as already mentioned, the possibly avoidable evils which arose from personal deficiencies in the government itself. I am bound to expose these with the same sincerity. The errors and defects of individual members of the Károlyi government arose partly out of the political situation. The coalition of the three parties brought together men with very different antecedents, convictions and political views. Our fate hung on whether the whole of the county and municipal administration could rapidly be taken out of the hands of the old corrupt and inefficient " Gentry," and modern-minded, energetic, trustworthy men placed in every post. The October Revolution itself showed the one thing that was needful. In the first few days the popular verdict drove from their posts one-third of the village notaries. The Ministry should have continued this cleansing process rapidly and on a grand scale. What happened was just the opposite. The expelled notaries were found employment in other parts of the country, fresh appointments came only slowly, and most of the persons appointed to important positions were unsuitable men, lacking any sincere sympathy with the revolution. The power also passed, as the current of Bolshevism grew in strength, increasingly into the hands of the Socialists, who insisted that only the Social Democratic organisations could successfully contend with the agitation fed from Moscow. This tendency was specially injurious as the Socialist party suffered from a serious lack of suitable human material for administrative posts. An end soon came to their supply of good and reliable men, and the period commenced of the rise to responsible positions of unknown adventurers and self-nominated candidates, by means of recommendations from local National Councils, and later by more drastic means, sometimes under an ultimatum from the workers. In this way a number of purely peasant counties, with hardly a trace of industrial Socialism within their borders, came under Socialist control.

The confusion and disunion were added to by the complete disorganisation of propaganda work. The two revolutionary movements flooded the country with the most varied placards and leaflets and pamphlets and other printed matter. It was a matter of the greatest importance for the October Revolution to secure popular approval of its ideas and efforts. But it completely failed. Not only did the Social Democratic party carry on an extreme Socialist, quasi-Bolshevist propaganda, as it had at least a formal right to do; but the propaganda bureau originally set up by the National Council, and very liberally supported by funds from bourgeois sources, did not advocate the common aims of the coalition, but published the most varied propaganda, from irredentist chauvinism almost to anarchism. It was not to be wondered at if no real revolutionary public opinion was evolved, to resist the extremists of both camps.

But incomparably the most fatal error of the Károlyi government was its failure to carry out, or to carry out in time, the reforms which were to be the justification of its existence, and on which its fate depended. I have already referred to the question of the public officials. I will only add that amid the bustle and noise and fine phrases of the various sorts of local councils, the old county and municipal organisation continued unchanged. Various considerations of home and foreign policy led the government continually to postpone the elections for the National Assembly, although a thoroughly democratic legislature was the only safety valve for the over-heated and dilapidated engine of the State. When we came at last to the elections, it was too late; a constitutional chamber cannot function amid open civil war. Still more fatal was the lighthearted postponement of the fundamental task of the revolution, the partition of the *latifundia*, until under the influence of the successful communist agitation no one appeared to want it. I will deal later with this crucial omission, not to say this unpardonable sin, of the October revolution.

I cannot end this list of the failings of the Károlyi government without mention of a serious defect of its chief. Apart from the duty of historical accuracy, I cannot give due weight to the moral greatness and the exceptional intuition of this remarkable man, without speaking plainly of his errors. A great weakness of Károlyi was his desire to show gratitude to all who had assisted him in his political efforts in the past, even in cases where these politicians were intellectually and morally of indifferent worth. He failed in consequence to withstand the onset of the placemen and adventurers who crowded round him, and failed all the more through his natural delicacy and courtliness. The atmosphere in which he lived more than once prevented him from obtaining a true idea of popular feeling. And in his aristocratic isolation from the common world he knew nothing of the unreliability and the low motives of the average man. Thus in his choice of men more than one blunder occurred which gravely injured our whole administration. Not that Károlyi was the easily influenced man of current legend ; the reverse would be truer. But he rewarded and overvalued men who brought news and material which bore out his pet ideas and convictions. He has paid so heavily for this defect that it may be hoped that he is cured of it. The politicians whom he set up in life all left him shamefully in the lurch, and many have since taken the lead in a campaign of calumny against him.

# Chapter V

# THE MASS PSYCHOLOGY OF THE BOLSHEVIST MOVEMENT

I HAVE frequently mentioned already in these reminiscences how the terror of Bolshevism had gripped the Hungarian public since the later months of the war. As the family in Maeterlinck's "L'Intruse" is obsessed by the approach of death, so the more impressionable members of the public continually seemed to be hearing the rapping of the spectre of Bolshevism at the gates of the tottering structure of class rule. I remember that more than once I had veritable visions of its approach. I still remember the time when the papers gave the first news of the departure of Béla Kun and his comrades for Hungary. It was in one of the first weeks of our government. Nothing was known of Béla Kun save that before the war he had been a subordinate official in a provincial office of the Insurance Department. I have never seen him, either before or since, and at that time I had never discussed him with anyone ; but I realised as distinctly as though my eyes had told me, and I said so to friends at the time, that this was the man who would bring the October revolution to destruction.

This nervous expectation and anxiety was not surprising in a country in which there was perhaps more inflammable material, both social and national, than anywhere outside Russia. It would be a mistake to suppose that the theories of Bolshevism are purely a product of national defeat and dissolution and famine; but without doubt these conditions are a soil in which the seed of Bolshevism strikes root. The actual process of striking root depended both in Russia and Hungary on the introduction into the daily life of the people of conditions which predisposed them to accept the Marxian doctrine of communism, which had become even before the war almost the sole spiritual nourishment of many millions. The central idea of this doctrine is the belief in an inevitable process, independent of our wills, from capitalism to communism through the concentration of industry into fewer and fewer hands, with a progressive depression of the mass of the people to proletarians, and with recurring crises producing more and more intolerable conditions of poverty; culminating in an anti-capitalist revolution, the dictatorship of the proletariat, the explosion of the old order of society and the emergence of the embryo of communism ripened within it. But this process, doggedly prophesied for more than half a century by Marx and Engels and their followers, had refused absolutely to materialise. The Marxian theory of revolution, of the violent eradication of capitalism and the armed dictatorship of the proletariat, had steadily lost ground both among leaders and rank and file. Socialism had grown reformist and developed in the direction of co-operative and parliamentary activity.

This unmistakable waning of the revolutionary tradition had its mourners. They were the orthodox theorists of Marxism, the Syndicalists who gloomily predicted that there would be an end of the labour movement in the corrupt atmosphere of Parliament, and the " full-blooded revolutionaries." These last belonged to a type of which we had almost forgotten the existence in the quiet decades before the war, but quickly rediscovered it in this period of chaos. They were the unbalanced, the hysterical, the degenerates, for whom Revolution was an art for art's sake, the means of quenching a thirst for violence or of witnessing the materialisation of Messianic fantasies. But not one of these revolutionary groups had been able to initiate any powerful or widespread movement. Militarism had proved sufficient to keep down the turbulent minorities everywhere, as these minorities had found no support in the elementary instincts of the masses. Marx had shown sound judgment. Nothing will spur the masses to drastic and effectual revolutionary action—to such action as could overthrow the capitalist order *by force*—save the very extremity of misery and embitterment, destitution in mind and body and spirit. These were the conditions necessary to world revolution, and they existed nowhere in the years before the war.

The war changed everything.  Bolshevism is simply the revival of the doctrine of the Communist Manifesto in an environment in which all the conditions of the Marxist prognosis were combined, not, as Marx expected, through the free development of economic forces, but by an external factor, the war.  The war provided his postulates of general impoverishment, hunger and morbid tension, of the decay of the middle-class and the glaring contrast of extremes of fortune ; it produced the complete destruction of economic liberalism by the various organisations of State control, and yet other factors which Marx could not foresee and which, as we shall see, rendered the advance of revolutionary Communism irresistible.  The trumpet call of the Communist Manifesto now appealed for the first time, not to a working-class élite, but to dispossessed and starved masses driven from their employments and brutalised by five years of war.  The dæmon lying in wait behind the Marxist dogma now had for the first time perfect conditions for starting the conflagration.

And, as in every true mass movement, he owed his inflammatory power primarily to elements of a religious character.  Let us not be deceived by the materialistic and hedonist characteristics of Marxism !  The essence of religion is the subordination of self to an external, all-powerful directive and the effort to attain spiritual harmony with this outside power, to assist it and serve it and bring sacrifices to it, to the death if need be ;  to be indifferent to present and future in the service of the final purpose of this creative will.  If this be admitted, then whoever lived observantly through the months in which the dictatorship of the proletariat was being prepared, could see that the country was full of men and women permeated with religious fanaticism.  In the streets and the cafés, in theatre or lecture room, one was continually witnessing hot and earnest debates in which blazing-eyed controversialists prophesied and discussed with emphatic gestures the approach of the new world order :

" The days of capitalism are numbered, the world revolution is marching in thunder towards us, Lenin will soon have the workers of all Europe united in a single revolutionary alliance."

The new deity was incarnate in these people, in their faith in the inexorable nature of the economic development which was to destroy capitalism and create with the inevitability of natural law—the law of God—the new society dreamed of by all the prophets, the land of peace and equality and brotherhood, the communist social order. For them, let fools try to fashion the future out of thought, let madmen set themselves in opposition to the irresistible course of social development. For them the only wise man, and the true priest of the new God, was the man who despised theoretical hypotheses, ideal or moral, and bowed down to the new order which was in any case at the gates, the new order of world communism.

It is impossible to fail to realise the unprecedented propagandist force of this new religion. It invests what might have seemed the most tentative, materialistic " scientific " theses with the absoluteness and the emotional appeal of old-world religion. The coming of the Kingdom of God, the victory of Good over Evil, the time when there shall be one Shepherd and one flock, the humbling of the rich and the exalting of the poor, and many another moral and social judgment of positive religion, step down from supernatural mysticism and announce themselves as scientific truth. This new religion, moreover, makes none of the demand for asceticism of the other-worldly religions, it demands no restraint and disciplining of our evil passions, neither humility nor self-criticism ; it preaches the doctrine of unrestrained liberty for the passions of the masses. We were constantly hearing this sort of exhortation :

" What ! Do not be deceived by bourgeois religion and morality. Morality is anyhow only a reflex of economic conditions which cannot be amended without the destruction of capitalism. . . If you are vicious or unmoral, that is not your fault, but the fault of the system. So give us the class war, the stirring up of hatred, the accumulation of resentment and embitterment ! And no Geneva convention in this war !

Every means is justified, every atrocity and deception, murder, arson—so long as the end is the destruction of the modern Satan, Capitalism."

Thus it was no mere chance that provided in Eastern Europe a much more fruitful soil for the Leninist neo-Marxism than in Central or Western Europe, despite the virtually complete absence of the conditions favouring communism which Marx had postulated : namely, the decline of agriculture relatively to industry, the concentration of industry in gigantic concerns and the failure of the smaller ones, the enormous spread of a soulless technique. Mass movements are not primarily rational and deliberate : they are the promptings of religious instincts. The unorganised proletariat of Eastern Europe and its industrially in-experienced leaders, the enormous masses from the villages who had stumbled through war into revolution, and whose superstitiously nationalist mentality, intricately entangled in tradition, was only superficially affected by Bolshevist propaganda—this was an environment in which the new religion could flourish. The primeval religious susceptibility of the masses, and the patriotism drilled into them century after century, suddenly exploded under the pressure of Bolshevism as hatred of capitalism and enthusiasm for communism. The good Ruthenes of the Carpathians requested the government to appoint Bolshevist priests and even bishops ! The main support of the old order, the dynastic army, had crumbled away, and no other social restraint had taken its place. And the propaganda of the tiny Bolshevist minority was more reckless than any other in aims and methods, in pace and intensity.

Apart from these general psychological influences, there were three immediate causes of the Bolshevist revolution. The first was the accumulation of social grievances and the backward state of political organisation for which the old régime was responsible. The second was the destitution produced by the war, the influence of the Russian revolution, and the example of war-time communism at the front and within the country. The third was the policy of the Entente.

It is no exaggeration to say that the war provided a telling object-lesson in Bolshevism for a public all too ready to draw facile conclusions and uncritical generalisations. It seemed to have taught the relativity of all moral law, and justified naked force. All was fair in dealing with enemies, and the Sun of war-time ethics seemed to shine most kindly on those who succeeded best in murder and arson and the robbery called requisitioning. Thus when Lenin and his colleagues passed the word not to stop the war but to direct it against the enemy at home, the advice appeared natural and common-sense and unanswerable to the war-tortured masses, who had lost the habit of productive work and were impregnated already with the doctrines of hate and violence. And all the more so since this Messianic religion of hatred not only appealed to material interests and animal appetites, but to primitive religious associations of ideas, almost literally fulfilling the old prophecy :

" But when ye shall hear of wars and commotions, be not terrified : for these things must first come to pass. . . . . Nation shall rise against nation, and kingdom against kingdom: And great earthquakes shall be in divers places, and famines, and pestilences ; and fearful sights and great signs shall there be from heaven. But before all these, they shall lay their hands on you, and persecute you, delivering you up to the synagogues, and into prisons . . . for My Name's sake." (Luke xxi. 9-12).

But not only in teaching and instinctive suggestion did the war powerfully support the Bolshevist case, but in its economic and administrative example, both at the front and in civil life. The common soldier saw at the front little else than a communist organisation. Common supplies, sometimes common production, common distribution. He had no need to take thought for material things : a higher power provided everything, food and drink and fuel, clothes and amusements and sometimes even sexual indulgence, and all on a strictly regulated plan and scale. This com-munism in consumption had its shortcomings, especially when the war was nearing its end, but there was nothing in his sufferings and privations to set the simple soldier against the system ; frequently it functioned admirably and supplied him amply with meat and drink, in contrast with the hungry and precarious existence of the civil population. Thus under the influence of the Bolshevist propagandists he concluded that the system was perfect, and the only thing wrong with it was that it was being worked in the interests of generals and "brass hats." The system must be reversed like the front, and a communism set up that served the interests of the common soldier.

The economic life of the country also influenced the masses in favour of communism. All over Central Europe the old freedom of exchange, the direction of economic life by the laws of supply and demand, had virtually disappeared. Central Europe became more and more a blockaded and starving fort, and in such conditions, with food supplies growing continually scarcer, free competition would have meant death for whole populations. The limitations of freedom of trade and industry, and the organisation of State control, became inevitable. The moment the production of munitions and of food supplies began to become precarious, Central Europe began to turn over to rationing, State production, official distribution, requisitions, price-regulation, and the limitation of freedom of labour and commerce. Independent enterprise was gradually being eliminated.

This was the process well described as the militarisation of the economic system. But instead of seeing in it a necessary evil, the theorists of the war period acclaimed it as the epoch-making discovery of the German genius, destined to replace the indolent old liberal system. Most of the Socialist writers joined in the chorus of praise, to defend or palliate their support of the war. Their argument generally ran as follows :

" This war which has been forced upon us [for it was, of course, a dogma raised high above all criticism from the very first moment that the war had been forced upon us !] would in any case demand our support, apart from the right of self-defence, for the simple reason that it represents the triumph of socialism ! Can you not all see that the war is destined to bring the complete socialisation of the constitution and the communisation of economic life ? This development is making gigantic strides forward. Manchesterism, the child of English selfishness, has been destroyed, and we are on the threshold of the Marxist régime.   The Socialist system of law and the communist economic order are, of course, as yet only half-fledged ;  they have been introduced primarily for war purposes and in the interest of the ruling classes.   But after the war it will be in your hands, comrades, to forge the communism of the militarists into the communism of the workers ! "

The Bolshevist coup in Hungary signified the acceptance of such advice and appeals, at all events among a wide circle of intellectuals.   But for matters to get as far as this, a spark was needed to set fire to the inflammable accumulation of social and national discontent.   The spark came, as already mentioned, from an external political act.   But before dealing with the situation created by the final note from Colonel Vyx, we must survey the principal events of the last weeks of the Károlyi government and the main stages of the Bolshevist attack.

# CHAPTER VI

## THE LAST MONTHS OF THE KÁROLYI
## GOVERNMENT AND THE BOLSHEVIST ASSAULT

SUCH, then, were the psychological conditions during the last months of the Károlyi government. The conditions described, and the national exasperation they caused, grew daily more acute. Perhaps nowhere in Europe was there a more favourable soil for Bolshevist propaganda than in Hungary, and its potentialities were exploited by Béla Kun and his comrades to the utmost, in true Russian fashion. They were no mere theorists of communism ; they preached very practical violence, and some, even general robbery and murder. Arm at once, forcibly secure the control of the State, transfer every industry and all landed property, without compensation, into the possession of the proletariat —then every problem would be solved ; there would be bread and work and uniform prosperity for all ! Rob the bourgeois of his property and his political privileges, take over the factories, shops, banks, businesses and landed estates for control by the proletariat—and the problem of poverty would be solved, and even the problem of the cruel imperialism of the Entente, against which the bourgeois members and the renegade Socialists in Károlyi's cabinet were incapable of effective resistance.

Budapest had become the very type of the *ville tentaculaire* of Verhaeren. During the war and the revolution its population had nearly doubled. It devoured and exhausted the produce of the countryside, with hardly any return but to shake the land with political convulsions. Officials and workers fleeing from the frontier territory swelled its ailing, restless, disorderly, excitement-craving mob. Soldiers returning from the front and from internment added to the army of unemployed, crying out for food and shelter. And the more the economic life of the country suffered and collapsed under the occupation of foreign troops, the more the old Austro-Hungarian unit of commerce and transit fell to pieces, the more distress and unemployment grew in the capital, the more irresistible became the communist propaganda, with its quick panacea, ready to hand, for evils against which the government was doing nothing, and its spirit in tune with the fury and covetousness and murderous hatred stored up in men's souls by the war.

This propaganda grew menacing even in countries of age-long culture and with firmly-planted democratic institutions. In our Hungary, uncultured, illiterate, totally deficient in social and political institutions worthy the name, it set the old order in flames like a match in a hay rick dried in the August sun. The first number of " Vörös Ujság " ("The Red Gazette") appeared on December 10, and within a very few days we experienced the first of a long series of mutinies among the soldiery, disorders in the factories and sporadic acts of terrorism. The communists' tactics were as simple as could be : whatever the " bourgeois " government promised or did, was denounced as a worthless crumb of reform, and in place of it the communists promised everything : universal prosperity and freedom for the proletariat. They not only promised this, but a new form of class-rule government in the interests of the workers, transferring their burdens to the capitalist and the land-owner, but retaining all power in the hands of the people.

Sacrifices in blood and money counted for little with the communist propagandists. Money came in plenty from Russia, and what were the lives of a few hundred or thousand men after the millions sacrificed by capitalism ? If millions of men could be thrown, with the blessing of Church and State, to the Moloch of sordid class interests, what should prevent, who could condemn the sacrifice of a few thousand more lives, a few tens or a few hundreds of thousands even, for the liberation of humanity ? " It is merely a change of front in the war," but the reversal of the front had left untouched the spirit of militarism, of violence and contempt for individual rights. The mutinies in the barracks of the first Honvéd infantry regiment and in the Maria-Theresa barracks, the mutiny in the prison on the Margaret Boulevard, the rioting and bloodshed in Salgótarján, the attack on the offices of the Socialist party organ, the disturbances in Szeged and a number of other definitely revolutionary movements week after week, were ominous evidence of the increasing hold of the Russian religion on the soul of the people.

It is true that the revolutionary masses were not at first recruited from among the disciplined body of the old social democracy. In all civil wars the leadership has lain not with this class but with the *Lumpenproletariat*, the tag, rag and bobtail. In any case we are living through a period in which the line of demarcation between these two categories is a shifting one ; day by day thousands are cast down from relative prosperity to complete destitution. The Marxist prediction of impoverishment has become vivid and dangerously widespread reality. On the other hand, the communist movement won over more and more of the young and energetic enthusiasts. " Young and twenty " sees only ideas, is blind to objections and difficulties. These young people were completely under the influence of neo-Marxism. They had been taught for years that the transition to communism is an irresistible process, that the new order of things ripens of itself, and cannot ripen before the moment which the natural laws of economic life appoint ; that to take thought for the creation and organisation of the new order is "utopian Socialism"; that the true Marxist knows that " the new world does not proceed out of the mind of man " ; that morality, religion and justice are merely bourgeois conceptions, which it is the task of the proletariat to destroy utterly. Can anyone wonder if it was precisely the best and the most enthusiastic of the young men who regarded the tactics of the Socialists as hesitating and opportunist, at a moment when the ripe fruit of power was dropping into the lap of the proletariat, and when the "splendid" example of Russia heralded the approach of the Kingdom of God ?

Nor was it mere coincidence, but philosophically an exceedingly important contributing factor, that the metaphysical standpoint of this young generation was an altogether unique mixture of materialism and idealism, of mysticism and the belief in violence. On one side they fed from Marx, Lenin, Trotzky, Bucharin, on the other from Fichte and Hegel, the mild Rickert and Windelband, Kierkegaard, Husserl, even the mediæval mystics !

The situation, then, was exceedingly dangerous. The old order had been caught between the millstones of the animal appetite of the mob and the transcendental enthusiasms of the young men.

Nothing could avert its destruction. The forces of tradition, even where they were of real worth, no longer possessed either practical or moral efficacy. They were represented to begin with, by no political organisation. With the dissolution of the old army and county administrations, the old parties had no more substance left than soap bubbles. They had proved destitute of any social or moral sanction : they had rested entirely on armed force, absolutist Lord Lieutenants, usurious bankers and a following of paid vote-catchers. The oppressive policy of the Hungarian oligarchy and its indifference to the needs of the people were visited on it now in bitter vengeance. The people would have nothing to do with the old parties which for decades had abused power in the interest of the great landowners, the Roman Catholic Church and the usurers. Apart from the defects already mentioned, the Radical party was of too intellectual a type, too careful to avoid any taint of demagogy, to be able to gain wide support for its programme. The organisation of the peasant farmers had hardly begun. None of the churches had shown any serious concern for the needs of the people, and in this chaos and uprooting of society they offered not the slightest moral basis of support. There did not exist in Hungary a bourgeoisie in the Western European sense. Capitalism stood on a level with the old colonial régime of the Western Powers, living mainly on extortion and corruption, and was a fit tool and accomplice of the political machine. The middle-class had always been

content to remain in complete subservience to feudalism
and clericalism.  No one had dreamed of the protection of
so-called bourgeois interests.  It was only when the hurricane
of Bolshevism was howling around it, that the middle-class
realised the peril to which its lack of organisation had
exposed it.

At the last moment Martin Lovászy, who was Minister
for Public Worship in the Károlyi government, did make the
attempt to achieve some sort of fusion of the bourgeois
parties.  He acted in good faith and with the best of
intentions, but it was too late.  Amid the revolutionary
deluge his action created the impression of a counter-
revolutionary effort.  And it would in fact have developed
into that.  For amid the chaos of the revolution the demand
for a bourgeois concentration came primarily from the great
capitalists, the landowners and the reactionaries who stood
in terror of agrarian reform and a capital levy.  Thus
" the sacredness of private property " became a purely
reactionary cry, aimed at preventing all radical reform.
Even among the propertied classes, therefore, all the
progressive elements regarded these plans of concentration
with mistrust, if not with antipathy.  I saw at once that
despite his obviously good intentions, Lovászy's plan must
inevitably produce violent collision between extremes of
opinion, and assist the counter-revolution into the saddle.
Even Michael Károlyi at first gave his blessing to the idea
of fusion, but I insisted that fusion would mean confusion,
restoring the old inchoateness and absence of principle in
Hungarian politics.  We of the Radical party also rejected
the dogma of the sacredness of private property, claiming
that the only purpose of the cry was to block all serious
social reforms.  I expressly stated that I regarded as sacred
all property acquired by genuine labour, but not property
accumulated by force and fraud, speculation and exploitation.
Such accumulations should be appropriated wholesale for
public purposes.  The Socialists, of course, were still more
pronounced in their opposition to this reactionary concentration, and in the end the effort to form an united
bourgeois front failed.  Lovaszy's ill-success had proved

once more that in politics everything depends upon the element of timeliness. A few years earlier his plan might have been an epoch-making step forward. But amid the clash of revolution and counter-revolution it was no more than a provocatory move towards reaction, doomed beforehand to failure.

The result was that the Social Democratic party, persecuted and despised through decades, and unrepresented by a single member in parliament, counties or municipalities, proved during these months of crisis to be the only organised political force in the country, the only party with a large and disciplined following, the only party with clear political ideas ; and it is fair to say that the fate of the country lay in its hands. Had the party been able to show a wise moderation, to avoid abuse of the almost dictatorial power which the momentary collapse of feudalism had given it, Hungary might have grown into a very promising workers' and peasants' republic, and might have escaped the horrors of the Red Terror, and of the White Terror after it, which have ended in the dictatorship of feudal and clerical militarism.

Unhappily the Social Democratic party proved unequal to this great historic call, although its best leaders tried to obey it. They failed for two main reasons, one arising out of the nature of international Socialism and the other out of the special conditions in Hungary. The international Socialist movement fails entirely to recognise the limitations which should be imposed on political action by what may be called inter-party or inter-class ethics. Each class owes justice, loyalty, and humanity to the others ; any policy aiming genuinely at the liberation of a people, must recognise the supreme duty of serving not merely class interests but the advancement of the whole community ; there are natural rights which must at all times be respected. Marxism has not only not inculcated these principles, but has emphatically rejected them as bourgeois notions. (Though, to do it justice, the bourgeoisie itself has never observed them in relation to the classes opposing it !)

Still less was the Hungarian party able to work in this direction for a special reason : it had in its midst no leader enjoying the absolute confidence of the masses, such as Friedrich Adler or Otto Bauer in Austria. Apart from his great talent and purity of character, Adler staked his life at the blackest moment of the war for the cause of the people. Bauer had taken his share with the people in all the hardships of the trenches and of imprisonment in Russia. No-one could suspect such men of opportunism or lack of courage when they set themselves against the popular demagogues. Even before the war the leadership of the Hungarian party was much inferior, both morally and intellectually, to that of the Austrian party.

Political forces are still blind forces, obedient to nature's physical laws. In the parallelogram of Hungarian political forces, all the old historic parties had ceased to act upon the body of political thought and will, owing to the dissolution of the army and the administration. It followed as by natural law, that the whole system was propelled irresistibly in the direction of the only force left acting upon it, towards the dictatorship of the proletariat.

In other words, the Social Democratic party could only have saved the situation and withstood the Bolshevist advance if it had not taken full advantage of its unrestricted power over the masses, but had acted as though peasantry and bourgeoisie were actually organised. It failed to realise that in present-day Hungary the town proletariat cannot rule alone, but must allow at least equal weight to the will of the peasantry, and that it is impossible either to destroy the middle-class at a blow or to herd it in a day into the Social Democratic party ; it should be a matter for satisfaction if the middle-class were organising in progressively minded parties. The Social Democratic party should have said :

" You, Szabó of Nagyatád, will have a free hand to organise the small peasants, on condition that you array the whole of the rural population against the feudal landowners. You, Károlyists and Radicals, shall be free to organise the middle class elements and intellectuals who for one reason or another are not yet ripe for socialism, but are perfectly ready to support a policy of opposition to the landowners and the great capitalists. Even you, Alexander Giesswein, and your section of the Christian Socialists, must be admitted into our coalition if you are really prepared to pursue a Christian Social Policy, that is, a democratic policy in the face of the nobles and the prelates. The Socialist Party will use neither force nor terrorism against your organising efforts."

This was the only platform on which the essential aims of the October Revolution could have been realised. But it has only to be defined to show clearly the tragic situation into which the Hungarian democracy had fallen, owing to its complete lack of organisation. Those conditions were virtually political impossibilities. Political parties in our day are still non-moral, selfish, predatory ; they are organisations aiming at taking full advantage of any opportunity of serving their immediate interests. To keep a class from using its supremacy for its own exclusive benefit needs an altogether exceptional personality, an anti-Leninist Lenin.

Thus the October Revolution inevitably veered away from the path of a democratic coalition. The Social Democratic Party soon realised that it had no need to abide by its compromise, that it could get much more, perhaps everything. And its capacity for restraint, loyalty and tolerance steadily diminished when its own followers, under the influence of Communist agitation, began to denounce its " feeble, opportunist and corrupt policy." The air grew thick with accusations against the old Socialist leaders. The agitation against " Garami-Scheidemann " and " Garbai-Haase" grew more and more reckless. So, almost imperceptibly, the Bolshevist spirit invaded the Social Democratic Party itself. " Everything is yours which you can grab, either by means of propaganda (propaganda of any sort you like !) or by terrorism ! "

The government fell more and more under the dictatorship of the Socialist Party, which was continually demanding more portfolios, and those the most important—namely, the Ministries of War, the Interior and Education. The Ministry of the Interior remained in " bourgeois " hands, but it was an open secret that Vincent Nagy was compelled to give way before the pressure of the local Socialist party leaders in every important question, and that the administration fell more and more completely into the hands of the Socialists, and very often not genuine Socialists, but mere adventurers and *arrivistes*. The army, as already mentioned, was completely under Socialist direction, but its rank and file fell more and more under the influence of Communist propaganda.

The capitalist and commercial Press worked subtly to undermine the government. It did not dare to attack the Socialists, but tried to crush the bourgeois elements in the government, correctly divining that this would destroy it. The tactics of the reactionaries were therefore to make no attack on the land and taxation policy of the government, though they specially dreaded the latter, but to work upon irredentist and chauvinist feelings ; if they could discredit the government on national questions, they would at the same time be wrecking its social reform policy. This manœuvre proved more and more effective as the country drifted towards civil war.

When the writs were issued for the elections for the National Assembly, the signs of Socialist terrorism grew ominous. There were bloody conflicts with the Christian Socialists; and the Peasant Farmers' party, and even the two bourgeois parties allied with the Socialists, continually suffered from attempts to wreck their demonstrations. The Minister Vass was insulted at an election meeting, and Radical professors and teachers and public and private officials were " punched " into the Socialist party—that was the official phrase[1]—by threats that their official careers would be ruined unless they joined it.

The party openly attacked the government's land law, and carried on a passionate agitation for the socialisation of the land instead of its partition. At the same time opposition to the distribution of the land was stimulated by recklessly screwing up the wages of the agricultural workers. Under the new wages agreements it seemed a much pleasanter and easier life to remain as a farm servant or day labourer,

[1] Literally " boxed on the ears into the party."—Trans.

than to undertake the risks of an independent small farmer !

So the spirit of dictatorship and terrorism grew, even in the Socialist party itself. The " Népszava " flatly declared in its leading articles that if the elections did not produce a Social Democratic majority, the armed workers would make short work of the National Assembly. It had become clear to everyone with eyes to see that there was no longer any distinction between Bolshevism and Socialism in Hungary, and that the elections would be simply a farce. Events were, indeed, racing irresistibly towards Bolshevism At the extraordinary congress of the Socialist party on February 10, which voted the exclusion of the Communists, Wagner, the delegate from Székesfehérvár (Stuhlweissenburg), declared that in the county of Fejér and in the town itself a dictatorship of the workers had actually been set up.

Amid these disturbing symptoms nothing alarmed me more than the fate of the land reform. I saw from the first that this was the central problem of the whole revolution, the complete satisfaction of the land hunger of the poorer peasantry and the agricultural workers, mainly through the partition of the church and other *latifundia* now under extensive cultivation. In this reform I saw the only way to secure the needed increase of production and development of co-operation, to lay the foundation of democratic progress, and above all to lift from the people's backs the heavy yoke of feudalism.

From the first I was deeply concerned at the government's evident under-estimation of the crucial impotence of the land reform. Barna Buza was an alert and well-intentioned man, but entirely lacked the broadness of outlook needed for so epoch-making a reform, and the fanatical energy which could alone overcome the extraordinary difficulties it presented. The feudal interests lay low for the time and made no serious effort to hamper the reform, and the bishops even made a theatrical gesture of offering to give up their land. But behind the scenes there were great efforts made to moderate the revolutionary pace of the government.

For the time, however, there was no serious danger from the counter-revolution. All the more disturbing was the propaganda begun by the extreme left against the distribution of land. The propaganda was carried on by two schools of thought, and both were confined for the time to highly theoretical reasoning. The disciples of Henry George desired to see reform concentrated on the taxation of ground rent. The orthodox Marxists, who still swore by Kautsky's intransigent agrarian theory, desired to save the " superior " large-scale farms at any price, all the more since they were bound to look upon the peasantry as a reactionary class which should on no account be gratuitously strengthened.

The great landowners were plainly delighted at the introduction of the single-tax propaganda, and later viewed the Bolshevist agitation also with benevolence, on the principle of supporting anything which tended to weaken the government. The propaganda against the distribution of land grew gradually to a mass movement ; and the Bolshevist agitators, with their very sharp eyes for a practical advantage, at once divined the point at which to apply the lever which could overthrow the reform. As already mentioned, they screwed up agricultural wages to a level at which it was much pleasanter for the landless man to be the pampered slave of the soil, than to be bent beneath the endless hardships of an independent peasant farmer. (Naturally they never mentioned the impossibility of permanently retaining these abnormal wages.) The large landowners, immensely relieved, laughed in their sleeve as they joined in the attack upon the " backward peasant farmer with his primitive technique."

Farm servants, supporters of the large estate system, Communists and single-taxers united in declaring that the partition of the *latifundia* would bring famine and would ruin production ; and that in organisation, technique and marketing opportunities the large estate had a great advantage over the isolated peasant holding. This argument overlooked two important points. In Hungary the majority of the great landowners go in so largely for extensive culture, that the most backward of peasant holdings can compete successfully against them ; and the co-operative system, combined with small ownership, is able everywhere to beat even progressive large-scale farming. As for the Communists' panacea of socialisation, it had not occurred to the fanatical supporters of this system that the nationalisation of the *latifundia* involved the cessation of the order and discipline and the spur to effort produced by capitalist control, and would thus end in quite as acute an agricultural crisis as partition. The true line of progress would have been to deal separately with the intensively and extensively worked *latifundia*. The former, a vanishing minority of the *latifundia*, should have been converted into true producers' co-operative organisations, not into State capitalist concerns ; and should have been placed under the direction of conscientious and highly qualified experts. It is possible that we might have found a sufficient number of competent managers for such of our large estates as were really being intensively cultivated. The latter should have been partitioned among the landless, such forms of co-operation as can be carried into effect at once being simultaneously introduced. The liability could not be escaped under any radical change, of a transitory decrease in production (which is not by any means the same thing as famine) ; but this liability must be accepted in the interest of a future increase in productivity.

Unfortunately nothing of this was realised by the revolutionary leaders. The concentrated attack made jointly by the extreme reactionaries and the extreme revolutionists visibly perplexed the Minister for Agriculture ; and instead of increasing his efforts to bring his proposal safely into port, he began to set up committees of enquiry, thus placing himself at the mercy of the obstructive tactics of the supporters of the single-tax on one side and of those of the big estate system on the other. Meanwhile, the Bolshevist agitators sounded the alarm up and down the country : this cowardly bourgeois government was going to permit the existence of large estates up to 500 yokes (this was to be the extreme limit exempt from expropriation),

and even to compensate the owners (no mention, of
course, of the fact that in fairness the pre-war prices were
to be the basis of compensation) ; while if they, the true and
exclusive revolutionaries, had their say, they would take every
field without a penny of compensation ; and would give it
over, not to " isolated, stupid, reactionary peasants," but
to powerful Red " producers' co-operatives."

I felt instinctively that if this propaganda succeeded it
would deal a mortal blow to the October Revolution. I
was already overworking on the nationalities question, but
gave myself up, to the limit of my powers, to battle also with
this movement. In the Council of Ministers I was constantly
urging progress with the land reform, and I pointed out over
and over again, that without it no solution of the nationalities
question was possible. I laid great emphasis on the hopelessness of any preservation of Hungarian integrity except
by one means : the immediate partition of the large estates
in the frontier territories among the peasant farmers and
landless men of the national minorities. Had this measure
been rapidly and energetically pushed through, it would
have attached enormous numbers to Hungary in the event
of the plebiscite for which we hoped. Unhappily it proved
impossible to increase the slow and sleepy pace of our government. Twice I tendered my resignation " on account of
the general lack of energy of the government and its
indifference to the progress of the revolution." I was
constantly urging Buza to stand fast, and to remember
always that the Hungarian peasant was the Archimedean
lever of the October Revolution. I tried to persuade the
Socialist Ministers not to be influenced either by the noisy
single-taxers or the Communist demagogy. And rarely have
I experienced such happiness as on the night when Radical
and Socialist Ministers had arrived at complete unity upon
every essential point in the land reform, and a means had
even been found of bridging over the extreme differences
of view between the Radical expert, Arnold Dániel,[1] and the

---

[1] Dániel had for years been issuing a series of important works dealing
thoroughly and luminously with the Hungarian agrarian question from the
free socialist point of view.

Socialist expert, Eugene Varga (later People's Commissary for Economic Affairs). The Land Reform Law virtually embodied this compromise. It would have been an admirable solution, but it came too late. It proved no more possible to carry through the law than the elections for the Assembly. There was only one actual instance of partition : Michael Károlyi's distribution of his own estates.

But I did not content myself with this activity behind the scenes. In many speeches before the party and before the public I urged the immediate settlement of the land question. I emphasised that we were living in extremely revolutionary times, and that we could not afford to ride off on theories or make Hungary a laboratory for social experiments ; if the land hunger of the peasants were not satisfied at once and completely, there was no escape from counter-revolution. I showed the extraordinary dangers hidden beneath the party cry of socialisation of the land, the impossibility of setting up producers' co-operatives amidst an agricultural population which arbitrary government and bureaucratic oppression had kept in a mentally and morally backward condition, and the certainty that the catchword of socialisation could only mean the salvation of the existing *latifundia*. I quoted the example of Lenin, who was certainly as good a Communist as Béla Kun and his comrades, but who was also a politician with insight and intuition, and accordingly had not hesitated, despite all his Communist fanaticism, in practice to partition far the greater part of the *latifundia* among the Russian people. Finally I predicted that if we did not at once provide the settlement of the land question which public opinion in Hungary was demanding, by partitioning the *latifundia*, the feudalism which we had beaten would sooner or later recover from its defeat, regain its old power and reduce to nought every conquest of the Revolution.

Unhappily it was in vain to contend against the swelling tide of demagogy ; the more the Bolshevist pressure grew, the more the Socialist party lost its self-discipline and its sense of realities. The order of the day was the forcible " socialisation " of the big estates. It was clear to me in

December that disaster was inevitable, and as there was
for the time no possibility of any serious progress in the
nationalities question owing to the arbitrary partitioning
of Hungary, I resigned and took no further part in the
Berinkey Cabinet.   I hoped that release from the burdens of
office and from the obligations of cabinet solidarity would
enable me to put forward my views more energetically.   I
hoped also to be in a position to work more successfully for
the furtherance of my plan for a Danube Confederation.

Meanwhile, however, conditions were growing wilder,
not least through the mistaken tactics of the government
and the Socialist party in relation to the Communist movement.   I was in agreement with those who held that no limit
should be set to the Bolshevist propaganda so long as it
used, no matter how recklessly or with what demagogy,
the normal means of political controversy ; I agreed that
the Bolshevists must be respected as the pioneers of a great
though unrealisable idea.   On the other hand I considered
that energetic steps ought to be taken against those
Bolshevists (and they were many) who threw off the restraints
of law and morality, and advocated not merely revolution
but anarchic resort to force and even sporadic robbery and
murder ; these men should be arrested and kept within four
walls, for it was better to maintain a few wild fanatics in
honest custody than to shoot on the unfortunate, misguided
masses.   It was clear that this would become unavoidable
if events were allowed to develop further.   We also believed
that this measure would be effectual if it were adopted at
the outset, provided always that the government entered
upon the path of energetic revolutionary reforms by an
immediate settlement of the land question.   It is possible
that we were mistaken, and that it was already completely
impossible to stem the Bolshevist advance.   But certainly
the government chose the most hopeless of tactics.   During
the early months of the Bolshevist propaganda it professed
not to interfere with it.   Some members of the government
underestimated the strength of the movement, and were
unwilling to inflame it by unnecessary attention ; others as

revolutionary Socialists, had conscientious scruples against the imprisonment of Bolshevist agitators ; there was also a general hope that the Social Democratic party would be able to fight the Bolshevists with exclusively intellectual and moral weapons. The Socialist leaders did in fact develop a feverish agitation against the Bolshevists, the party organ, the " Népszava," denouncing them as evildoers and robbers; and finally the party excluded the Communists from its ranks. But all this was of no avail. Thanks to the foreign situation and the social and economic crisis at home, the Bolshevists, with their greater consistency and their apparently closer faithfulness to the Marxist doctrine, were visibly gaining the upper hand. In the end the situation became so acute, and the violence of the mob against the " Népszava " attained such threatening dimensions, that the government finally resolved to act " energetically"; and on February 22 the leaders of the Communists were arrested. But this action, which two months earlier—always provided it had been accompanied by energetic and revolutionary reform—might have saved the situation, came now at a time when the government had gradually lost its popularity, and only aroused resentment. The extreme brutality of the police, who beat Béla Kun until he was half dead, and Kun's manly behaviour in the face of his persecutors, immediately attracted the sympathy of every generous nature to the side of the Communists. The pressure of public opinion forced the government so greatly to modify its treatment of the prisoners that their confinement was reduced to a farce.

Grist came also from other directions to the Communist mill. The merciless attitude of the Entente towards us grew steadily worse. Hardly a week passed without fresh blows against the nation from its foreign invaders. Professor Apáthy, a biologist of world-wide repute, at that time the Hungarian High Commissioner for Transylvania, was imprisoned ; Szeged was occupied ; and it became clearer every day that we were to suffer a " Vae Victis " peace. The humiliated people of Hungary turned away with disgust and hatred from the Wilsonian hypocrisies, and the intelligentsia saw in Lenin the only hope for the future. This feeling spread to the higher officers of the army. Lieutenant-Colonel Zombor wrote a memorandum glowing with patriotic indignation, and held up the patriotism of the Russian Bolshevists, who were destined to save their country from the predatory imperialism of the Entente, as an example to follow. At the same time news was continually coming in of the enormous spread of Bolshevism in the West. It must not be forgotten that there was an idealist section of the Bolshevists which showed a close analogy with early Christianity. Thus a considerable section of opinion in Hungary looked more and more kindly on the theories of Bolshevism.

Finally the hold of Bolshevism was greatly strengthened by the growth throughout the country of counter-revolutionary movements. It had become evident that feudalism and plutocracy were recovering from the heavy blow which had been dealt them, and were organising and awaiting their chance to strike back. In some of the principal country towns public opinion had been greatly irritated by counter-revolutionary demonstrations. The government showed itself as hesitating and undecided in face of the Whites as of the Reds. The chief conspirators were allowed to continue their work undisturbed, while Szterényi, a man then of no significance whatever, and Szurmay, by no means a prominent leader, were interned by way of assertion of the revolution and to counter-balance the arrests of Communists. Public feeling grew more and more hysterical, and hardly a day passed without the unearthing of a dangerous counter-revolutionary conspiracy. Revolutionary Hungary stood in fear and trembling; it was generally felt that this government was no longer able to save the October Revolution; and if a choice had to be made between White and Red counter-revolution, the Red was preferred.

Moreover, as already mentioned, the demarcation line between Socialists and Bolshevists had been gradually disappearing. The leaders of the two parties mortally hated one another, and their papers vilified one another on every possible occasion; but the Socialist party itself began to use Bolshevist methods against the middle-classes, and even against the bourgeois parties in the coalition. The atmosphere grew heavy with forebodings of open civil war and responsible opinion was unanimous in agreeing that it was no longer possible to carry out the elections for the National Assembly; they would have been a signal for the actual outbreak of civil war. Károlyi made one more attempt to compose differences, and summoned the leaders of the coalition parties to a joint discussion of means for ensuring the orderly conduct of the elections. This conference showed clearly the stage at which matters had arrived. It showed that the Socialist party was determined to stop at nothing to secure a majority, while its revolutionary section, of which Joseph Pogány was the centre, made no secret of its view that the whole " farce " of the election was now behind the times. In private talk Pogány had been suggesting that the next event would not be the elections but the " real " revolution. There was great depression at the conference. The bourgeois parties had all declared that they would take no part in the elections in existing circumstances, since the Socialists were openly resorting to terrorism. The Radical party was the only one which had no complaint to make on this score, partly because it was not a serious rival to the Socialists and partly because the revolutionary feeling of its leaders was well known to the masses. But even for the Radical party there was no longer any reality in the elections, as the process of the " punching " of brainworkers into the Socialist trade unions had already been carried a long way. I showed the error of these tactics at the conference, contending that they were not only incompatible with the principle of liberty of thought, but likely to be fatal to the Socialist party itself, as it could not be in its interest to be swamped with renegades or Socialists-under-duress. In any case this was an old trouble ; we had had frequent negotiations for the neutralising of the brain-workers' trade unions, an idea which was supported by a number of earnest Socialists.

The Socialist party was, however, unprepared to make

any concession. Amid the general utilitarian intransigence, only one proposal for a compromise emerged—a proposal which has its psychological interest. One of the leading personalities in the party advised the Radicals to join the Socialist trade unions, and then, as the ballots were secret, to vote for Radical candidates. I declared at once that this would be incompatible with the moral principles of my party. Stephen Szabó of Nagyatád, the Minister, was in a similar position. All he asked was freedom for his followers to speak at meetings without disturbance, and the cessation of the Communist agitation against the execution of the land law. I took the opportunity to re-emphasise the danger of opposition to the distribution of land, as likely to drive the country people into the arms of the counter-revolutionaries. But all argument was in vain. Károlyi not only obtained no guarantees, but no serious promise that the elections should be honestly carried out. It was evident that the Socialist party was determined to get a majority at any price. It fought against Tisza's ideas of morality in public life only so long as it suffered from them ; now that it stood to gain from them, it adopted them without a moment's hesitation. Here again the front had merely been reversed, and only one Socialist voice was raised in protest at the conference, that of Ernest Garami, the leader of the Right Wing Socialists. Everyone with eyes to see left the conference with the conviction that there would be little reality in these elections. If this was the attitude of the Socialists to us, their allies, how would they treat the opposition parties, the reactionaries ? There seemed no way out of bloodshed and civil war. On the way home I said to John Hock, with whom I had for months been in entire agreement that there was no way of avoiding the catastrophe,

" What do you think now ? How long will this sort of government last ? "

Hock answered after a moment's thought, with his characteristic prophetic gift,

" Say until March 20. About then we shall be thrown down."

The Radical party was the first to act. Its executive

resolved by a large majority to take no part in the elections " in view of the latent civil war," and recommended the members of the party to give their votes to the Social Democrats in order to support them against the reactionaries.

Our whole position was on the verge of collapse ; it needed only the final blow, and that was not long in coming. I will describe it in the next chapter. But in concluding this account of the agony of the Károlyi government, I must devote a few words to my work as President of the Foreign Affairs Committee in collecting and arranging our material and our case for the approaching peace negotiations. The time was very far advanced and no serious step had been taken in this matter. Before taking up the task I agreed with Michael Károlyi, who had by then been elected President of the Republic, on the main lines of the argument which we should advance at the negotiations. I proposed to put forward as our conception of the best solution the plan of a Hungarian Eastern Switzerland, as part of the plan of a democratic Danube Confederation. If we failed with this programme, and there proved to be no way out of the partition of Hungarian territory, we would insist on two principles : that of the plebiscite and that of the maintenance of free trade between the lost territories and the territory left to Hungary. " If we fail even with this, we will at least hold to the plebiscite as a last compromise. Without that we will not sign the peace ; if it is proposed to determine our fate by simple force, we will refuse to sign, appealing to the Wilson principles and to the higher sense of justice of the workers of the world." Michael Károlyi approved my standpoint in every respect.

# CHAPTER VII

## THE TRANSFER OF POWER: THE SCAPEGOAT

INTO this flood of anger and embitterment, increased by hunger and unemployment, national humiliation and unbridled demagogy, there now came a thunderbolt from without : the well-known note of Lieutenant-Colonel Vyx, handed to Károlyi on March 20 in the name of General de Lobit. This note laid down fresh and much worse lines of demarcation, which cut off some purely Magyar districts. In the presence of several witnesses, Vyx added the verbal commentary that the new line was not to be regarded as merely an armistice line, but as a definite political frontier. Subsequently, of course, when faced with the general indignation which the remark had aroused, he denied having made it.

The cup of despair was filled to overflowing. Berinkey resigned to make way for a purely Socialist cabinet, the only power with which there could still be any hope of warding off the threatened anarchy. But even this desperate effort was overtaken by the peculiar fate which dogged the steps of this revolution throughout. It proved impossible to control the course of events. The greater part of the Socialist masses went over to the Communists, the old Socialist party leaders capitulated, and the proletariat proclaimed the Soviet Republic.

Public opinion was left uninformed as to the course of events and the intentions of the leaders at this stage, for the simple reason that the complete suppression of freedom of the Press under the proletarian dictatorship made it impossible to publish any account of facts unwelcome to it. Thus arose the fable that Michael Károlyi not only voluntarily and deliberately influenced events in such a way as to enable him to hand over power to the Communists, but also carried through this intrigue by basely misleading the whole Council of Ministers. Károlyi disposed of this tale in an article in the Vienna " Arbeiterzeitung " of July 25, 1919, " The Story of my Resignation," in which he describes in detail those two disastrous days. Communism was then, however, at its last gasp, and in those fevered July days Károlyi's article failed to secure full publicity in Hungary. Subsequently the Whites have, of course, done everything possible to prevent the truth from reaching the Hungarian people ; their efforts have been directed to creating an impression of Károlyi as a traitor to the popular cause, a paid agent first of the Entente, then of the Communists, a mere adventurer of limited intelligence, ready to be swayed by anyone. In conversation with Hungarian refugees, whether from the Whites or the Reds, I have been surprised to find that this important historical statement of Károlyi himself has remained almost entirely unknown. Whenever I have asked those who were most bitter against him whether they knew his own account, they have answered *without exception* that they had not read the article. I feel bound, therefore, to reproduce its essential passages—the more so as I was present during the latter part of the decisive meeting of, the Council of Ministers. Before the final decision was taken I was myself asked, as President of the Foreign Affairs Committee, to state my view. I am, therefore, in a position to check the main points in Károlyi's statement. He writes :

" Finally Lieutenant-Colonel Vyx declared that if by six o'clock in the evening of the next day (March 21st) an uncon-ditional affirmative reply had not been received, that is a reply completely accepting the terms of the Note, the Allied Missions would at once leave Budapest. This last statement could only be interpreted as meaning that the Entente threatened us with the renewal of a state of war."

Károlyi at once replied that it was impossible to comply with these demands, as they meant fresh and cruel amputations of purely Magyar territory, in gross con-tradiction both with the letter and the spirit of the Belgrade armistice agreement ; they robbed us of age-long national possessions and would completely prevent the economic restoration of the country. The conditions were also impossible of acceptance because the narrow time-limit set by the French note, or ultimatum, and the proposed immediate dismemberment of Magyar territory, prevented any reference of this momentous question to the decision of the country.

Károlyi also saw at once, as he said in his speech before the Council of Ministers, that the existing coalition government could not continue, since the deep humiliations imposed on Hungary robbed the bourgeois parties of all moral support.

"None but a purely Social Democratic government can maintain order in the country in face of the grave disturbances threatened. The actual power has, indeed, for months been exclusively in the hands of the organised workers. If we are not prepared to fulfil the murderous demands of the Entente, we need an united army. In this period of economic crisis and exceedingly bitter class conflicts " (Communist riots were already the order of the day), "only the Social Democratic Party can secure this united army. Our Western orientation, our policy of reliance on Wilson, has definitely been wrecked. We must have a fresh orientation, which will ensure us the sympathies of the Labour Internationale. In such circumstances the existing coalition government can only make things worse, since the first essential is moral and social unity in the government. And only a purely Socialist government can stand against the more and more ruthless attacks of the Communists; the present coalition is being robbed of all popular support by the charge levelled by the Communists against the Socialists of being in the pay of the bourgeoisie and fighting Bolshevism in its service."

In Károlyi's view the new Social Democratic government should now come to an agreement with the Communists, to ensure that there should be no disorders in the country so long as it was conducting this life and death struggle against the imperialist invaders.

He concluded his speech by saying that he would not resign the Presidency of the Republic, but would continue to steer the ship of State in these difficult waters. If the Council of Ministers accepted his point of view, Colonel Vyx would be informed accordingly on the morrow, and he would nominate the new Premier, who would then communicate to him, in accordance with the desires of his party, the names of the Ministers of the new Social Democratic Government. Future decisions would lie with the new government.

Károlyi proceeds to give a full account of the debate which followed his statement, and declares that all the Ministers present shared his view, and the following was announced by the Premier to be unanimously resolved by the Council of Ministers : That the cabinet resigns, and that Károlyi remains at his post and on the morrow will appoint a purely Social Democratic cabinet, which will in turn refuse to comply with the demands of Colonel Vyx.

Károlyi then relates his negotiations on March 21 with some of the opposition party leaders, who also shared his views ; and he mentions that on this day, under the influence of the Vyx Note, thirty thousand ironworkers joined the Communists.

Early in the afternoon of this day, continues Károlyi, the Social Democratic executive met. A Council of Ministers was held later, but not a word was spoken by the Social Democratic members of the government as to what had happened at their party meeting. He inferred, as did the bourgeois ministers, that it had met in connexion with the cabinet resolution of the preceding day and had been discussing personal matters and matters of detail regarding the coming Social Democratic cabinet. The Socialist Ministers were equally silent, both with him and with their bourgeois colleagues, concerning the fact that, as early as 3 p.m., the leaders of their party had concluded a written agreement with the Communists, under which the two parties were to amalgamate, and, in contravention of the Resolution of the Council of Ministers, were to form not a Social Democratic but a Soviet government.

Here Károlyi relates some striking facts which prove that at this final meeting of the Council of Ministers, as at the preceding one, business was conducted in the belief that the government was to be replaced by a Social Democratic cabinet.

Instead of this, continues Károlyi, the situation had already been dealt with in quite a different way. In the afternoon the Soldiers' Council, on the proposal of Pogány, its president, had resolved to support the Communists; and at 5 p.m. he had every motor vehicle, even those of the Ministers, requisitioned. The town guards fell entirely into Communist control, and at 7 p.m. Garbai informed the Workers' Council that a Soviet government was already being formed. By then the soldiers and sailors had the power actually in their hands; and Károlyi and the Cabinet, who were still deliberating, had heard nothing. As Béla Kun stated later, four guns had been placed on the Blocksberg and trained on the central government offices in case of resistance.

He, the President, had received not a word of information from anyone about all this. At 7 o'clock the decision of the Workers' Council was already public property, and Károlyi was invited by a journalistic confidant of the Communists to renounce his former standpoint and the resolution of the Council of Ministers, and to reckon with the new situation. After what had happened he could only resign, and in order to avoid useless bloodshed he signed the proclamation resigning the presidency and " handing over the power to the proletariat," which had already taken over. There was no organised force in existence except that of the Socialists, and the whole of the armed forces—national guards, police, army—were under Socialist and Communist control.

" I made this sacrifice," concludes Károlyi, " instead of assuming the cheap martyr's crown of arrest, to avoid a massacre of citizens, to prevent the useless shedding of blood in the streets of Budapest, and to save the country from the worst horrors of a civil war. . .

" I had good reason to hope that the workers, under the guidance of the former Socialist Ministers, would avoid the shady sides of the Russian experiment if developments proceeded smoothly and without resistance from the bourgeoisie. I had good reason to hope also that the united proletariat would now take up with the moral strength of its unity the war of defence against the amputation of the country."

At the end of his historical survey, Károlyi makes a confession of Socialist faith, and points out that the fate of Hungary will ultimately be decided by the organised workers of the world.

Thus far Károlyi. Returning to the events he narrates, I can only add that when I reached the Council later in the evening of March 20, its decisions had already been made. The excitement was great. Károlyi explained the situation anew to me, and told me of the resolution. I associated myself unreservedly with it. After the Council I talked with many of the Ministers, and they gave me in all essentials the same account of the course of events as Károlyi in his article. The attentive reader will agree that the events of this final Council of Ministers were no more than the logical outcome of those already described. The responsibility of the Socialists, at least for their apparently double-faced activity, must be assessed by the future historian. At most I can establish the inconsistency of their undertaking to form a joint government with the very people who for months had been abusing them in every conceivable way. This is equally true of the Communists, who must bear their share of moral responsibility. Their gains in the deal were incomparably the greater, for they came into power with a sense of victory and as professional revolutionaries.

John Hock and Paul Szende have told me that they fully agree with Károlyi's account. Sigismund Kunfi also agrees with it in essentials. There can be no room for a shadow of suspicion that Károlyi's account is written with anything but complete sincerity.

The Communist leaders have themselves given public confirmation of the fact that the Communist revolution was the immediate result of the Vyx Note. In the meeting of the Workers' Council which proclaimed the Soviet government, Alexander Garbai, later president of the Soviet republic, said " Entente Imperialism inscribed on its banner Democracy and the Right of Self-determination, but now that it is in a position to carry these principles into action it belies them." He proceeded to show that the new demarcation line placed us in an impossible economic situation, " for it must be obvious to all the world that this fresh evacuation will drive further tens of thousands of refugees towards Budapest, while the whole of the food supplies of these territories will fall into the hands of the Entente, and our population will be even worse nourished than up to now. We placed our trust," he continued, " in the intention of the Entente to aim at a just peace. Our trust is entirely destroyed by this new ukase. The Entente is bent on an imperialistic peace. . . . This aim is proved by the theft of our Danube. . . . We have nothing to expect from the West but peace by dictation, and this compels us to abandon the election of a National Assembly. . . . *The new policy for us must be to look to the East for that which the West has denied us.*" Finally he repeated once more, by way of disclaimer of responsibility on behalf of the new leaders: "*Looking coolly at the matter, we are bound to say that what is happening now is happening because the Entente has forced events into this channel.*"

Two days later Béla Kun threw upon the same event the direct responsibility for the dictatorship, in his wireless message " to the workers of the world " : " The reply of the Hungarian people to the ultimatum of the Entente demanding the immediate and final surrender of Hungarian territory to the Roumanian oligarchy, is the proclamation of the Dictatorship of the Proletariat."

It is impossible therefore to deny the immediate connexion of cause and effect between the Vyx Note and this dictatorship. There will be those who now, looking back on events in the light of the horror and suffering of the years that have followed, will say that the Károlyi government was guilty of a grave dereliction of duty when it abdicated amid the paroxysm of national embitterment. There will be those who will add that it was too soaked in the spirit of genuine pacifism and internationalism to entertain for a moment the thought of a war, even a war of self-defence. There will be others who will contend that the very worst peace would have been better than all that was entailed by its resignation. These are complaints which are entitled to a hearing when made by sincere pacifists and democrats. But when complaints of this sort come from the jingo agitators whose motto was, " We will not give up a single acacia tree "— the people who helped to make the Károlyi government impossible by their blind and unscrupulous opposition, and were themselves largely responsible for the undermining of its position, and who yet afterwards signed the Peace of Trianon and used it to further their selfish class interests— the only possible reply is that the Károlyi government may have incurred a tragic responsibility in abandoning power, but at least it acted honourably and in good faith, and was in earnest in the patriotism which for these people is merely a basis of profitmaking.

Never, perhaps, have I felt the magnetic fields in popular opinion so distinctly as on this fateful night. All of us, Károlyists, Radicals, Socialists, even the majority of the Communists, felt in these hours that it was out of the question to accept the crude violence of the Vyx note. We knew the intentions which underlay it. The despair and humiliation, all the meannesses of these six months, had come now to a climax of bitterness. It was a tragic collision between the necessities of the situation and our pacifist commonsense on the one side, and on the other our outraged national instincts and sense of justice.

For the rest, I do not believe that the most servile complaisance before the demands of Colonel Vyx would have altered the situation in any way. The bourgeois Ministers would have been carried away by the flood of indignation let loose by a chauvinism partly sincere and partly prudential. No other Cabinet could have succeeded us but a purely Socialist one, and in that fatal cabinet meeting Kunfi rightly said that " a Socialist cabinet would inevitably mean in the end an accommodation with Communism." There is a general tendency to attribute great historical changes to the last link in the chain of a long series of causes. This is over-simplification. The Vyx note was not the real cause of Hungarian Bolshevism ; it was preceded by a long causal process : the centuries of class domination, the poisoned nationalities policy and social policy of the past half-century, the violence and corruption of the Tisza era, the five years of war, the anarchy which followed closely upon the disintegration of the army. It was these and many other factors which led up to the dictatorship of the proletariat. However, those who must at all costs connect an epoch of change with a personal cause, may without much exaggeration be told that the father of Hungarian Bolshevism was Stephen Tisza, and its godfather the foolish Colonel Vyx who was stationed, through the criminal shortsightedness of the Entente, at the most critical point in Central Europe.

Public opinion, however, naïve, misled, maddened, knew nothing of this long and intricate historical process. All it knew and appreciated was that Michael Károlyi had " handed over the government," and that it was thus on him that the whole responsibility fell for all the suffering and humiliation through which the country was soon to pass, for the agony of the Red Terror, even for the enormities of the White Terror. So in hardly more than a few weeks Michael Károlyi passed from a legendary hero to a hated and despised evildoer. Every great national misfortune demands a scapegoat, and it is a fact that since the first weeks of the Red government the life of Károlyi has been permanently in danger ; it is so still. I remember visiting him at his villa on the Schwabenberg at the beginning of the Red dictatorship in order to warn him of a conspiracy which was being planned against him by some of the aristocratic officers. I remember how oppressive already was the sense of the general hatred, as violent as it was uncritical, which was felt against him in bourgeois circles. I begged him to leave Budapest and Hungary, as his life was no longer safe here. Károlyi stood in gloomy silence. A lean cow, which had been grazing by the hillside, swung slowly past us. She was kept for the President's little children. There was something symbolic in the picture. Károlyi seized upon it : pointing to the poor beast with a bitter smile, he said, with the ironic self-criticism of a Balzac hero, " Look ! *les derniers restes d'une fortune jadis presque princière.*"

The paroxysm of hatred of the mob against him grew continually, and reached its culmination in the first months of the White régime. The Budapest " Christian Nationalists " and their Jewish scribes connected him with every conceivable scoundrelism and disgraceful action. The howls of slander, against which no word of reply could find a paper to print it, greatly distressed Károlyi at first ; he was very near a breakdown, and there was a time when I was afraid that he would die. I could not look on in silence at this barbaric campaign of abuse, and at the end of 1919 I endeavoured to show the true features of this much persecuted man in a literary portrait. It is a characteristic fact that I could find no Vienna paper, and no paper anywhere in Germany, which would publish the article, though I tried a number ; so widely had the bourgeois hatred of Károlyi spread beyond the borders of Hungary. I may add that even the Socialist Press refused him the protection which this single minded protagonist of popular rights had well deserved. This article has remained unpublished. I think it has a historical interest, in that it sketches not only the hero but his environment, and I will therefore reproduce the essential parts of it here.

CHAPTER VIII

MICHAEL KÁROLYI: A PSYCHOLOGICAL STUDY

A YEAR ago acclaimed the hero of his nation, the last hope of a sorely tried country, the conquering symbol of every creative element in the October Revolution; to-day, denounced by those now in power as a murderer, thief and speculator, driven from his home by the danger of lynch law at the hands of the mob, betrayed by most of his friends and comrades in the struggle: this is the history of a personality that should indeed interest all thinking persons, all students of human nature. From the point of view of mass psychology there is still more food for thought in his career, for it throws a light far into the hidden depths of the brusque metamorphoses of public feeling.

From my personal experiences and observation I will try to elucidate this riddle for those who have neither hatred nor love for this outstanding personality of modern Hungary. His enemies desire to discredit him permanently, for they well know that when Károlyi returns to the country the revolution will have recovered its leader. There is every reason why progressive circles in Europe should form a right judgment of the character and the qualities of this remarkable man, for history is something more than mass movement, economic determinism and religious synthesis; it is compounded also of the sufferings, initiative and character of individual men.

This problem of Károlyi has been reduced by most of my foreign friends to an all-too simple formula. They paint themselves some such picture as this of Hungary's late President: an incompetent and excessively ambitious politician, ready, with his sporting and gambling nature, to hazard everything in order to achieve a personal triumph.

He was unable to compete with the strong genius of Tisza in the field of traditional politics, and he was aggrieved because Tisza had subjected him to brutal insult in Parliament at the hands of the gendarmerie. Rivalry and ambition, hatred and revenge, drove him into the arms of the Radicals. Thus the Tory developed into a Whig coquetting with Socialism. For his mediocre personality this was the only way to a political career. So he became automatically, almost unconsciously, the leader in the revolution. But he failed to make any impression on his Entente friends, and the situation in Hungary steadily became more intolerable. The gambler awoke in him again ; his inherited chauvinism was deeply wounded ; and he plunged his country into the hell of Bolshevism. In a word, Károlyi is represented as a man without ability or character, a sporting and gambling politician, a sort of cross between Coriolanus and Catiline.

If such a caricature as this can be drawn by the progressively minded intellectuals, it is not difficult to imagine the judgment passed on the work of the first President of the Hungarian Republic by the jaundiced class-politicians and the simple man in the street whom the Bolshevist régime afflicted so sorely for months, both within and outside Hungary. But those who have any thorough acquaintance with history will reject this view at first sight, even without knowledge of the circumstances ; for narrow as is the vision of the masses, it would be impossible for anyone who had not some greatness of personality to occasion the floods of love and hatred which beat around the figure of the fallen revolutionary.

The very starting point of this crude picture is completely wrong. If Károlyi's only aim in life had been a " career," all the roads to the Hungarian Parnassus lay open before him ; he was already President of the Hungarian Agricultural Union, the most influential Conservative body in Hungary. With a little judicious subservience Károlyi could have made certain of a prominent place in any cabinet. As for his abilities, it is no particular compliment to him to say that he would have had an easy task in competing with the great

majority of Hungarian politicians.  Károlyi has not only all
the outward ease of the old diplomacy, he is not only an
elegant man of the world, but he is also thoroughly acquainted
with Western languages and literature, has read widely and
deeply, and is thoroughly acquainted with the main problems
of current world politics.  Such qualities are not to be met
with every day in Hungary ;  and as we shall see, Károlyi
has other and more important gifts.

But, say his critics, if it was not pique which impelled
Károlyi, what is it that suddenly converted Saul into Paul,
the protagonist of petty vested interests into the champion
of the most modern type of universal suffrage ?    It is curious
that the date of his political conversion corresponds with
that of the blows inflicted on him by Tisza's hirelings, at the
time when the obstructive tactics of his party were beaten
down by armed force.

This again is entirely mistaken.  Several weeks before,
when Tisza was using armed force against Parliament,
Károlyi was already the soul of the Opposition, and it was he
who frustrated every attempt at small compromises or private
" deals."  It was moral, not physical, blows which drove
the conservative aristocrat into the democratic camp.
Shortly after Tisza's *coup* he gave this analysis of his feelings :

" Tisza has destroyed my whole political past.  Only now do
I see that the much-vaunted Hungarian constitution is a mere
farce.  It had no popular support.  With this constitution
anything can be worked.  If to-morrow it is desired to create a
Greater Austria or a military absolutism, all that will be needed
is to send down a new Tisza, and this Parliament will agree to
anything.  No one will move his little finger to defend its rights.
It is a nerveless, corrupt body.  Only a people's Parliament can
remedy the present situation.  The national cause must be
identified with democratic aims."

His more intimate friends were always aware of what
lay beneath the surface of this Conservative magnate.  As
far back as 1910 the secretary of a reactionary corporation
said to friends of mine, " You gentlemen do not know
Károlyi ;  he is a revolutionary, a republican."  This was
of course totally disbelieved at the time, and the speaker
was only laughed at.

Once he was won over to Western democracy, there could for a man of Károlyi's stamp be no further hesitation and no stopping. He took consistently and with passion the course which his changed convictions indicated ; he took it, indeed, with the nerve and recklessness of the sportsman and the gamester. Philistine public opinion instinctively divined that this is the pivot of his character, though, of course, not in the sense of those who label him to break a stick over his back, but in that of a just psychological estimate.

In every genuine personality there is a fundamental energy, there are certain dominant characteristics which remain unchanged whatever the course through which his life runs, as the mountain stream retains its vigour of movement whether it is dashing in turbulent freedom from rock to rock or is shackled to a saw mill wheel or to an electro-turbine.

This Hungarian aristocrat brought to the service of democracy all the imagination and intuition, the recklessness and imperturbability, the knightly romance of the former sportsman and gamester. And it is just this adventurous quality which the man in the street everywhere hates in him —that same man in the street who is prepared to prostrate himself before every successful adventurer.

The great pioneers of to-day were the adventurers of yesterday. Were not Cromwell, Napoleon, Bismarck adventurers ? In popular opinion it is always material success which distinguishes the famous statesman from the wretched adventurer, but the true difference does not lie in these externals but purely in the ethical motive of the individual.

This does not, however, provide the clue to Károlyi's changed attitude. To understand this we must take into account two other fundamental qualities in his character. The first is his patriotism. The service of one's country must go before all else ! Hungary must gain her independence ! Károlyi could never forget that Count Louis Batthyányi was taken prisoner in his family mansion and that his calvary began there. The other is his natural and ingrained tenderness of heart. Democracy for him is not a mere political principle but the formulation of his love for humanity.

A small episode will show his sensibility in the presence of any human suffering. It was two days before the revolution. There were disturbances in the street, the military intervened brutally, a few men were killed. Immediately after this Michael Károlyi came into the National Council, pale and agitated. We feared something tragic had happened to him personally. His voice broke as he asked, " Have you heard, there has been blood shed by the Suspension Bridge, and everywhere they are shouting ' Long live Károlyi ' in the streets. If only I might not hear my name ! "

In a man of this moral and spiritual calibre it is only natural that his new democratic convictions should not stop at the ordinary Liberalism, but should quickly lead him on to Pacifism and even Socialism. His big American propaganda tour before the outbreak of war had a great effect on his imaginative, artistic, highly-strung spirit. The tide of democracy in public life in the United States strengthened and matured his new political convictions. And the mean and hateful war invested his pacifism with passion. He stood his ground firmly and courageously, was not in the least intimidated by the brutal terrorism and the ugly espionage system, or the high treason proceedings instituted against him. And on the battlefield his conviction was yet more unshakably reinforced, and he continued his peace policy with growing exasperation, even amid the rejoicings over victories gained.

There is in him somewhat of Dostoyevsky's " Idiot," who, of course, was so called because, in childlike simplicity, he took principles and human characters at their face value. Democracy, socialism, pacifism, were no mere political tags for him, but moral realities—powerful and almost personal entities with which he lived in a sort of mystical intercourse. It was a fatally dangerous situation indeed for a politician who had never had to do with the actual realities of life, and had always seen men and things from the exterritoriality of his aristocratic home. And once he had arrived at a principle, he would hear no more of obstacles.

I will describe elsewhere his part in the revolution. Here I will only put the following simple question to those who have accused Károlyi of weakness and indecision, or charged him with promoting Bolshevism:

If Vienna or Berlin had had six months' supplies of food, that is, had they been economically independent of the Entente, would they have avoided Bolshevism? Was not fear of the blockade the most powerful of the means of holding popular passions in leash?

What has followed since belongs to the history of the present, in which Michael Károlyi can play only a passive part. He is not allowed to speak, he is unable to defend himself. The nobles, usurers, agents, and lawyers now once more in power are crucifying him in effigy. They even charge him with ordering the murder of Tisza—when the truth is that he nobly sent the garland of reconciliation to be placed on Tisza's coffin, while the party of the fallen giant had not the courage to attend his funeral.

And the hungry people of our unhappy country are apparently looking on with complete indifference while their former exploiters proclaim their desire to execute with ignominy their former hero. *Qui mange du Pape en meurt.* A pioneer of the fight against feudalism rightly applied this phrase to the system of *latifundia.* We ourselves need not be reminded of the Gracchi; there was in Hungary a typical victim of feudalism, George Dózsa, whom the infuriated magnates burnt to death on a red-hot throne because he dared to agitate for land and freedom for the peasants. The present rulers have to content themselves with a figurative execution.

But why does not the people move? The Labour movement has been crushed out of existence, and the peasants are still terrorised by the memory of the blood tribunals and the "rounds-up" of the White officers. And the independent intellectual elements in the country, even those who had nothing at all to do with Communism, are all silenced by the dictatorship of the White officers' detachments. Everywhere the true Russian type is dominant. Michael Károlyi can hope for no satisfaction so long as the peasants of the great plain, the factory workers and the creative intellectual workers are not allowed to raise their voices. The thesis of the Reds has been followed by the antithesis of the Whites, and we can only wait for a just and sensible synthesis to assert itself. This is the external process of world dialectics before which even the most outstanding personality is impotent.

\*     \*     \*     \*

So I wrote at the time, and the many opportunities I have since had in exile of becoming intimately acquainted with the character of the first President of the Hungarian Republic, have given me no ground for altering anything in this sketch. All I wish to do is to add a few fresh details to complete the picture from later experience.

I should greatly like some day in quieter times to describe the proud endurance with which the former petted and sought-after master of the Károlyi Palace, and his wife, bore their trials as proletarians ; how for weeks at a stretch their evening meal consisted of cheese, and how the Countess herself washed their clothes. I should like to describe how they broke finally with the past and with all their relations (with only one exception) ; and how there awoke in their souls a new solidarity, broader than the old one, a solidarity with suffering humanity.

The terrible spiritual crisis which brought Károlyi near to death found its outlet in a wonderful process of κάθαρσις through which he came steeled and ready for battle as never before. He has faith in the cause in which he was the leader, even if he has not always faith in his own personal fate. To those whom he loves he has often insisted that his children should be brought up in that same spirit, and that he would rather see them in poverty than that they should accept even a crust from the clique who had left him in the lurch so shamefully.

He has made some special provision, too, for the contingency of the old economic order remaining intact. If he should again come into possession of his property, only sufficient would be allotted to his wife and children to provide a moderate competence for brainworkers ;

the remainder of his property would serve as a great educational endowment, to be devoted to the furtherance of the well-being and the education of the people.

But the most significant spiritual change which he has undergone is the final determination of his views on life. He has told me himself how, under the influence of sleepless nights and spiritual self-mortification, and of discussions and studies in exile, he has developed from an amateur Socialist into a Marxist revolutionary. And being a man unable to do anything by halves, a man who carries everything through to its final stage, like Dostoyevsky's heroes (I always think of Dostoyevsky's characters when I try to find a parallel for Károlyi's spiritual build), it is natural that he should tend to visualise this conception in an intransigent rather than an opportunist spirit. I have often said to my friends :

" Owing to the peculiarity of his personal and social situation, Károlyi underwent at the age of 45 that inoculation with the Marxist serum which we underwent in our twenties. The reaction which has showed itself at this later period in life is evidence of an extraordinary youthfulness. But its dangers are correspondingly great and undeniable."

# CHAPTER IX

## THE DICTATORSHIP OF THE PROLETARIAT

FROM now onwards I personally played no part in the revolution. As I am not writing a history of it, but merely setting down my reminiscences and direct impressions of it in order to expose the aims and the interplay of the main cross-currents of the revolutionary period, I cannot offer a chronological narrative of the Hungarian Commune, but must limit myself to an estimate of the more important events in this second revolution—events which live still in the hearts of the people as factors in the building up of the future. I was only able to observe the first weeks of the dictatorship on the spot ; on May 1, 1919, I left Hungary, as I was unable to tolerate the complete denial of freedom of thought and conscience which characterised this system, and also because I expected the collapse of the Commune, and its inevitable sequel of White anarchy, two months before it actually came. But my stay in Vienna did not prevent me from obtaining direct and trustworthy information concerning all the principal phases of the process.

I had not a moment's doubt on the general question : it was clear as day that this breakneck adventure of the Hungarian proletariat was doomed to disaster from the outset, and that it would bury beneath its ruins all the cultural and democratic gains of the past quarter of a century. I remember how in the first days of the dictatorship, when everyone was jubilant and the whole of the Press was hysterically competing in submissiveness to the new rulers, one of the leaders of the new régime asked my view of its prospects. I replied : "The dead ride hard."[1]

[1] That is, disasters would soon come, riding as hard as death.—The quotation is from Bürger's " Lenore."—Trans.

This was also the view of all the more clearsighted among the Socialists ; in their own circles they made no secret of their one reason for taking part in the government : to prevent the worst conflicts if possible, and so perhaps to save the Labour movement from final destruction.

In commenting on the course of the proletarian dictatorship I was able to go beyond general impressions ; I had frequent opportunities of stating my views in detail in the circle of my colleagues.    I claimed that while the method of the dictatorship might serve to bring the capitalist system by main force to its end, it was completely unsuited to the task of building up a fresh system of production and distribution, of any intricacy of organisation, that would work.    If as the result of the insane policy of the Entente, there was to be a further spread of Bolshevism, that development could only plunge us again into mediævalism.    Despite all its horror and madness, it would still be an advance, in the same sense in which the early Middle Ages brought an advance by destroying the slave-capitalism of antiquity, itself incapable of reform from within.

For this reason I gave to the members of the Radical party on its dissolution the final word of advice that they should accept neither political nor moral responsibility for the Communist régime, but should on no account attempt to copy the sabotage of the Russian intelligentsia ; leaving politics aside, they should bend their minds to assisting the new system in the administrative and economic fields.    In giving this advice I had in mind not only the absolute hopelessness of opposition on the part of the brainworkers, which could only add for no purpose to the merciless brutality of the system, but also the immense advantage of using the opportunity to put the Communist system to a practical test.    I was aghast at the hold which Lenin's extreme application of the mechanical, fatalistic Communism of the Marxists had obtained over the masses, with its extraordinary surface simplicity and lucidity, and at the completeness with which it excluded all possibility of a footing from any other, and in my view more fruitful, conception of Socialism.    The cause of the liberation of humanity has come to a *cul-de-sac* from which there is no way out except through practical experience of the lessons the difficulty offers. I was anxious, therefore, that the Communist experiment should have the fairest possible chance, and that no one should be able to say that it had failed through the sabotage of the brainworkers. If it succeeded, so much the better ; it would have opened the way to a new world order. If it did not succeed, then, though at the price of terrible sacrifices, the Russian and Hungarian examples would at least have " freed humanity from the tyranny of a dogma which is at present discrediting every other conception of the liberation of the human race."

To-day I can see that once more I had over-estimated the good sense of humanity. The most brutal facts are powerless against strong popular feeling. I had soon the paralysing experience of seeing that the monstrosities of the Russian and Hungarian experiments had hardly any influence on the ideas of those who were carrying them out. Instead of correcting their theories to bring them into correspondence with facts, the facts were twisted to fit the theories ; instead of saying " Marx or Lenin went wrong here," search was made for traitors, and some scapegoat was found. Once more Dostoyevsky's words came true :

" It is not sufficient for people to show the error of our fixed ideas, they must also offer a substitute for them, they must be able to replace them with something else on the same scale ; otherwise in my heart I refuse to be convinced ; let them bring what demonstrations they will, I will not give up my pet ideas at any price, even if I must do violence to my own sense of logic to preserve them."

But I was not alone in my rationalist optimism. Rudolf Goldscheid had the same view when he hurried to Budapest in the first weeks of the commune, to study on the spot the methods of the dictatorship. It encouraged me to see that this Marxist Social Democrat judged the situation of the moment in every essential respect precisely as did I, the anti-Marxist. It was clear to him also that the methods of the Commune could lead nowhere; that there would be a bitter vengeance for its contempt of all considerations of individual justice and of all moral scruples; that it is not possible simply to wipe the old economic order off the slate in a single night.   The final judgment of Goldscheid was that even if no international complication came to upset the dictatorship, the organised workers would themselves over-throw it ; for the proletariat of the Western countries there was only one lesson to be drawn from its policy : how Communism must on no account be introduced !

My unfavourable judgment of the Commune rested mainly on three groups of facts and considerations :

My studies in recent years led me to the deduction that a number of the fundamental theses of Marxism will not stand criticism.   Economic life without markets, price regulation by government dictation instead of through the free play of supply and demand, the State regulation of production and distribution—all this, in an economic system of any degree of development and differentiation, is either altogether impossible, or only possible with the aid of such a development of State omnipotence, militarism and bureaucracy, that in comparison with it the corresponding evils under capitalism are but infantile ailments.   I came, therefore, to the conclusion that the mechanical State Communism of the Marxists cannot be a higher stage of development, as it would completely absorb the freedom and self-direction of the individual.   Finally it became clear to me that some other method of abolishing unearned incomes must be found, and that the searcher for the true Socialism of the future must follow in the steps of Smith, Carey, Proudhon, Dühring, Henry George, Kropotkin and Oppenheimer ; he will find it in a co-operative system that allows a wide field for competition and initiative, and narrows down the sphere of activity of the State.   Otto Bauer has rightly summed up the ideals of Western as contrasted with Prussian Socialism, but, it seems to me, in anything but an orthodox Marxist spirit : " In contrast with Prussianism " (and how much more in contrast with Russian Bolshevism) " we must set up an entirely opposite ideal of the State, rooted in the need of individual liberty, nourished by the active work of the mass of mankind, and pointing to the ultimate aim of self-government by the workers." This ideal is not to be found in the Marxist doctrine of a blind catastrophic process ; it belongs to the line of thought of British Guild Socialism, which builds upon good sense, education and moral discipline.

The second group of facts from which I deduced the inevitable collapse of Communism, was concerned with economic organisation and social life in Hungary. Even viewing things with the eye of the sternly orthodox Marxist, it seemed to me to be unquestionable that in view of the primitive condition of agriculture in Hungary, in view of her undeveloped industry, her poor technical equipment, the overwhelmingly peasant character of her population, and above all the extraordinarily low moral and intellectual level of her proletariat, to expect from her the great step of the transition to Communism (or for that matter to expect it from Russia !) would be a social illustration of the fable of the frog and the bull. Even the Marxist doctrine would suggest that true Communism could only commence in Europe among the leading Western industrial States.

The third group of facts was furnished by the Bolshevist experiment in Russia. Although at that time there were few reliable reports of events in Russia, such few credible data as I had made it quite clear to me that there was no question of any true development of Communism in Russia; that what was in progress there was nothing but the extirpation of feudalism, the partition of the great estates, and the abolition of mediæval privileges under a Communist banner and with the aid of the iron broom of the dictatorship of the proletariat. At that time this view of mine was intuitive ; now, especially after the masterly investigations of Otto Bauer and the account of such eye witnesses as Bertrand Russell, Peter Kropotkin and Wilhelm Dittmann and the exceedingly cautious reports of the British Labour Party, it has proved to be a well-grounded judgment. Russian Communism has performed two gigantic tasks. The first was the final partition of the *latifundia* among the landless classes—a pre-eminently individualistic, anti-Com-munistic act. The second was the destruction of Western capitalism in Russia and the attempt to replace it by a despotic Socialism, a sort of State capitalism.

These deductions and observations were all confirmed by the experience of Communism in Hungary. The experiment was, of course, too short-lived to enable its logical results to develop to their final consummation, but anyone who passes them in review without fanaticism or prejudice has the clearest possible picture of Bolshevist doctrine in practice.

It is only possible to note briefly the outstanding events of the proletarian dictatorship in Hungary as they affected men and things, the events which account for the endless mass of hatred and false witness which grew up around the dictatorship, and those which have played a part of more or less importance in the chain of historical development.

The first fact to note is that in its first weeks the proletarian dictatorship was thoroughly popular, strange to say, among the middle-class and the petty bourgeoisie. There were two reasons for this. The first was the complete ignorance of matters political and economic among the middle-class in Hungary. It had not the faintest notion of the significance of Bolshevism, or of the dangers involved in the Communist experiment. And day by day it read in its papers (for the whole of the Press was compelled to support the Bolshevist policy) of the marvellous age which was dawning, of the ending of poverty and of great wealth, of the care of the State in future for the provision of a decent livelihood, free from anxiety, for every one of its honestly working citizens. A lady of my acquaintance was, for instance, informed in dead seriousness by a quite well-educated dressmaker's assistant, on noting the enormous defects of her post-war wardrobe, that in future every woman who worked would get from the Soviet fatherland, among other things, two good blouses a year.

But it must not be supposed that the Hungarian Press was merely performing forced labour for the dictatorship, at all events in the first weeks. I make bold to maintain that on the contrary the great majority of the journalists

were at first serving the commune with enthusiasm
Hysterical by nature, the Hungarian journalists hastened
to prostrate themselves before the new rulers ; prostitute
by habit, they served now as in the past the interests of the
men who paid them.   And not only the journalists.   Nearly
the whole of the Hungarian intellectual middle-class showed
the same lack of character and backbone, and served the
dictatorship as they had before served capitalism, or Tisza,
or the war spirit, or the October Revolution.   Let me not be
misunderstood.   I am not reproaching the Hungarian
intelligentsia for its active support of the commune.   On
the contrary, that is just what I advised those among the
brainworkers who belonged to my circle to do.   Nor
were there only the higher reasons I mentioned for their
support ;  their personal position justified it, inasmuch as
the tendency of the ruling system was to starve to death all
who did no work in the proletarian State.   I could therefore
offer nothing but praise if the Hungarian intellectuals had
performed honest and decent work, if they had advanced the
cause of order and conscientious citizenship, and with their
superior education and self-control had endeavoured to
soften the needless brutalities and excesses of the system.
But what happened was the direct opposite of this.   The
majority of the Hungarian intellectuals not only associated
themselves with the dictatorship but tried to out-howl the
wildest of the wolves.   The usual Hungarian chase for
government posts began, and of course the most reactionary
and clerical and militarist elements became the loudest
shouters, and the most merciless and uncompromising
executioners for the Communist system; while persons who
for decades had been selflessly serving the cause of social
progress, were pushed everywhere into the background by
these greedy bands of placemen.   We had been made to
witness the third prostitution of Hungarian intellect within
five years, and this third episode outdid in loathsomeness
all that we had experienced in the war and the October
Revolution.   Yet it is intelligible, as subservience to the
ruling clique not merely represented the chance of a fat
job, but was necessary for a bare living, since to be without a

trade union card meant to run a considerable risk of death by starvation.

The second reason for the popular acceptance of the dictatorship lay in the demagogic, unprincipled way it played upon the popular chauvinism, and awakened in the masses, after their national humiliation, a belief that the Soviet Republic would enter into hostilities against the new and imperialistic neighbouring States and would quickly reconquer the lost territories. This enthusiastic readiness for *revanche* accompanied the conflicts with the Czechs, and the great successes of the Red army were attributable at least as much to nationalist as to Socialist feeling among the soldiery. The glamour of this war of national liberation was only destroyed when Béla Kun gave way before Clemenceau's ultimatum and abandoned the recovered territories again to their conquerors. Nothing shows better the strength of the nationalist element in the Bolshevist movement than the fact that everyone recognised the fatal nature of this step taken by Béla Kun, even those who regarded it as unavoidable. Thus in a public sitting of the Soviet the Commissaries Pogány and Szamuély called the attention of the proletariat to the fact that to order the victorious Red army to give up again the territories which it had won back, was to run the risk of its speedy demoralisation.

In any case the rosy views of the dictatorship to which I have referred did not last long, and every day the gradual revulsion of public feeling, both among the middle and working classes, was more plainly visible. Cautiously but inevitably, compulsory military service was introduced again, and the population was plunged once more into all the personal suffering of war; while the economic situation grew continually worse through the blockade, the increasing industrial and commercial disorganisation, and the growing passive resistance of the peasants. But the genuine Bolshevists at the head of affairs were far from abandoning their glowing optimism. They clearly felt that they had burnt their boats, and that their group was now master of the situation. If, on the other hand, the system crashed, they would not only lose everything but would quite possibly not even escape with their lives. Next to this instinct of self-preservation, the principal food of their revolutionary fire was the myth of the imminent world-revolution. They played a thousand variations on this prophecy in all their literature and at all public meetings. Whoever dared to doubt this article of their faith, was set down at once as a counter-revolutionary. If the most insignificant strike or disturbance occurred abroad, they at once concluded that the collapse of the capitalist order the world over was only a question of weeks or even days. Thus the People's Commissary Hamburger proclaimed on April 7 at Kaposvár, with a prophetic fire which brooked no opposition, " We have a deep conviction that in a few weeks the whole of Europe will be in flames, and everywhere the proletarian dictatorship will take the helm ! "

An element which added to the ardour and uncritical nature of this revolutionary faith, was the fact that the true Communists remained to the end a tiny minority of the population, bound together by the bonds of personal contact, friendship, and comradeship, shut off from all outside influence and criticism, and so enabled to preserve their moral and intellectual cohesion. If I were to set the number of the determined leaders, those capable of initiative, at fifty, and those whom the Jacobins would have called " citoyens actifs" (that is to say, those who had absorbed into their blood the propaganda of the Russian dictatorship, and who consequently stood in decided opposition to the old Social Democratic party) at five thousand[1] for the whole country, I should certainly have overstated rather than understated the number. (Incidentally, the Jacobin period of the great French Revolution constantly shows extraordinarily close and enlightening analogies with the proletarian dictatorship.)

This tiny minority was the driving force of the proletarian dictatorship. It was able up to the end to impose its will over the heads of the old Socialist and trade union leaders,

---

[1] A Socialist critic of my book who had himself been a people's commissary *malgré lui*, commented on this that my figures are greatly exaggerated, and that the real Communist camp was much smaller.

and even of the masses. Its dictatorship within the
dictatorship is to be accounted for by various circumstances,
by the prestige of victory over those who had been associated
with the bourgeois government, and were now being represented to the revolutionary masses as semi-traitors; by the
anathemas of the Russian Soviet Papacy against the "Social
Traitors," and by its blessings on Kun and his friends;
by the firm faith and boundless energy of the Communists,
in contrast with the more critical spirit and more hesitating
tactics of the trade union aristocracy. A yet more important
element in the strength of the Communists was their power
at all times of mobilising the great masses of the tag, rag
and bobtail in opposition to the moderate Socialists. This
actually occurred at one moment during the dictatorship,
towards the end of May, when it was feared that the
infuriated masses would set aside Béla Kun as too moderate,
and deliver over the power to a Terrorist dictatorship under
Szamuély.

For the rest, the leading Bolshevists were of very different
types, and a close acquaintance with the various species is
necessary for an understanding of the psychological
atmosphere of the Communist revolution. There were, to
begin with, the orthodox, fanatical Leninists, bolshevised
by the war and the Russian revolution, swearing by the
revolutionary and subversive passages in Marx as the faithful by the Koran. These were men who knew no doubts
or scruples, intellectual or moral. For them the problem
was portentously simple : all private property must be
confiscated without more ado, all production and
distribution become the business of the State, the bourgeoisie
must be ruined politically and economically (this class being
taken as including the widest circles of the lower middle-
classes and peasantry), or if it resisted it must be literally
exterminated ; finally all capitalist States must be set
ablaze by propaganda and by force, until the World Soviet
Republic emerged. Nothing could prevent the realisation
of this programme, as under the Marx-Leninist natural laws
of economics it must inevitably come to fulfilment. This
was the most active of the groups, the most robust and

untiring; it was the actual directing element of the Communist revolution. Alongside its extremist utopism it was quite ready to haggle and compromise and make shady bargains, in short to follow all the old methods of capitalist politics.

The second group was as dogmatic and fanatical as the first, but differed in that it was composed of the intellectually unhinged, a group totally incapable of any comprehension of the situation and the conditions. The central obsession of these people was the idea of massacre as a simple and rapid panacea. If the bourgeoisie were exterminated in a night, there would be an end once for all of the danger of counter-revolution. These people were completely under the influence of the *idée homicide* of which Taine has given a masterly description. Fortunately the more sober elements in the dictatorship were able to hold this group in check. During the four and a half months of the dictatorship its victims numbered at the most four hundred. Four hundred deaths is a terrible thing in the eyes of the moralist, but the figure is small in comparison with the loss of life in civil wars in the past, especially when it is borne in mind that it includes those killed in armed counter-revolutionary risings. It is also certain, though this does not absolve the Red Terror from its heavy responsibility, that the White counter-revolution which followed it claimed at least ten times as many victims.

The third type of Bolshevist experimentalists was a complete contrast to the other two. Its representatives were primarily religious, even mystics, numbers of them were nurtured upon German idealism, and ethically set themselves a rigorous standard ; but they saw no way of release from the sins and enormities of capitalism and war except through ruthless force. Their attitude was Messianic. During the dictatorship several of the more loosely attached members of this group were driven by the shock of their experiences to Christian Tolstoyanism.

This Messianic faith was so strong in the whole movement that it did not shrink even from a baptism of blood. Thus there were elements who demanded the continuation of the hopeless offensive, even at the cost of the total destruction of the Hungarian Labour movement. It was to these elements that Sigismund Kunfi referred in the Soviet session on June 19 :

" In my view the conception advanced by comrades Pogány and Szamuély of the rôle and function of the Hungarian proletariat in the international revolution, amounts to this, that they ascribe to the Hungarian proletariat the rôle of saviour of the world, and that if necessary they will have it bleed to death in performing its part. This conception of Messianic Socialism . . . I do not share."

In any case the apostles of this pseudo-Messianism recommended it for others to follow, not themselves. Thus Béla Kun shouted on May 3 that " We must fight to the last round of ammunition." But the same Béla Kun, when the proletariat of Budapest was suffering appallingly from the raging White Terror, had not the slightest hesitation in taking a special train, not to take his promised place at the barricades, but to escape to Vienna.

At the same time it is a duty to recognise the self-sacrificing character of some of the Bolshevist leaders. I have credible authority for the statement that Otto Korvin, who had been brutally tortured by the Whites, gave his brother this farewell message before his execution : " If you come back to power, forget what was done to me." If this proves true, it shows at least one case of genuine heroism. There were many instances of enthusiasm for their ideal among the simple combatants in the ranks. I myself know young girls who to this day are suffering the slow death of perpetual internment, though one word to belie their convictions would set them free at once. These women, delicate and in feeble health, have preferred the dirt and privations of the internment camp to a denial of their Communist faith. I know of scenes which are truly reminiscent of the faith and enthusiasm of the early Christians.

In this atmosphere of ardour and fanaticism and intolerance, it was only natural that the dogma should materialise that all means were permissible which would help on Bolshevism and world-revolution. The end justifies the means : this Jesuitical principle was the crux of the moral system of the Bolshevists ; even their humaner and more moderate elements did not venture to attack it, so intimately was it bound up with the movement.   Thus there were none to protest when in the session of the Workers' Council on May 3, Béla Kun proclaimed the new ethics : " I do not admit the distinction between the moral and the immoral ;  the only distinction I know is the distinction between that which serves the proletariat and that which harms it."  Never was moral relativity in the economic field more openly proclaimed.   The nationalist ethic of " my country, right or wrong," was replaced by the proletarian ethic of " my class, right or wrong."   The former brought us in the end to a world war.   The latter, if it really gains hold over the masses, will bring universal civil war.

On the intellectual side a dogmatic faith in an inevitable catastrophic collapse of the present-day world order, on the moral side the rejection of all moral restraints as mere bourgeois narrowness ;  on the political side an uncritical trust in violence and terrorism and in compulsion as the basis of organisation—these are the essentials in the Bolshevist synthesis.   The Bolshevist type may safely be described as a purely town product ; it has lost all association with nature and the soil.   It not only knows nothing of the village, that is, of at least three-quarters of Hungarian social life, but instinctively it hates it, as an unfamiliar and a foolish and backward world.   In the peasant it sees merely stupidity and reaction, and the youngest and the longest-haired propagandist youth feels for him much the same contempt as the white American for the negro. Naturally it must be a very low type of humanity which still wallows in the traditional religious and national super- stitions, and whose thick skull is impenetrable by the saving truths of Marxism and the mysteries of Freudism, that new idol of the Communist youth !

This partly solves the riddle why at least 95 per cent. of the Communist leaders were Jewish.  The predominantly rationalistic and non-moral quality of the average Com- munist is strikingly similar to that of the historic Jewish type. Both types show the same lack of instinctive and natural promptings, the same lack of tradition, the same proud exclusiveness, the same call to deliver a Messianic message, the same impatience of other ways of thinking, the same over-development of materialist hedonism in some, and absolutely oriental, life-spurning mysticism in others. It is clear, too, that this was the first opportunity which the Jewish nation had had of unconfined activity in a movement of worldwide importance, and of giving free rein to powers which had slumbered in it for centuries.

But the theory frequently put forward in reactionary circles, that Bolshevism is a purely Jewish product, is altogether mistaken. All that can truly be said is that the Jewish mind proved peculiarly receptive to the twin ideas of a catastrophic revolution and a Communist kingdom of Heaven. It should not be forgotten that the opposition between Jewry and Christendom is much more acute in Eastern than in Western Europe. The Hungarian people is much more attached to the soil, more conservative, more mentally indolent, than the Western peasant populations. And the Hungarian ghetto is much less assimilated than in the West, it is virtually an independent body in society, which has never been really in contact with the traditional spirit of the country. The opposition between the villages and the town ghettos in Hungary has almost a mediæval hue. The Magyar peasants, with their Turkish-Turanian origin, their racial phlegmatism, their rustic torpor and their concentration on pigs and crops, increased by the oppression of the feudal lord and the moneylender, were little fitted to assimilate Western ideas ; this task had been accomplished mainly by foreigners among them, and above all by the Jews, who with their great receptivity, their international outlook, their exclusion (more through antipathy than actual legislation) from the governing classes, had taken into their own hands the development of intellectual commerce, as formerly they had led in the commerce in goods. The Hungarian Jews played a leading part not only in Bolshevism but in every economic and intellectual movement, and also in spheres which had been closed to them for centuries. They had begun, for instance, to take a leading place in agriculture as great landowners and directors of large-scale agricultural enterprises, and similarly in the Press, in politics, in art and literature, in every walk of life, so that it might have been supposed that 90 per cent. of the population was Jewish, instead of a tiny minority.

CHAPTER X

A CRITICAL ESTIMATE OF THE PROLETARIAN
DICTATORSHIP

THE Soviet Republic was mainly concerned with three
problems :

1. The socialisation of production and distribution.
2. The destruction of class rule, bureaucracy and
   militarism.
3. The creation of an intellectual and moral atmosphere
   of Communism.

The best course will be to consider the work of the
dictatorship separately in connexion with each of these
problems.

Under the communalisation of production every banking
and exchange institution, every concern with more than
twenty employees, all landed property exceeding 100 yokes
and every building not included in the category of workmen's
dwellings, was converted into " common property." The
undertakings and properties taken over were " socialised."
This socialisation is the central principle of Soviet economic
organisation, and came next in importance to the belief in
the world revolution among the myths of the dictatorship.
But there were the most confused ideas as to the nature of
this principle ; one may recall, for instance, the angelic
naiveté of the following dictum of Commissary Hevesy,
*four days* after the dictatorship was proclaimed :

" In the People's Commissariat for Socialisation, by working
twenty-three hours a day we have in the past four days organised
nearly every section of industry.   And even where it has not
been possible yet to complete taking over the concerns, they are
already working under the direction of a Commission of Control."

With no less optimism, Commissary Böhm declared on April 18 that :

" We have the advantage over Russia that we have been able to begin reconstruction at once, and have succeeded within four weeks in socialising more than 1,000 concerns, while the Russians socialised no more than 513 in a whole year."

These and similar declarations reveal the mechanical and arbitrary tendencies of the dictatorship. It failed to take account of the fact that socialisation is primarily a moral recasting, a product of education and organisation ; it went on the assumption that the problem is to be solved by taking an inventory and appointing a number of commissaries for production and control commissions.

Nowhere was this paper socialisation more superficial than in agriculture. This was perhaps the one and only field in which the Hungarian dictatorship departed from the Russian model, though it was the very one in which it would have done better to follow it. As already mentioned, Lenin recognised, with statesmanlike intuition, that in an agricultural state *par excellence* it is out of the question to make a revolution against the will of the peasantry, and that the land hunger of the landless peasants must be fully and immediately satisfied. Accordingly, after doing formal honour to the " principle of common ownership " by proclamation, he permitted the peasants and the agricultural workers in practice to share out among themselves the great bulk of the *latifundia*, and energetically resisted the fanatics who were for forcing the dogmas of Communism upon the rural population. At the 8th congress of the Communist party Lenin declared roundly that :

" The very idea of trying to alter the economic conditions of the decently prosperous peasants by force, is perfectly absurd. . . . We have to bring conviction to the peasants, and we can only do it by force of example. . . . The one thing necessary is to give actual proof that collectivisation is better and more profitable."

The Soviet farms and the co-operative farms in Russia set out to offer the refractory peasantry an object lesson in Communism. The Hungarian dictators chose exactly the opposite method, the method characterised by Lenin as the height of absurdity.  They pushed their dogmatic obstinacy and their hatred of the peasantry to the point of refusing to hear of the partition of the *latifundia*, and turning them instead into so-called productive co-operative societies. These societies, however, had nothing in common with true co-operatives ; they neither followed the principle of genuine self-administration nor that of participation in profits in proportion to work done.  At the same time they stirred up ill-feeling against the small-holders and peasant farmers; as though they had not class wars enough already against the capitalists, the big landowners, the rich farmers, the clergy, the old army and the old bureaucracy, they did their best to add to these yet another, against the agricultural day labourers and the small farmers.  Béla Kun himself, in the session of the Soviet on June 21, let loose a flood of demagogic denunciation of the small farmers and called on the agricultural labourers to make an end of them !

In a word, the *latifundia* simply became State concerns, in most cases with the former owner as manager.  Feudalism in Hungary owes a debt of eternal gratitude to the Hungarian Bolshevists; for it was they who discredited the land distribution policy of the October Revolution and saved the big estates by painting them red, and indeed not only preserved them but formally released the great landowners from their social liabilities.  A friend of mine, a Transdanubian landowner, gave me figures showing how in the worst period of economic difficulty, when the isolated landowners could no longer have borne their burdens, with wages artificially forced up to a fantastic level, and a more and more acute shortage of industrial products and seeds, they were saved by the Soviet Republic, which took over the payment of wages and the provision of floating capital and improvements.

Socialisation in practice soon justified the objection always made by anti-Communist thinkers, that it necessitates a rigid and all-embracing State centralisation.  It soon became clear that no limit can be set to the process of socialisation.  The Communist system tends to swallow up all individual enterprise. In many works employing less than twenty men the workers themselves arbitrarily socialised the concerns. Thus most of the barbers' shops were socialised. Apart from this, it became impossible for small works to continue, as the proletarian State, the sole distributor of raw materials, was disinclined to make any issue from its meagre supplies to the small employers. It reserved its supplies for the socialised works. The workers' aristocracy also viewed these small concerns, working for the " bourgeoisie," with disfavour. In these circumstances the condition of the small employers grew more and more wretched, and the middle-class in the towns accumulated a boundless hatred of Communism. This hatred is still one of the main strengths of the White Terror.

The development was similar among the small land-owners. In contrast with the socialised big estates, the small farm was the home of the old order, of private property and individual initiative. Much against the grain, the Communists were led by tactical considerations to exempt properties of less than 100 yokes from socialisation, but no one made any secret of the fact that the turn of the small farms would come ; indeed there was a very general belief that the small peasant farm would die out, either of its own accord, from inability to exist alongside the socialised large farms, or with the assistance of a " prudent policy " which would make it impossible for the small farmer to get machinery and raw materials. These fanatics for the removal of class domination would not have hesitated a moment, had they had it in their power to make it impossible for the peasant farmer, the hardest worker in the country, to survive !

Even apart from this attitude, the exigencies of distribution made it inevitable that the Communist State should interfere more and more drastically with the economic situation of the peasant farmers. " We cannot allow the small farmers," said Commissary Hamburger in the Soviet session of June 17, " the farmers with less than 100 yokes, who account for half our tillage, to dispose freely of their produce, to profiteer and perhaps ruin the industrial population ; we are bound, therefore, to place the tillage of properties of less than 100 yokes under the control of an agricultural board." The leaders, who knew the situation, were aware from the first that in consequence of what they regarded as the obstinate conservatism of the peasants, and their objection to Communism, this measure would be of little real effect. The essential factor in the situation was that the fundamental condition of the division of labour, exchange, had ceased to exist. For his agricultural produce the farmer was getting fewer and fewer industrial articles, and during the dictatorship he did not even receive the old money (the so-called " blue money ") but only the white notes of the Soviet Republic, which from the outset were regarded even in the capital as of no value. The psychological conditions for normal exchange were thus absent, and exchange could only be maintained by the use of force. The dictators realised this, and Hamburger announced that without strong armed forces it would be impossible to assure either the production or distribution of agricultural produce. " We must organise a very strong armed force," he said, " or we shall fail to maintain the public food supply of the industrial workers. It is not only a question of the unfortunate conditions among the agricultural workers (they are refusing to work on account of wage reductions) but also of smugglers, hoarders, middle-men and so on. Against all these, armed force is necessary. We must set up harvest defence bands, as during the war. These are hard nuts for us to crack, but there is no other way out."

The truth was that these problems were not " hard nuts " but gaping wounds in the Soviet Republic, from which it was doomed to perish. Every month, every week, every day, the discord became more acute between town and country ; bloodshed became more and more frequent. And not only on account of the economic conflict of interest, but because of the unbridgeable moral gulf between town and country. The dictators had no conception of the mentality of the countryside, and offended it even without economic occasion for doing so. Thus Béla Kun's plan (propounded in the executive committee meeting of the Budapest Workers' Council, May 23) of sending unemployed town workers into the villages to organise propaganda and requisitions, could not but make the situation worse instead of helping towards a solution. Anyone who attended a meeting of a provincial soviet and heard the violent attacks of the delegates on the " long-haired Ikes," who were incensing the village populations with their conceit and ignorance and their anti-religious indiscretions, could see clearly that there had never been a more audacious Utopia invented by a politician than this one of the orthodox Marxist who despised all Utopias !

It is clear that this irritation of the country with the town showed itself first in anti-Semitism, of which there was a rapid and threatening growth in the time of the Soviets. The subject began to dominate private conversation, and came up frequently in Soviet meetings. A few examples will illustrate the general feeling. At the Soviet assembly on June 15 Béla Somogyi, himself a Jew, spoke as follows, with bitter irony : " In the meetings of all the organs of the Soviet republic I have noted a tendency for a small clique of prayer leaders to claim the whole of the time, and to shut out the remaining members from any active participation." In the meeting on June 16, Louis Jankovics, the delegate from Veszprém, violently denounced the invasion from the towns : " Impossible people have been coming into the country districts.   .   . The agitators came in like a swarm of locusts and have upset everything. . . . The agitators went out to the villages, and each one began by advising us to turn the church into a cinema." On June 21, Louis Tóth, the Somogy delegate, used similar language : " We are discovering that any Ike or longhaired youth is regarded by the central organisations as reliable, and the only elements which are not reliable are our rural directories."[1] M. Nyisztor, People's Commissary for Agriculture, himself frankly declared the danger at the same meeting : " I am convinced that if anti-semitism gains the upper hand it will be the death of the proletarian dictatorship. . . .

[1] The directories were local Communist organs for the control of production and distribution.

Whatever contributes to this anti-semitism must be got rid of. . . . Yesterday was Corpus Christi day, and a certain Leo Reisz actually burst into the church and spat at the Host." Several of those present cast doubt upon this statement, and Nyisztor continued : " Still worse things have happened in the country districts, and it is not enough to imprison the guilty persons ; the matter must be made public. It is not enough to say that there shall be no anti-semitism in this country ; every young ruffian who does not obey must be punished. . . . We must refuse to be content to say idly that anti-semitism is spreading and at the same time to give free rein to any rogue who chooses to flout the religious convictions of thousands of people."

Despite these warnings, the leaders of the dictatorship underestimated the enormous danger represented by the yawning abyss between town and country, although it was obvious that the moment the commune made the peasantry its bitter enemies it was doomed to destruction.

But let us return to the economic side of the story. It was not only necessary to set limits to the economic liberty of the country districts, and to compel them, in common with the factories, to regulate their production according to the Communist needs; it soon proved that the Communist State cannot even tolerate the existence of the co-operative movement among the industrial proletariat. At the Soviet sitting on May 28 Béla Kun said, quite rightly from his own point of view, that, for instance, a well-organised consumers' co-operative society can hardly exist at the same time as the Communist order, since it guarantees to its members privileges over non-members. Accordingly, Kun quite logically included in his programme the nationalisation of the co-operatives, and their conversion into a system of compulsory co-operation. And when an expert in the co-operative system, again quite rightly from his own point of view, described the nationalisation of the co-operatives as squaring the circle, Béla Kun, in his best Russian Dictator style, replied : " If that is so, we shall be performing the miracle of squaring the circle, for the co-operatives have got to be nationalised."

Thus every independent industry or organisation, every autonomous authority outside the proletarian State, was antagonised by the Communist dictators, and it was no accident, but a logical consequence of the whole system, that the trade union and co-operative leaders of the organised workers themselves came to feel the pressure of the Bolshevist dictatorship to be intolerable.    Next to the peasant farmers and the small employers, the most advanced section of the industrial workers became the hottest opponents of those who were applying in Hungary the methods of the " proletarian Tsardom " of Russia.

Thus the catchword of socialisation was applied in every field in the form of a dictatorial absolutism which was completely incapable of solving the difficult problems of the new economic order.    Every Communist ordering of society is a beast with four heels, all of them Achilles' heels !    It can suffer mortal injury through the failure to secure industrial discipline, through the abandonment of free competition in determining prices and wages, through the abolition of the old monetary system and the introduction of a labour-time currency, and through the centralised State direction of production and distribution.    In practice, of course, these defects are inseparable from one another, and they were all felt from the outset in the Hungarian experiment.

Industrial discipline is secured in capitalist society mainly by two means :  the power to discharge the unsuitable workman, and the dependence of the wages of the workman upon his industry and his qualifications.    From the first of these methods the Communist order of society is shut out by its first principles, which include the general duty and right to work; from the second both by principle and in practice : by principle because it would be an anti-Communistic proceeding to make any distinctions whatever in the reward of labour—everyone must work according to his capacity and be provided for according to his reasonable needs—and in practice because only demand and supply can construct the exceedingly complicated and shifting wage scale which passes from the mass of unskilled workers, through the better trained and better qualified categories, up to the workers of the rarest intellectual capacity. A central administration is only able to construct a very incomplete wage scale, and the bureaucratic division of workers into the various categories leads to the worst injustices. In the industrial life of to-day supply and demand determine automatically the distribution of the workers and their movement from works to works; but the Communist order has no means at its disposal other than juridical, and in the last resort physical, compulsion. The Communists, of course, announced from the outset that they would not need either a wage scale or means of compulsion, because in the happiness and liberty of the new society everyone would work freely and with joy, and at most only overtime would need to be paid for. Perhaps it is superfluous to mention that this payment would be an application of an anti-Communist principle.

Experience under the Soviet dictatorship brought the Communist dogmatists the most unpleasant surprises. From the very first day there was evidence that industrial discipline had been most gravely disturbed. The old capitalist, militarist organisation of control had come to an end, and the workers lacked the needed insight and moral self-restraint to obey even the authorities of their own election. They had become masters and had no knowledge of the way to make proper use of their position of domination. In the Soviet sitting of June 16, M. Gelinsky, a provincial delegate, spoke despairingly of the condition of the agricultural " producers' co-operatives " : " In my view," he said, " it is impossible to let part of the workers carelessly squander the wealth of the Soviet Republic simply because they were used in the past to work with a man with a knout behind them, and now no longer have this spur. Some equivalent spur we must provide for ourselves. The proletarian dictatorship must apply to itself in its workshops the same or even greater severity than it is applying to the bourgeoisie."

In industrial production the evil was even greater ; here the contrast between the new and the old order was still more glaring, and the advantage to the workers still greater. Active Socialists and trustworthy technicians joined in deploring the complete shattering of industrial discipline. Even the Commissary Hevesi, who as a rule was inclined to over-optimism, bitterly denounced the reduced productivity of labour in the Soviet sitting of June 18 : " The members of the Workers' Councils are unable sufficiently to maintain discipline at work because of the insecurity of their position as councillors. If in the interests of production a member of a Workers' Council or a Commissary for production shows any energy in tackling the workers, he exposes himself to the risk of a new councillor being at once elected in his place by the workers as a body." As is well-known, exactly the same situation was produced in Russia, and this fact moved Lenin to proclaim on top of the political and military dictatorships an economic one.

But complaints and warnings were in vain. An ineradic-able defect of Communist industry showed itself more and more plainly : the impossibility of allowing the workers a free choice of occupation in the new order of society. Commissaries Lengyel and Varga both emphasised the necessity not only of restoring industrial discipline at all costs, but of providing a government body to assign workers to particular works in accordance with the needs of the moment. But how could discipline be restored ? With what means ? Commissary Lengyel showed in the sitting of June 17 that the workers were refusing to take up the work assigned to them, and cried in despair, " Either the reserves of labour will obey their leaders, and then there will be an end of unemployment; or we shall throw out from our society of workers those who are unwilling to work." But this threat was obviously an unconscious return to capitalistic ways of thinking. The proletarian State cannot expel the non-workers from its industrial organisation ; the most it can do is to throw them into prison.

In addition to restoring, by force if necessary, the needed industrial discipline, it soon became essential to apply the other despised methods of capitalist industry. One after another there were tried the hated methods of differentiation

in the wage scale, of overtime payment, of the Taylor system ;
even of piecework.   The old rhyme

Akkordlohn
Ist Mordlohn

("Piece-work pay is a murderous way") was entirely
forgotten.

Unhappily, owing to the industrial and financial crisis
which overtook the proletarian dictatorship, even this
wholesale return to capitalist industrial methods was of no
avail.   In vain were wages raised, when with the enormous
inflation the purchasing power of money continually
decreased, while no goods of any sort were to be bought.   The
free market for goods had had very largely to be allowed
to continue in existence, but owing to the State-fixed prices
the few goods that there were found their way more and more
into underground trade channels.   Thus, by one of the ironies
of fate, the money problem became one of the most difficult
ones in the Communist order—the money problem of which
Communism by definition does not recognise the existence,
as it should operate only with labour values !   The dictators
tried by a brutal system of judicial punishments to force
the circulation of the valueless " white money," and to
prevent that of the old " blue money."   Of course with no
result.   No dictatorship in the world can alter the elementary
laws of the circulation of goods.

The enormous wage increases in industry proved entirely
illusory, while in agriculture, where they were effectual
(for they were largely payable in kind), they threatened the
very existence of the Soviet republic, the substantially higher
real wages of the agricultural workers endangering the
provision of the needs of the town workers.   The government
was compelled to order the reduction of the excessive wage
rates, and this gave occasion for disturbances here and there.
The order proved insufficient.   At the sitting of June 17
Commissary Hamburger was compelled to demand that
agricultural wages should also be paid in cash, and that the
agricultural workers should receive no higher wages than the
prescribed amount per head.   A still more serious trouble
was that the wages policy of the Communists made it

impossible for them even to obtain the labour they needed for their socialised properties. The farm hands in receipt of fixed rates of pay earned considerably less than men who did seasonal work as independent workers on the exceedingly high wage rates. Under these conditions, Hamburger pointed out, it was impossible to get the most urgent work carried out. "We must at all costs find a remedy," he continued. "We shall have to organise a very strong armed force, or we shall fail to secure the food supplies necessary for the industrial workers."

Thus the question of proletarian discipline in industry and of wage fixing worked itself out to the bitter end : the proletarian dictatorship was forced, in order to ensure production, to appeal to armed force against the proletarians themselves. The remorseless logic of the system defeated the system itself all along the line : after the small employers and shopkeepers and peasants, after the trade union and co-operative leaders, the masses of the agricultural proletariat came into conflict with the Communism which was to save the world. At this stage the situation had indeed become disastrous. The wretched food supply of Budapest, of this increasingly unemployed, feverish, hysterical, and hungry Budapest, was only to be ensured with the aid of armed force, employed against the agricultural proletariat in order to force it to work and against the peasant farmers in order to force them to give up their produce. Day by day the situation of Budapest grew more critical, and if the dictatorship had not fallen, by midsummer there would certainly have been a sanguinary civil war between town and country.

No less were the difficulties arising out of the problem of price fixing. They grew in proportion as the Communists stopped the operation of free exchange and the play of supply and demand, working upon their theory of social cost instead of costs of production, and endeavoured to pursue a class policy in regard to prices, favouring the proletariat at the expense of the bourgeoisie. Commissary Erdélyi, the co-operative expert, and a capable observer, was perfectly clear as to where it would all lead. In the sitting on June 20 he said, bitterly, " Comrades may be interested to know that in the conference in the People's Commissariat for Agriculture we had information of cases in which the manuring of a single yoke of tilled land cost 8,000 crowns. I know of market gardens here, in the neighbourhood of the capital, which have cost impossible sums. The system we are following of continually selling under cost price, is more than we can keep up. There is not paper enough in the world to cover the deficit it will accumulate. Comrades, it can only bring us to starvation ! " The absurdity of the prices became steadily more evident. Commissary Lengyel said (June 20) : " It is a hopeless position that 10 crowns should be being asked to-day for a kohlrabi and 50 crowns for a kilogram of pumpkin ! "[1] But all the dictators could see in these phenomena was smuggling and profiteering; they could not understand that the root of the evil, the morass in which the rank weeds of corruption were growing, was the stoppage of production, the endless printing of banknotes, the irrational price and wage fixing, the complete extermination of the decent traders. Meanwhile a regular aristocracy of profiteers had grown up in Vienna, often doing a smuggling trade with Hungary on account of the Soviet government, at exorbitant profits. The conditions were similar in the provincial directories.

It is obvious that such a system must involve not only the complete destruction of the economic life of the country but a very serious moral crisis. Varga was evidently influenced by his realisation of this when he declared, in the sitting of June 16, that if the blockade were raised "we shall restore freedom of trade in many quarters." But how ? Is it possible to imagine the Communist State permitting free trade, that is, free competition, in many quarters ? It is conceivable that exceptions should be allowed to the general system of free competition, but it is a logical impossibility to free certain fields from a general State regulation of prices.

[1] Two things should be remembered in this connexion, that the prices given here were simply fantastic in 1919, and that even at these fantastic prices there was no kohlrabi to be got. Pumpkin and a little barley groats were the sole food of the town population.

The Communist State was not only ready to use methods of doubtful morality, but was even prepared for a logical somersault or two. For instance, in order to prevent the hoarding of paper money a regulation was issued on May 8 that in future the holders of fresh bank deposits would be able to dispose of them freely, and even that the State would also pay interest on these deposits. The interest-paying Communist State (on top of military enforcement of labour, the Taylor system, and piece-work wages)—the proletarian dictatorship which guaranteed unearned income—was certainly the severest conceivable self-condemnation of the system; and it was a poor excuse that was contained in the shame-faced remark in the preamble to the regulation, that all this was only to go on "until the use of money is finally stopped." For the same remark applied generally: terrorism, class politics, militarism, censorship, constraint of conscience, were of course to continue only until the State disappeared, until the class barriers fell away, until universal peace and complete solidarity between the workers arrived. But what was happening was just the opposite. State absolutism was extending its scope, class differences were as acute as they could be, society was being more and more militarised, and within the Labour movement ever more disgruntled groups were forming.

It was only a natural consequence of all this that production fell disastrously. The reports which came to me left no room for doubt as to that. There is no need to seek for evidence in regard to this acid test of the Bolshevist experiment. The highest economic authority in the Soviet Republic, Eugene Varga, perhaps the only leader with a thorough knowledge of economic theory, laid bare the situation with complete candour at the meeting of the Workers' Council on June 16. It will suffice to quote a few of his statements without comment :

" In general the productivity of labour has fallen greatly. A little less in agriculture than in industry, but enormously in some branches of industry. In the coal mines, for instance, it has fallen by amounts varying from 10 to 38 per cent. below the level of the period of the Károlyi government. I am not speaking of the output of the works, but of the output of the individual workers.  It is 50 per cent. below pre-war.  As regards industry, the fall in the Lang Engineering Works is 30 per cent., in the Mátyásföld lift factory 75 per cent., in the Röck factory 25 per cent., in the Wörner factory 50 per cent., and so on, a great fall in every single case.  . . .  I repeat, it is not a question of shortage of coal or raw material, but of a falling off in production due to the reduced output of the individual worker."

And Varga exposed the causes of the evil with equal candour.  He showed that this hopeless retrogression was primarily due to three causes : (a) the old industrial discipline had gone and a new one had not yet taken its place ; (b) piecework wages had been done away with and replaced by time wages ; (c) " men have not yet attained the higher type of Socialist mentality which will be the starting point of the coming generation."  Clearly this last cause embraced all others in itself : failing the ethical discipline appropriate to it, any Communist experiment will get no farther than a pseudo-communism, and no force or terrorism can alter this fact.  On the contrary, the Bolshevist method postpones the ultimate liberation of the workers, and produces more intolerable conditions than it found : compulsory labour, and the confiscation of the right to choice of employment and to freedom of movement.

The second main purpose of the proletarian dictatorship was the destruction of the State, of bureaucracy and of militarism.  The great Communist thinkers are unanimous in believing that the new economic order will have to relegate the State " to the museum of antiquities," will abolish the lazy and corrupt old-time bureaucracy—the workers themselves carrying on the administration as part of their daily work—and finally will make impossible any sort of militarism, save for the free and voluntary people's army for external defence.  Anarchist and Radical-Socialist thinkers have argued, both from first principles and from the history of Communist experiment, that Communism can only produce the opposite results to these.  The abolition of free markets, free competition and the principle of freedom of association can only extend the powers of the State and increase its bureaucracy ; and the maintenance of a system of compulsory labour organisation, compulsory production and compulsory distribution is only conceivable on the basis of a strong and ruthless militarism. Both the Hungarian and the Russian experience showed the accuracy of the conclusions of the Anarchist and Radical-Socialist schools.

It quickly proved that the Soviet State was compelled continually to add to its bureaucracy, to develop dictatorial rule in every field, and to set up a Red militarism differing ethically in no respect from the old one. It also proved at once that the idea of a bureaucracy which performs physical labour as well as its administrative duties is utopian, and that the Communist State has an even greater need than the bourgeois State of a cultured, instructed, qualified staff, predominantly technical, of officials ; obviously so, since the central State administration is to take over the economic functions formerly performed in freedom by the private citizen. Thus Varga was entirely right in his contention that the first and most urgent need of the State was the organisation of a new bureaucracy. Unhappily this bureaucracy soon reached fantastic dimensions. There were bitter complaints of the new officialdom, spreading with mushroom rapidity. The Communist experimenters, enthusiastic for their millenium, often used strange arguments in extenuation of this rank growth. One commissary, for example, whose puritanic dogmatism was beyond all doubt, was attacked in an open sitting of the government for his unmeasured increase of his staff of officials, and was told that he was infringing the fundamental principles of the Soviet States. He replied in some such words as these :

" It is quite true, comrades, there can be no doubt that it is our duty to reduce the bureaucracy to a minimum, and in the end, indeed, to nothing ; but we can only attain this high object by means of our well-tried and logical methods. The growth of the bureaucracy must first be artificially forced, so that later it may destroy itself by its own overgrowth."

But the worst evil was not the number of officials but their poor quality. The new bureaucracy, far from being an improvement on the old one, was crammed during the confusion of the revolution with all sorts of ignorant, grasping, unscrupulous elements. Without either selection by qualification or the control implicit in a free Press, there was no longer anything to prevent hungry and incompetent placemen from pushing their way into posts in which they abused their powers. The proceedings of the Soviet are full of indignant outbreaks against this thieving, looting, and arbitrary new bureaucracy. All the more decent and responsible elements in the Soviet Republic recognised the mortal danger to the dictatorship of the further spread of this system and this spirit ; for no form of State is the quality of its bureaucracy of more crucial significance than for the Communist State. Böhm, the commander-in-chief of the army, himself plunged into a heated philippic against the new bureaucracy, in the army debate in the Soviet on June 22, speaking with a passion which exceeded that of any of the persecuted Socialists in the days of the old bureaucracy. He charged the bureaucracy with confiscating the food parcels sent by the Red soldiers to their families in Budapest, and sharing the food out among themselves. In other words, in the days of the extremest danger the new bureaucracy was robbing the families of its own defenders ! The abuse of motor cars gave rise to special indignation, and was continually being denounced. Sometimes there was not a single motor available for the transport of sick persons, because the gentlemen of the government departments were driving to the theatre ! The megalomania of the officials and their mutual invasions of one another's spheres was another source of bitter and continual complaint. On May 5 Böhm had occasion to protest strongly against certain members of the Workers' and Soldiers' Councils who were requisitioning the homes of Red soldiery and commanders who were at the front— invading and searching their homes, insulting their families and confiscating their food ! If this was the way the families of the idolised soldiers of the Red army could be treated, it may be imagined what security common mortals enjoyed !

Unhappily the evil was too deep-seated for remedy. At the sitting of the Central Executive Committee, on

July 16, two weeks before the collapse of the dictatorship, the president of the committee, Jakob Weltner, denounced the arrogance and corruption of the new bureaucracy. I will quote only one sentence from his speech :

" To-day there are officials who treat the workers worse and more cavalierly than the so-called *gnädige Herren* of the past."

These administrative evils were further added to by the territorial and administrative disintegration of the country. The unifying forces, busy exchange, rapid communication, peaceful personal intercourse, were more and more weakened by the forces of disintegration, the ever growing pressure of food shortage, the increasing unemployment, the uncertainty of justice, the utterly neglected state of transport, the continual guerilla fighting on the borders of the occupied territories. A spirit of mistrust and ill-will spread everywhere. In every county and directory there grew up a tendency to ignore the central authority, to leave its regulations unobserved, and to retain for local consumption the rapidly falling food stocks. The country began to break up into small areas under the feudal domination of the proletariat. Many times the People's Commissaries complained in their speeches of this administrative anarchy.

With a bureaucracy of this quality, with a State in this condition of physical dissolution, it would have been a desperate task to put into operation the principles of Communism even under more favourable economic conditions, with industrial capitalism past its infant ailments, with industrial concentration farther advanced, and the country less predominantly agricultural. Even in a community economically more advanced, and even with the most perfect administration, it would have been impossible to make a success of the Communist recipe of abolishing markets and competition and individual responsibility and initiative ; still more was this disintegrating country, economically and morally in decay, unfitted for a task calling for the utmost self-discipline, the most perfectly adjusted organisation, and the most expert leadership.

It is one of the basic laws of sociology that a growing food shortage and a growing disintegration necessarily lead to the militarisation of society. This happened in Soviet Russia. Proletarian pacifism gave way to proletarian imperialism, not only in face of the danger from external enemies, but also because of the necessity of suppressing internal disorders, *putsche* and conspiracies, and also, as we have seen, of safeguarding the organisation of compulsory labour. The dictatorship of a tiny minority can only be maintained with the aid of military force, and the worse the situation of the Soviet Republic became at home and abroad, the more violent and ruthless became the spirit of militarism. The growing famine worked in the same direction : in the end the Red army was the only remaining institution whose servants had enough to eat, indeed enough left over, from the proceeds of requisitioning or looting, to send home to their families. The new militarism gradually adopted all the methods and characteristics and acquired the precise mentality of the old militarism. It relied at first upon voluntary service, but soon had to proceed to compulsory enrolments, and the Communists even armed their bitterest enemies, the old bourgeoisie and the old officers. The proletarian State visited draconic punishments upon every attempt to evade military service or to conduct propaganda against it. And with compulsory militarism the old methods were restored of subordination and discipline and executions without trial. An order of May 8 revived the cruellest provisions of the old Imperial Army Orders.

Nor was this all. Under the leadership of the officers of the old imperial army, themselves watched by secret police and political Commissaries, there were revived not only the external forms and methods of the old army, but the old military spirit, with all its arrogance and its worship of *la gloire*. Böhm, the commander-in-chief, declared without raising a word of protest that " after the Russian army there is no army better disciplined or readier for service than the Hungarian Red army." No feudal leader could have spoken more trenchantly : " We shall win or die. But we have no intention of dying. We shall win because win we must." (June 14.) And Béla Kun repeatedly declared that to doubt the victory of the Red army was a counter-revolutionary offence. He began a campaign against proletarian " defeatism," and in his denunciations he fell not a whit behind the famous oratory of Stephen Tisza ; the only difference between the two was that while the feudal leader added an appeal for peace and solidarity within the country, the proletarian tribune was not only concerned to organise a powerful army, but at the same time to work up the spirit of class war to boiling point.

The third of the principal aims of the Bolshevists was the creation of a new spirit in the community, a new popular faith and a new morality. This part of the activities of the Soviet dictatorship showed the new régime under its most attractive aspect. Unquestionably there was a certain greatness, and a consolation for much else, in the seriousness and the enthusiasm with which the proletarian dictatorship took in hand the things of the spirit. A small group of its leaders were filled with an apostolic fanaticism for a new religion, the first concern of which was for the spread of education and art. Of course, exclusively, Socialist, Marxist education ; all other intellectual interests would have found a welcome only in the esoteric circles of the universities.

The ultimate aim was the creation of a new religion of the State. The old doctrine of Socialism, to quote Kautsky's famous formula, demands Communism and State inter-vention in economic production, but complete freedom, complete anarchy in intellectual production ; the proletarian dictatorship decided without hesitation for total com-munalisation in both spheres. It cannot be blamed for doing so ; it was right, and the old theory was wrong. It is an impossibility to communalise production and distribution and to leave the realm of the spirit untouched. Universal compulsory labour can only be enforced on the basis of an appropriate intellectual synthesis. The Communists desired to create this new intellectual synthesis as rapidly as possible; with, of course, the same pious conviction as was held in regard to other liberties : once the Communist spirit had been developed, no restraint would be needed and the age of complete spiritual freedom would have dawned! Meanwhile, however, they introduced a Press censorship (Constitution, § 8), beside which the most oppressive of the war-time regulations appeared mild and liberal. In place of subjection to capitalism and militarism there was now subjection to the Communist State. The arbitrary domination of capitalism had, however, been greatly modified by the admission of free competition at least in some spheres, and by traditional liberties; in the end the capitalist order had failed permanently to suppress any single element of Socialist, Communist or Anarchist thought that had the germs of life in it. The new State made it a physical impossibility for anything but Communist thought to find expression, except with the gracious consent of the State. Every printing works, every publishing house, every ream of paper, every instrument of dissemination had passed into the hands of the State.

During the months of dictatorship every newspaper, every review and pamphlet trumpeted the virtues and the victory of Communism. Serious opposition of any sort was completely impossible. There were very few talented Communist writers or thinkers, and these were overwhelmed with commissions from the State. The whole of the Communist literature was made unreadable by its naïve and superficial and excited Communist phraseology. It is not to be wondered at. The same shallow and uneducated journalists who had been in the habit of reeling off ten or a dozen capitalist, nationalist or clerical clichés, now acquired ten or a dozen Communist phrases and worked them as before. In the atmosphere of universal intellectual slavery the more serious thinkers kept silence. This new Inquisition was not confined to politics; it was carried into scientific work, and the Communists applied it not only to their opponents but to their worshippers. Here is a typical episode in evidence of this. I have frequently mentioned Erwin Szabó, the revolutionary syndicalist thinker. The Bolshevists not only claimed him as one of themselves, but had placed his bust alongside those of Marx and Engels in the great May-day festival.   In his will, as was generally known in Hungarian literary circles, Szabó had requested me to revise for publication the MS. of his work on "Class Struggles in the 1848-49 Revolution."   The Soviet Republic refused to respect the last wishes of its idolised teacher.   Béla Kun sent to me, through an intimate friend, the following message : ‛The dictators were well aware that in his will Szabó had commissioned me to prepare the book for publication.   The government desired, however, to entrust the work to a Communist in whom they could place full trust. It would regard the compliance with Szabó's last wish as a piece of bourgeois sentimentality, and called upon me to give up the MS !

If this is the respect which a system accords to the liberty of conscience of the man to whom it set up a monument, it may be imagined how it treats its enemies and opponents !

So dawned the day of Communist freedom of thought. It was a poor consolation which the State offered in return, in its promise to guarantee a livelihood to writers and artists. A panel of writers was established, and was to be subdivided into a number of branches according to the special capacities of the writers.   Anyone admitted to the panel was provided for in proportion to his talent (a new form of class differentiation).   For instance, a first-class writer or artist could rise into the highest aristocracy, the class of the steel and metal workers.   This had not been officially announced, but the plan was under consideration, and active canvassing was going on among the writers' and artists' organisations for support for would-be mandarins of the first, second or third class.

Under the direction of George Lukács, the policy of the dictators in regard to education and art was certainly distinguished by many great ideals; but they were hardly more than experiments *in vacuo*, so ill-suited were the economic situation and the state of public opinion for carrying out any really important reforms.   But if the great ideas were condemned to remain on paper, it was so much the easier for the Talmudists of the system to spread their evil influence undisturbed.   They developed, for instance, their system of sexual instruction for young people with such criminal levity, that Joseph Pogány himself later stopped this section of their work entirely.

The brainworkers were soon filled with dissatisfaction and anxiety as to their future, and there was news from all parts of excited protests. Béla Kun made a speech on May 31 in the Engineers' Association which was little calculated to allay their fears. Not only did he support the primitive dogma of the essential identity of hand and brain work ; he extended it, claiming that the path of progress lay in the direction of abolishing the distinction even between skilled and unskilled work. In effect he boldly claimed that all labour should in future be regarded as of equal value.

But nothing was more damaging to the whole system than the exclusive monopoly it secured for the new religion. Writers and public alike grew disgusted with the reference of every published word to the basis of orthodox Marxism, Leninism or Bucharinism. The more serious writers wrote less and less, and made way for the chewers of the Marxist cud and the "class-war quacks." (The latter type I had discovered in Paris nearly twenty years before. When I coined that name for them, I little imagined that they would come to be the sole rulers in Hungary. I was startled one day to find this long-forgotten expression of mine reappear in the philippics of a provincial Soviet member). The new arrivals, ignorant and without any serious moral conviction, heaped phrase upon phrase of vulgar abuse. The loss of the freedom of the Press hung like a millstone upon the best of the brainworkers. In a speech unforgettable for its courageous good sense, delivered on June 7 in the Otthon Club, the association of the Hungarian journalists, Zoltán Szász gave expression to their feeling of resentment. Not all the howling of the Communist hooligans could rob this speech of its effect. The feeling of the brainworkers against the dictatorship grew steadily angrier ; the camp of the so-called counter-revolutionaries (I say " so-called " because everyone was called a counter-revolutionary who ventured to make use of his natural right of criticism) was added to by a fresh detachment.

This rack-renting of the economic system, this unreliable administration, the growing famine, the corruption, the more and more ruthless militarism, and the gagging of thought, steadily perverted the moral atmosphere of the Soviet Republic. The spirit of mistrust and ill-will, the nervousness and embitterment grew from day to day. Nowhere, perhaps, did it ever become truer that *homo homini lupus.* Every day had its *putsch,* its counter-revolutionary move, at all events in the imagination of the trembling tyrants. There were but few who realised the gaping wounds in the economic, political and moral order, through which the whole life of the State was inevitably being poisoned; attention was concentrated on discovering and punishing conspirators, counter-revolutionaries, profiteers and speculators, " defeatists " and traitors. The town saw in the country its mortal enemy, and the country districts replied to the regulations and requisitions and provocations from Budapest with a growingly dangerous mass movement : anti-semitism.

As we have already seen, anti-semitism was not originated by the White Terror, it had already assumed a threatening aspect in the last weeks of the proletarian dictatorship. Béla Kun and his colleagues delivered passionate speeches against it, and Kun himself, in a public sitting of the Soviet (June 21), charged a section of the workers with working up pogroms and anti-semitic demonstrations. And on top of the growing differences between proletarians and bourgeois, proletarians and peasants, town and country dwellers, Jews and Christians, on top of the fiery hatred of the small employers, shopkeepers and officials towards the dictatorship, and the denunciations of it as Antichrist and prayers to Heaven for its destruction from priests and faithful of every sect, there was growing up within the industrial working class a spirit of mutual ill-will and disunion. The opposition grew between Socialists and Communists, between the trade unions and the party, between the bureaucracy and the masses. Even the spiritual cohesion between the leaders, the unity within the government, had been undergoing dissolution, and the dictators were suspiciously watching one another. A very complicated organisation of mutual espionage grew up. Böhm, the commander-in-chief, complained in a public sitting of the Soviet that certain Communists were having himself and his Chief of Staff, Stromfeld, dogged and watched and reported on as persons of doubtful trustworthiness. This spirit of ill-will and mutual fear ruined the dictatorship. Its really trusted staff shrank to a few hundreds, perhaps no more than a few dozens. The revolution was to have stirred society to its foundations. In the end it had not as many reliable supporters to count on as would have served for the decent administration of a single county. Meanwhile the spirit of proletarian " defeatism " made disastrous progress. Böhm exposed the situation ruthlessly at a Soviet sitting. He showed that not only the " defeatism " of the old army had shown itself again, but the same abuses were spreading everywhere : the same desertions and dismissals from the front, the same idle swaggering at home at the expense of the front.

Anyone who reads the reports of the Soviet army debates is bound to see, if he is not blinded by prejudice, that the fate of the Red army was already sealed by the middle of June, six weeks before the collapse. Hence the growing spirit of " defeatism " and the policy of the moderate group, carefully elaborated by Kunfi : to make an end of purposeless bloodshed and to try to consolidate the proletarian State. But it was no longer possible to stop the progress of militarism. The dictatorship could only be maintained by means of military adventures. Sieyès' prophecy of the fate of the Jacobins came true again for the Communists: " *S'ils font la paix, ils sont perdus.*" The *salut public* became again the only argument by which the dictators could maintain themselves in power : the argument that their country was in the throes of a danger which continually threatened its existence.

Tempting, then, as it may be to some, amid the trials of exile, to hunt for scapegoats and perhaps traitors, it is evident that the Soviet dictatorship was destroyed by the disunion in its midst.

The tragic defeat on the Roumanian front was not a cause but an effect. Kun, who with all his dogmatism and lack of vision had a fine sense of the movements of popular feeling, was perfectly well aware that the dictatorship could only be broken from within. He failed to realise the causes of its moral debility, but the facts and the growth of the debility he despairingly admitted. At the sitting of the Central Executive Committee on July 16 he spoke out with surprising plainness : he declared that the Communist rule was being destroyed by internal paralysis : the leaders were showing themselves afraid to use their powers, the dictatorship was shrinking back from the consequences of its own principles. " The paralysis is plainly visible : there is everywhere a deadly fear of every symptom of counter-revolution, and yet we are shrinking back from every political or economic step which is required to set the dictatorship at last on a firm footing." His diagnosis was perfectly correct : the system had lost faith in itself.

This deep-seated moral crisis was exposed from another side and with a still firmer hand by Jakob Weltner in his presidential opening speech at the sitting of the Central Executive Committee of the Budapest Workers' Council. The speech had the air of a bitter denunciation, and concluded with these notable words :

" I will only hold this high office so long as the Budapest Workers' Council fights with all its strength against self-seeking actions, against looting and private violence, so long as it insists emphatically that the Soviet government was formed not to serve individual interests, but to promote the welfare of the whole community. Nothing does greater service to the counter-revolution than corruption and looting and robbery."

These words, spoken from that forum a week before the collapse, sound to us to-day like a pronouncement of the doom of the dictatorship.

But however great may have been the faults and mistakes of the proletarian dictatorship, we must not close our eyes to the fact that this despairing and heroic effort of the working class conveys certain moral lessons of great value for the future.

The first is a negative one : a warning of the way *not* to socialise, of the method which cannot succeed in freeing the workers. In the present disturbed times, amid the cruelties and abuses of the White Terror, this lesson tends naturally to be lost sight of by the militant workers, and they are inclined to forget the evils of their rash experiment and to remember only the wide freedom and unlimited scope which it gave the leaders of the Labour movement. But the time will come when the workers will be able to learn wisdom from their wounds, and it may be hoped that in the fights for freedom which are to come they will be able to avoid the tragic errors of the experiment which failed in 1919.

But the proletarian dictatorship has shown more positive results. It must not be forgotten that despite its eccentricities and its conflicts and bloodshed the Soviet dictatorship maintained a measure of order and organisation during a period in which there was no alternative to it but the horrors and anarchy of mob domination.

But the most important effect of the proletarian dictatorship will certainly be found in the radical change of outlook produced among the proletarian masses. It had the character of a violent moral explosion in the Hungarian social order. It planted in the minds of the great mass of semi-brutalised slaves perhaps the first seeds of faith and hope of liberation. To this day there lives in the hearts of millions the sense of the rights of the workers and of their superiority to the drones and idlers. Above all, the dictatorship shook out of their age-long apathy the unhappy helots of Hungarian society, the agricultural workers.

No less important was the service of the Soviet Republic to the idea of internationalism, made vivid and real in the minds of the people by the memory of hard and bloody conflicts.

Finally, through the spirit of the Soviet constitution, despite much childish naïveté and many violent outbursts, the Republic did pioneer work for the ideals of more advanced types of democracy and self-government. It did this by its exposure of the defective organisation, the shortcomings and hypocrisies of the bourgeois democracies of to-day, and its proclamation for all time of the ideal of the State in which only those who work and produce shall have the right to control and govern society.

These philosophical gains were certainly bought by the Hungarian workers at a terribly heavy price : at the price of the temporary destruction of their economic, political and moral existence.

CHAPTER XI

# THE COUNTER-REVOLUTION AND THE WHITE TERROR

THE economic and moral bankruptcy of the Soviet Republic at home spurred the dictators to a break-neck foreign policy. To escape from their hopeless internal difficulties, they commenced the fresh foreign adventure of an offensive against Roumania. This foolhardy attack was quite welcome both to the Roumanians and to the counter-revolutionaries (particularly the White government of Szeged), who had for months been supplicating the foreign diplomatists, and especially the Roumanians, for military intervention against Hungary. The demoralised Red army fell to pieces on the Theiss, and the way to Budapest was open, not only for the Roumanian army, but also for the White counter-revolution.

Everyone saw the approaching danger, but it was no longer possible to guard against it. Béla Kun's resignation just succeeded in saving his bare life and that of his fellow-dictators ; it could not avert disaster from the working class or from the Hungarian democracy. In vain were the whole of the Soviet laws repealed, in vain did the Workers' Council hand over the government of the country to a moderate Socialist cabinet ; with no army, this Peidl government was quite incapable of resisting the rising White flood, and Friedrich's officers had no difficulty in thrusting it aside. Only a determined and sustained intervention on the part of the Entente could now have averted the White counter-revolution. If the Entente had wished it, legality and democracy in Hungary might have been preserved. Sir George Clerk, the plenipotentiary representative of the Supreme Council in Hungary, appeared at first to be working in this direction, seeking a solution in which the Socialist and progressive movements would have played the leading part. He was kept informed by Socialists, democrats and Pacifists as to the steps which needed to be taken. I know that various memorials were submitted to him indicating the clear path of peaceful settlement on democratic lines. It was made clear to him that, if the settlement of the Hungarian crisis were left to Horthy's White officers and army, not only would there be an unexampled White Terror, but a permanent centre of monarchist and feudal infection would be set up which would make peace in Central Europe impossible. The Entente, he was told, should not dream of negotiating with the pseudo-political parties in Budapest, the leaders of armed bands and the various " business politicians " ; it should at once disarm the White officers' army, replacing it for the time by a reliable Entente force of 10,000 to 20,000 men, until the new Hungarian government had succeeded in organising a reliable army recruited from peasants and workmen. The new cabinet should not be formed from the membership of the various demagogues' clubs and officers' organisations, but from officials of long service and reliable and progressive character, not belonging to any party : these, with the support of the Socialist party and the peasant farmers, and with the assistance of the Entente police, could easily ensure the proper conduct of the elections. If this were done, there could be no doubt that Parliament would contain a strongly democratic and progressive majority, which would be able to prevent a new civil war and to secure the fruits of the October Revolution.

Sir George Clerk at first showed a good deal of sympathy with these plans, but not for long ; he changed his attitude in a very few days. He had dined and hunted with the nobles until in the end he had completely assimilated the mentality of the Hungarian *ancien régime.* He was, moreover, so disgusted with Hungarian conditions that he wanted to get out of this Balkan chaos as soon as possible, and was only concerned to produce some sort of order, real or apparent. In the end he obtained the assent of the leaders of the armed bands, the chiefs of the coffee-house cliques, and the

Socialists who had remained in the country, to a patched-up compromise. The basis of this compromise was the concession of universal and secret franchise and of political liberty in all other respects, with a plebiscite on the question of the form of the State ; but a blind man could have seen that any solution behind which there stood the White officers' army and the terrorist organisations of a Horthy, could lead only to bloodshed and anarchy. But all this was of no interest to the diplomatists of the Entente. They were interested in only two things : that the Hungarian Treaty of peace should be signed *sans phrase*, and that the country should be kept a close preserve for foreign capitalists and profiteers. Horthy and his associates agreed to both conditions with the generosity of true Magyar gentlemen, and the foreign missions accorded such obliging goodwill and hearty support to the White system of mass murders, internments, pogroms, castration, torture and rape, that if the Hohlers and the Troubridges had offered a tithe of this goodwill and support to the democratic and pacifist government of Károlyi, the disaster which befell our unfortunate country could have been avoided. However that may be, history will lay upon Sir George Clerk and upon the policy of the Entente a heavy responsibility for all the horrors which were revealed by the very circumspect delegation of the British Labour Party.

Before I pass to a discussion of the Horthy régime, and to a description of its terrorist activities, I must analyse in a few words the state of public feeling amid which the White counter-revolution developed.

Enfeebled by the world war, reduced to a third in size, exasperated by the brutalities of the Bolshevist experiment, the country still remained in a condition of latent revolution ; political democracy and land reform, the basic aims of the October Revolution (which must in time inevitably be realised), were still unattained : instead, the old feudal tyranny had been let loose again as a result of Bolshevist absolutism, which had proved even more intolerable for the great majority of the population, for the reasons detailed in the previous chapters. The public was therefore in revolt above all things against Bolshevism, and was demanding real democracy. In the judgment of the great mass of the people, who tend always to simplify and symbolise issues, the Bolshevist domination had the appearance of the domination of the town proletariat over the countryside, and of a foreign race, the Jews, over the Christian community; it is not unnatural, therefore, that popular feeling grew violently anti-town and anti-semitic. The country was maddened by the humiliations and persecutions which the peasantry, the middle-class, and large sections of the brain-workers had suffered under the dictatorship of the proletariat. The newly enthroned *condottieri* and caucus leaders (I have already pointed out that in Hungary no popular force had been created and no democratic organisation achieved except by the Social Democrats) had divined this popular feeling, and they fabricated appropriate catchwords to cover their rapacious designs : " Christian, National, Agrarian Democracy," was what in a thousand variations they promised the country.

The White counter-revolution was in this sense an inevitable reaction from the dictatorship of the proletariat, but it soon belied its own programme, and pressed forward to the realisation of aims quite alien to those of the tormented masses. In order to understand this change, we must briefly pass in review the general staff of the White counter-revolution. In it we can distinguish three principal elements. First of all, the mass of adventurers and soldiers of fortune who swam on the surface of the counter-revolution, irresponsible coffee-house and tavern orators, depraved and predatory creatures without culture or political education, who now suddenly found themselves lords and potentates, and whose efforts were directed solely to their personal advancement and enrichment. The representative man of this group was that same Stephen Friedrich, who during the Károlyi revolution was an ultra-revolutionary and a pro-Semite flirting with Zionism. At the beginning of the White counter-revolution this group became the loudest and most influential one. Secondly, an important part was played by the officers and public officials who, in consequence of the disbanding of the old army or the partition of Hungarian territory, or through the revolutions, had lost their occupations and now lounged about in coffee-houses, and whose main object was to recover their old positions in the governing class. Only third in importance were the actual representatives of the *ancien régime*, the nobles and landed gentry and the higher clergy and the bankers, slowly recovering from the sledge-hammer blows of the two revolutions, and now advancing again, treading delicately, in the hope of regaining their nearly lost paradise of feudalism.

Under these leaders public opinion, still fundamentally revolutionary, still demanding land and democracy, gradually became demoralised, and gave ear to a hollow and noisy demagogy. The old feudalism and the old plutocracy stepped aside for the time, knowing well that the influence of demagogues unsupported by any organised masses could not last.

All the leading positions were filled by the most philistine section of the population, people whose mental horizon was no wider than that of the starving and embittered subordinate officials, ready victims for phrasemongers. The Swabian lower middle-class in particular, whose anti-semitism and narrow nationalism was always the most violent, played a leading part (Friedrich, Huszár, Haller, Schnetzer, Bleyer, etc.). The more serious among the Conservatives and the educated elements among the aristocracy and gentry were not sufficiently popular in style to counter the influence of the wild coffee-house orators. In the past these latter could rarely bring themselves to the front ; for their crude atavisms, their provincial ignorance and mediævalism there was no room in the division of public opinion between progress and conservatism. But in the first period of the Horthy domination this type secured itself the sole mastery of the country. Hungary to-day is like a being whose brain has been partially destroyed : its consciousness has clouded over, and the intelligence has been displaced by reflex action. The shallowest nationalism, the most insane anti-semitism and jingoism have swamped public life after ten or twenty years of gravitation towards Western ideas. The empty-headed swagger which cares nothing for international relationships, and the simplicity which tries to abolish famine by whippings and pogroms, are shouting their folly in the market-place.

Starting in this unreasoning, hectoring mood, which was a product of the abuses and cruelties of the " Jewish dictatorship of the proletariat," the White counter-revolution soon entered upon a course of action which could no longer be accounted for by the passions aroused by the Commune, but which served more and more the positive ends of the old Hungarian class-domination. The " Exter-mination of Communism " became the cloak for systematic terrorism, applied more and more openly for the realisation of its definite aims : to make impossible any democratic progress, any land reform, any democratic administration, and to re-establish the economic and political system of pre-war days, rescinding every social reform which the October Revolution had brought. Hence the White attack was directed with much more rancour against the October Revolution than against the Commune ; and a campaign of calumny, lavishly supported, was organised to discredit the October Revolution and its leading personalities.

The old order, which had been rendered nearly impotent by the two revolutions, raised its head again, and began to strive openly to restore its old monopoly in economic and political life. The control of the country fell more and more into the hands of the old feudalism and the old plutocracy, and the planks of the " National and Christian Agrarian Democracy " were steadily pushed into the background. In the first period of the Horthy régime rude demagogy, the grievances of the lower middle-class, and public-house anti-semitism were the dominant influences ; in the second period, which still continues, the political system and methods of the *ancien régime*, and above all of the Tisza era, are being restored.

This process of complete restoration of the old order is marching under a triple banner. Three main planks are continually being emphasised : anti-semitism territorial integrity, and the restoration of the Habsburgs. (The Whites split later on the Habsburg question, but at first Horthy and the whole of the White counter-revolution were legitimist, and they would be again the moment the pressure of the Little Entente were removed). Anti-semitism is the pet idea of the mob, territorial integrity, of the lower middle class and the officers' corps, and the Habsburg restoration, of the great landowners and the higher clergy, who see in the crown of St. Stephen the mightiest bulwark of the integrity of their *latifundia*.

But for all their differences of emphasis, the counter-revolutionary groups were essentially in perfect agreement, possessed by a single crowning desire, the desire to preserve undiminished their former political domination, the old " leisure class standard " and all the old privileges of social position. `The spirit of the two revolutions is to them a continual nightmare. Their every thought and deed aims at making impossible, once for all, the great ideas of democracy and reform of the October Revolution. Communism they already fear less to-day, since, as we have seen, it failed seriously to infect the economic and moral organism of the country.

The first effort of the Horthy system was therefore to sweep away all who might seriously hinder the work of the counter-revolution.

The country was covered with a network of bloody assizes, which wreaked vengeance not only upon the greedy adventurers of Communism, but also upon those whose only offence was their political faith. The " Christian Course " made the cross, that shining symbol of the love of man, into a gallows, and used it with a wild fury which in the end disgusted the Entente missions, who tried to moderate this hanging mania. Thousands of innocent persons, among them women, students, young girls, and even children, were sent to the prisons and the internment camps.

But this " legal " retaliation was not enough for them. It was too ceremonious and controllable. Throughout the land there were formed "armed detachments," of the White forces, and other bands, which hunted down all who had excited their suspicion or ill-will. It may be said that the whole so-called upper class took up arms and joined one or another of the military organisations. Hungary became a veritable Eldorado for the disbanded Imperial army. All the officials and the university students were distributed among the armed formations, as one of the most uncomfortable questions for the new lords was how far the common soldier was to be relied upon. These detachments shot up and multiplied like mushrooms, and certain of them, under the leadership of particularly determined chiefs, almost secured legal status. A Hejjás, an Ostenburg, a Prónay, became real States within the State, imprisoned and tortured and murdered whom they would, and went about levying contributions. Especially on the further side of the Danube there were sanguinary " hold-ups," often of whole villages, mainly directed against the Jews and those compromised in the revolutions, and the total number of the victims of these raids is estimated by independent observers at many thousands. Often the political point of view dropped quite into the background, and the armed bands abandoned themselves to unvarnished robbery and extortion, cruelty and lust.

This raging of the White Terror makes one of the darkest pages of Hungarian history. A whole literature has been devoted to it. In excuse of its horrors, the statement is often heard that the White Terror really only continued the method of the Red. I have no desire whatever to palliate the brutalities and atrocities of the proletarian dictatorship ; its harshness is not to be denied, even if its terrorists operated more with insults and threats than with actual deeds. But the tremendous difference between the Red and the White Terror is beyond all question. During the counter-revolution the decreased spread of the Terror was compensated by increased brutality and by an entirely different psychological and moral quality. The Terrorist actions of the Reds usually revealed the primitive cruelty of coarse and ignorant men ; the Whites worked out a cold and refined system of vengeance and reprisal, which they applied with the cruelty of scoundrels masquerading as gentlemen. The worst atrocities of the Red Terror were usually the wild acts of depraved and semi-bestial proletarians : those of the Whites were the deliberate actions of elegant officers. I have no space even for a brief sketch of these horrors. In order, however, that the uninstructed reader may have a rough idea of its dimensions and its character, of the mentality and morality of this period, I will venture to select a few characteristic facts from the chronicle of crime of this so-called "Christian and National" system.

On the entry of the White officers into Kaposvár, Alexander Latinka, Stephen Szalma, Irma Levin, Ladislaus Tóth and Joseph Farkas were dragged from prison and executed with frightful torture. August, 1919.

In the prison in Pápa an old man of 89 named Hoffmann was beaten to death by the officers. Lieutenant Antalovics put out the eyes of Dr. Epstein, District Medical Officer, Raab. September, 1919.

In the presence of the Public Prosecutor Lányi, at Veszprém, five prisoners awaiting their trial were executed by soldiers of the White forces. One of them was mutilated beyond recognition. The names of the other four were Andrew Kovács, Frederick Láng, and the brothers Schwarz. September, 1919.

At Sopron, the writers Ladislaus Bors, Alexander Salzberger, and Desider Enzbruder were executed by the soldiers of the Whites without trial. On account of an alleged attempt to escape, Alexander Kellner and Gabriel Knapp were shot. August, 1919.

At Dunaföldvár, a "People's tribunal," consisting of thirty-five soldiers, was set up under the control of Paul Prónay, an intimate of Horthy's ; a merchant named Alexander Stein, who lived there, was hanged in place of his brother-in-law, who had fled because he was unable to pay the contribution levied on him by Prónay's gang. August 8, 1919.

At Balatonfökajár, an old Jewish merchant, Emanuel Rosenthal, and his son-in-law, Rudolf Bergmann, were also murdered by Prónay's gang, who prevented the doctor from

giving treatment to other Jews who had been half-killed.
August 17, 1919.

At Celldömölk, the local White force organised a pogrom ;
the Jews were almost beaten to death. The Jewish schoolmaster, Simon Kemény, was killed with a butcher's cleaver.
The authors of the bloodshed then forced their way into the
house of a merchant named Schöntag, who was murdered
before the eyes of his wife and six children, and his head
thrown out of the window. August 7, 1919.

A Prónay detachment entering Tolnaozora murdered
Bernard Weiss and his son-in-law, Hermann Weiss. The son
of the former, hastening to save his father, was mortally
wounded. The officers killed, with horrible tortures, a farmer
named George Turós, who had protested against their
brutality. August 20, 1919.

White guards came to the parish of Vörösberény and
demanded, as on government authority, that the Jews living
there should leave the village. The lieutenant in charge of
the band had Ignaz Reimand, who had been condemned to
several years' imprisonment during the dictatorship as a
" counter-revolutionary," released—and shot. August 20,
1919.

The Commandant of the White forces, Count Salm, had
a landowner named Anton von Tószegi-Freund, whom he
had been dragging from place to place for days, and his
son-in-law, an estate agent named Albert Graner, hanged
at Balatonfonyód. The rope broke three times under the
weight of Tószegi-Freund's body. Meanwhile his wife
arrived with a letter from Horthy, and implored Salm to
spare her husband's life. Salm dismissed her with these
words : " Horthy instructed me to listen to you. I have
done so." Then he had her dragged away and the execution
carried out. August 20, 1919.

The officers of the White forces at Sátoraljaujhely brought
out of the prisons those awaiting trial, and executed six of
them without trial. August, 1919.

The White guards entering Marcali (Somogy county)
committed many horrors. Twelve corpses, mutilated beyond
recognition, were found near a tile factory. August 27, 1919.

George Szmrecsányi, vice-president of the Union of Awakening Magyars, delivered speeches at Tapolca and Diszel, inciting to pogroms. Thereupon the White formation which had been brought up commenced a systematic extermination of the Jews. The landowner Desider Korein, the inn-keeper Maurus Singer, Alexander Singer, Moritz Breuer, the schoolmaster Gartenau and his son-in-law, and the landowner Géza Weiss were killed. The Roman Catholic schoolmaster at Dorog, Ernest Kiss, was taken for a Jew and killed. In the morning, three corpses of men mutilated beyond recognition were found in the road. The inhabitants were deeply indignant at these outrages, but had not the courage to oppose the armed bandits. September 8, 1919.

In the parish of Gyönk (Tolna county) the shopkeeper, Simon Fischl, was dragged out of the synagogue and shot. September 6, 1919.

According to eyewitnesses' testimony given by Stephen Hayden, who had served as staff sergeant-major at Siófok and had fled from the service of the White Terror, Horthy's troops were guilty of frightful bloodshed. At Siófok, under the leadership and at the command of Paul Prónay and Captain Freiszberger, more than 200 people, including John Kövess and his young wife, were executed with the most horrifying torture. One of the officers condemned the execution of the young woman as inhuman, but Captain Freiszberger ordered her to be hanged, on the ground that " this woman has seen everything." August—September, 1919.

On the railway between Lajosmizse and Kecskemét, Eugene Wertheimer, Director Neubeuer, Professor Nemes, and a shopkeeper named Fodor were taken out of the train by a party of soldiers led by Michael Francia-Kiss, a subaltern of the Héjjas detachment. All four were shockingly tortured, hemp yarn was thrust into their throats and their mouths were closed with wires, so that two of them died in agony; the other two were buried alive. November 17, 1919.

Under the leadership of Lieutenant Ivan Héjjas, his two brothers, the Kecskemét Captain of Police, Tibor Barna, and Michael Francia-Kiss, a Terrorist detachment appeared at the Kecskemét prison, dragged out the political prisoners, and then seized one by one all the officials, farmers, etc., in Kecskemét and the neighbouring farms, who had played any part, however small, in the revolution, as well as a number of Jews who had in general taken no part. These people were brought into the Orgovány wood, where some of them were hanged, some buried alive, some dismembered or flayed alive. This mass murder claimed more than 200 victims, amongst them the University Professor Dr. Desider Buday, the barrister Dr. Fritz, the journalist Franz Berkes. November, 1919.

Baruch Reich, a forty year old Viennese merchant and a Polish subject, who was travelling to Hungary on business, was taken out of the railway carriage at Komárom by two officers, on the ground that his passport was forged. They took his gold watch and his fur overcoat, and then murdered him. His body was found on the Komárom road. Reich's family, and even the Polish Legation, did everything possible to secure the identification of the murderers, but failed through the obstruction of the Hungarian authorities. December 15, 1919.

Lieutenant Dionys Bibó, with the assistance of his detachment of officers, arrested the Szeged engineer Stephen Müller from motives of private revenge. Müller was beaten with Horthy cudgels until half dead, his eyes were put out, and he was beaten again, until he lost consciousness. His testicles were destroyed by blows with iron-pointed knouts. A few hours before his death, the poor fellow was handed in to the Public Prosecutor's prison at Budapest, where a receipt was given for him as " in good health " by its director, Albert Váry. (January, 1920.) Müller died of his tortures. The criminal, Lieutenant Bibó, is to-day the proprietor of a motor-car works. It is believed that it was in these works that the infernal machines were made with which the Awakening Magyars committed the outrage against the Democrats' Club.

Mme. Alexander Hamburger received from her brother-in-law in Vienna, who had been a People's Commissary during the dictatorship, a letter on purely private affairs. For this she was imprisoned, together with Martin Vadas, the bearer of the letter, and Adalbert Neumann, a friend of her husband who happened to be on a visit to her. She was taken to the Kelenföld barracks, and at the command of Héjjas and Prónay was violated by the whole of the troops in the barracks. Her old acquaintance, Adalbert Neumann, was ordered to violate her, and refused. On this he was castrated before her eyes. Regent Horthy was himself aware of the bestial treatment of Mme. Hamburger, since just at this time he was inspecting Héjjas' barracks at Kelenföld and Héjjas showed Mme. Hamburger to him. The British Labour Party deputation enquired very fully into this case ; Colonel Wedgwood's report also states that Héjjas and Prónay thrust the handles of their riding-whips into the unhappy woman's womb, and thereby maimed her for life.

The letter was brought from Vienna by Martin Vadas and Gabriel Kohn. Both were arrested. Andrew, the sixteen-year-old brother of Martin Vadas, was also imprisoned and all three were horribly tortured. After about two months of long-drawn-out torments they were thrown into the Danube. January, 1920.

Paul Prónay, Baron Alexius Nopcsa and George Sefcsik carried off in a motor car at night the editor of the Social Democratic daily paper, " Népszava," Adalbert Somogyi, and a contributor to the paper, the poet Adalbert Bacsó, and threw them both into the Danube. Somogyi's eyes were put out beforehand. This murder was committed in revenge for the revelation of the atrocities at Orgovány. The murder excited the greatest indignation among the Hungarian workers, and as the foreign Press began to give credit to the reports of White terrorism in Hungary, the then Prime Minister guaranteed the arrest of the perpetrators within two days. More than two years have passed, but the murderers are still at large and picking further quarrels. Not a hair of their heads has been touched. February 20, 1920.

Joseph Bottlik described in the National Assembly the atrocities at Miskolcz. In that place the Ostenburg detachment carried off twenty of the forty prisoners awaiting trial, and these have never been heard of since. February, 1920.

Officers of the White forces, hearing that Michael Gross, a wholesale meat dealer, was travelling on business with large sums of money in his pocket, intercepted him, took him out of the railway carriage, murdered him, stole his money, and threw his body into the Danube at Komárom. February 17, 1920.

At Enying, officers forced the carpenter Stephen Lénárd to dig his own grave, and then buried him alive with his hands and feet bound. March, 1920.

At Gyöngyös, lieutenant Meklényi, the commandant of the local forces, tortured Mme. Joseph Hegedüs until she died of her injuries. March, 1920.

At the farm of Jakabszállás the owner, Moriz Gróf, was murdered by men of the Ostenburg detachment. April 8, 1920.

Men of the Héjjas detachment, led by Ivan Héjjas and Lieutenant Michael Francia-Kiss, executed a sub-editor named Géza Hay at Szolnok. Then, in spite of the protest of the Public Prosecutor, they dragged the prisoners out of the Szolnok prison, and killed three of them on the spot. Several of the prisoners were bound with thin wire and beaten till the blood ran, and then brought to Abony, where, on the soldiers' own statement, they were all butchered, because, in the words of the perpetrators, they " attacked the sentry." April 2 to May 1, 1920.

Colonel Wedgwood, the leader of the Labour Party delegation, travelled to Abony in order to verify this report. The Awakening Magyars accused the rabbi of the Jewish Synagogue, Alexander Rechtschaffen, of asking Colonel Wedgwood to come to Abony, and beat him to death with Horthy knouts and rawhide whips on the threshold of his home, before the eyes of his wife and five children. May, 1920.

Emil Horovitz, a sentry on the Czech-Hungarian frontier, was carried off by Hungarian officers. According to the testimony of eye-witnesses, his teeth were knocked out, one eye put out, and he was then bound and thrown into the Theiss. May, 1920.

The Union of Awakening Magyars organised a novel pogrom in the Budapest public park. Promenaders were beaten till the blood ran, and seriously wounded with knives and knuckle-dusters. The badly injured were thrown into the lake. Amongst the latter was the young Budapest merchant George Kánitz, whose body, shockingly slashed, was found some days later on the bank of the lake. There were other victims of this raid who died of their injuries. June 1, 1920.

A dealer named James Fischof, who was in Budapest to make some purchases, was dragged by soldiers out of an inn in Laudon Street. Forty thousand crowns were taken from him ; he was brought to the Albrecht barracks, beaten until half-dead, and then, by command of the officers, thrown out of the window. June, 1920.

The infamous Jankovich detachment murdered the Budapest hotel proprietor Stephen Szabados at their barracks at Vác. The murder was committed at the command and in the presence of Count Jankovich. Szabados was first frightfully tortured. His offence was trying to expel a young woman from his hotel for improper conduct, and the officers who were her clients organised the murder. June 10, 1920.

A Budapest lady, the widow of Gustav Földváry, was arrested and kept for days in the police cells in the Mosonyi Street, where she lost her reason as a result of the prolonged and horrible torments she suffered. The reason for the arrest was that she had repelled the advances of a certain Lieutenant Biegler. June, 1920.

The notary of the municipality of Szalkszentmárton levied a contribution on the local Jews, to be collected by the senior member of their congregation, Alexius Rotter. One Jew refused to pay, and went to Budapest to report the matter. Thereupon the notary called the Héjjas detachment to his assistance. They kidnapped Alexius Rotter and murdered him, with frightful tortures, on the outskirts of the village. July, 1920.

In Budapest a detachment of officers of the Awakening Magyars carried out a pogrom on a plan laid down beforehand. The band of thirty men forced their way into the Café Club in the Leopoldsring, and cudgelled the persons present. Several of those who fled were severely injured. The fifty-six-year-old bank director, Arthur Verebély and the barrister Géza Varsány died of their injuries on the spot. Two of the murderers, members of the Ostenburg detachment, George Rigoczky and Ladislaus Illy, were condemned by the court, but amnestied a few months later by Horthy. July, 1920.

In September, members of the Héjjas detachment arrested a wine merchant named Adolf Landau, and brought him to Prónay's barracks at Kelenföld. Héjjas' officers tortured Landau for two weeks in the most horrible manner. They burned his rectum with red-hot irons, and compelled him to drink fifteen litres of water daily. Géza Landau, of Vienna, hurried there to free his father, and was imprisoned in turn, and a ransom of two and a half million crowns demanded for the release of the two. As the family could not raise the money, the elder Landau was so tortured by the officers that he died. The reason for the arrest was that Landau, who dealt in wine at Kecskemét, came into competition with the father of Ivan Héjjas in buying wine. October, 1920.

At Nógrádveröce the members of the Jankovich detachment murdered a dealer named Emanuel Löwy because he was unable to pay the detachment the 150,000 crowns demanded of him. October 3, 1920.

Complete anarchy reigned in the capital. The roving patrols of the Awakening Magyars assaulted peaceful passers-by in broad daylight so mercilessly that at last, in consequence of the unceasing pressure of the opposition members of Parliament, the government " tried " to produce order, and announced this intention in the National Assembly. As a reply to this announcement a detachment of Awakening Magyar officers shot down a policeman named Joseph Soltra, who was trying to do his duty by liberating an innocent passer-by from the hands of the rioting officers. November, 1920.

Three Awakening Magyar officers dragged the Budapest piano-manufacturer, Jacob Reismann, out of his house, robbed him, and then, at the orders of the detachment commandants, Baron Babarczy and Dionys Bibó, brought him to the Radeczky barracks, where he was tortured for months on end, and driven mad. This was not sufficient for the officers, and they murdered the poor madman in the barracks of the Ehrman Colony detachment. November, 1920.

At Miskolcz, a Jugoslav citizen, William Adler, was arrested on a charge of espionage. While he was under arrest his whole family was exterminated. Officers broke into his house at night, outraged his two daughters, and beat his wife terribly. Adler's son was roused by the noise, and shot at the officers from the next room. The shot killed a lieutenant, whereupon the officers revenged themselves by exterminating the whole family. November, 1920.

The authors of the wholesale murders at Orgovány continued their bloody work. Michael Francia-Kiss, one of Héjjas' ringleaders, happened to go to Oerkény to visit a relative. A few days later in Oerkény, Eugene Schwarcz received a threatening letter telling him that he had better pack off at once with bag and baggage to Palestine, or he would see what would happen to him. Schwarcz took the letter to the police station, and was promised at first that the miscreant's name should be ascertained. A policeman told him, however, in confidence that the writer of the letter was more powerful than the police, and they could do nothing. Before Schwarcz had succeeded in putting his affairs in order and getting away, he fell a victim to Francia-Kiss. One evening he did not return home, and since then no trace of him has been found. His wife searched in vain for news of her lost husband ; she could learn nothing about him or his fate. May, 1921.

The same Michael Francia-Kiss appeared in the market-place at Solt, and on the following night a dealer named Adolf Lederer was found robbed and murdered in his home. About the same time the house of a Jewish dealer named Rothschild, between Csengöd and Kiskörös, was broken into ;

he was robbed and beaten till the blood came. When his young daughter began to scream, he was shot. August 22, 1921.

In the spring of 1921 corpses showing clear signs of external injuries were taken out of the Danube at various places along its banks. At first the police began to make serious inquiries in regard to the victims and search for the criminals, but it was soon intimated to them by a superior authority that they must drop the matter. They were confidentially directed to draw up a report on each corpse, stating that no signs of external injury could be detected. In order that the public might not be convinced of the contrary, the bodies were not to be taken to the mortuary.

On April 28 the police of Szigetszentmiklós recovered the body of a man twenty-five to thirty years of age, with a gaping wound in his head; his body was bound with wire and bags of sand had been fastened on back and front. The bags had burst in the water, the sand had escaped, and the current had brought the corpse to the surface. The body was not allowed to be taken to the mortuary for identification. On May 3 a body was recovered in the neighbourhood of Ercsi.

A factory workman named Ladislaus Apostol was taken prisoner by a military patrol on the evening of May 1. He was brought to the Pálffy barracks and transferred thence with seventeen companions to the camp at Piliscsaba, where they were handed over to the officers' detachment of Jankovich-Bésán in Vác. The Jankovich officers tortured some of the prisoners to death, and soon afterwards the Danube washed up the corpses one after another. One body, recovered at Szigetszentmiklós on June 3, was recognised as that of Ladislaus Apostol. At the same time the Danube threw up two bodies at Szigetmonostor. Their throats were cut and heavy stones were found in their pockets.

In the camp at Piliscsaba a detachment was serving under the command of Lieutenant Arpád Galecski. Prisoners who had been pardoned and those about to be released were sent to this detachment from Budapest, by the Budapest Criminal Court, and from elsewhere. At the camp the prisoners were made to sign a declaration that they had been released and were leaving the camp. When, however, they started off, they were stopped by officers' patrols, dragged back to the camp, and most of them subjected to prolonged torture and finally thrown half-dead into the Danube near Budakalászi. Sefcsik, one of the Somogyi murderers, was a member of the Criminal Court for the district around Budapest, and conveyed the unfortunate people to the camp. Galecski had to report the fate of the prisoners to Sefcsik. Captain Baron Eugene Babarczy was in charge of the courier service. These terrible nights, on which the shrieks of the unhappy victims were heard even in the surrounding villages, were known to the people as the Bartholomew nights of Piliscsaba. Héjjas also came frequently to Piliscsaba, and during one of his visits Alexander László-Lauffer and the schoolmaster Anton Márkus were murdered. When their relatives inquired for them, they were shown the signed declarations that they had been released. The truth, however, came out, and Márkus' fiancée tried to shoot Lieutenant Sefcsik in the Café Royal, but the revolver missed fire. Thereupon the officers dragged the girl off to her room ; there they inflicted the most shameful outrages on her, and tortured her until she went mad. Then she was sent to the lunatic asylum at the Lipótmezö.

At St. Endre there was recovered the body of a young woman with bullet-wounds in the skull and other serious injuries. A body brought ashore at Margaret Island was recognised by onlookers as that of a factory workman named Ladislaus Kurta. May, 1921.

One by one the Piliscsaba corpses rose to the surface of the Danube. Thus at St. Endre on May 21 a body with a deep wound in the temple was taken out of the water.

On June 7 a corpse was taken out at the Buda end of the Francis Joseph bridge. A cord was wound round the neck and there were clear marks of strangling. On June 8 another corpse, which had been mutilated, was recovered between the Elizabeth and Francis Joseph bridges. The corpses were not exhibited, and *the Prime Minister's Press Bureau sent a confidential order* to all the papers to add nothing to the reports given by the Police of corpses recovered from the

Danube. This confidential order also directed that if individuals wearing officers' uniform were caught in any atrocity, they must not be described as officers but as civilians masquerading as officers.

The Danube continued to cast up its dead. On July 13 and again on the 14th bodies were taken out at the New-Pest Island, and on the 15th another came into the hands of the police at Szígetujfalu, and was duly reported as showing no marks of violence. Other Hungarian rivers also washed up suspicious corpses. Thus the newspapers reported from Györ on June 6 that the body of a man of thirty to forty years of age had been found on the banks of the Raab. Victims of the White Terror were buried wholesale in the forest at Acs, which became known as the Orgovány of Transdanubia.

When General Loós entered Pécs, the White Terror began to rage there also. The manager of the electric tramways, Ströhl, was hanged because he had headed the tramway employees' organisation. Detective Somogyi was also hanged, because he had remained at his post during the Socialist régime. A tailor named Löwy was tortured to death as an alleged Communist. September, 4, 1921.

At Kaposvár, Max Reisz was arrested, on suspicion of distributing Communist pamphlets, on July 28, 1921. His " examination " lasted two months. It consisted in beating him daily until he lost consciousness. On September 29 he was taken to Hadik barracks at Pest. There the tortures became yet more fiendish. Thumbscrews were fixed to his hands and feet, and his head was crushed into a similar instrument of torture. He was beaten till the blood ran, and the bleeding wounds were systematically sprinkled with salt. His tortures lasted until January 24, 1922 ; on that day he had the good fortune to escape. He is now living in Vienna. Formerly he was a man of giant constitution ; now he is a cripple and an epileptic, suffering daily from repeated fits.

Ivan Héjjas had Joseph Katz, an officer in the national army, and commandant of the Moson forces, arrested for daring to contradict him. In the winter, from November

22, 1921, to January 22, 1922, he lay naked in a cell at the Hadik barracks, where he was daily subjected to torture by being burnt with glowing cigars. In April, 1922, he succeeded in escaping. According to the medical report made in Vienna the marks of seventy-five burns remain to this day on his body. His kneecap is completely shattered, so that he cannot walk without crutches.

\*     \*     \*     \*

I repeat : The cases here quoted make up only a fraction of all the murders, robberies and torturings of the " Christian Course." These horrors were in great part revealed through the Press of the Vienna émigrés, which in the nature of things could obtain no information in numerous instances. I will add no commentary to this frightful picture. I will only stress one fact, that with one or two exceptions the whole of the miscreants have remained unpunished, although their names are known to everyone ; and the organisers of many deeds of horror continue to belong to the circle of intimates of the Regent Horthy.

Even this mediæval system of hanging, imprisoning, torturing and murdering was not enough to satisfy the counter-revolutionaries. The élite of the hand and brain-workers fled abroad in hundreds, but this exodus was furthered artificially by depriving of their living all who seemed dangerous to the Horthy system. *Ad hoc* disciplinary courts were set up, composed of the greatest bawlers of the régime (not least from among those who during the Commune were the noisiest of the Reds), and these gentry drove out the progressive professors, teachers, and officials, from their posts without any serious proceedings or evidence.

The best industrial foremen and scientific, artistic, and intellectual workers were driven from home or deprived of their livelihood, or so terrorised that they were robbed of all spiritual freedom and means of constructive work.

I will quote a few instances only. Julius Pikler, in the truest sense one of the pioneer minds of Hungarian science, whose investigations in psychology and biology are known throughout Europe, was driven from the University of Budapest, of which he had for three decades been one of the principal ornaments. Bernard Alexander, the eminent historian of philosophy, another pillar of the University of Budapest, fled to Switzerland. The well known experimental psychologist, Géza Révész, was robbed of his chair. Theobald Péterfi, the distinguished anatomist, and Michael Polányi, the eminent chemist, are to-day working in foreign institutions. From the ranks of the best workers in Hungarian culture, the following, among others, went abroad: George Hevesy, the physicist; Paul Liebermann, the biologist; Gustave Rados, the professor of medicine; Paul Dienes, the mathematician; Max Goldzieher, the professor of pathological anatomy; and Joseph Madzsár, the professor of hygiene, formerly Secretary of State.

A similar fate befell the best in Hungarian art. The three most advanced painters in Hungary, Karl Kernstok, Robert Berény, and Louis Tihanyi, are now working in Berlin. The two best caricaturists, Marcel Vértes and Henry Major, are having great success in Paris and London. Béla Uitz is also in exile. The best brains in Hungarian literature, Louis Birô, Louis Kassák, Béla Balázs, Ignotus, Alexander Bródy, Louis Hatvany, Edward Kabos, and the well-known dramatic actor Oscar Beregi, have been forced to flee abroad. Among the leading Hungarian publicists in exile are John Hock, Martin Lovászy, Ernest Garami, Sigismund Kunfi, Zoltán Rónai, Paul Szende, and George Bölöni. I have only mentioned the best-known names, but I could name scores of capable industrial foremen, medical men, technicians, chemists, artists, authors and playwrights, who are now scattered far and wide and engaged in a desperate fight for their daily bread.

Yet more pitiable perhaps, is the fate of those brainworkers who, from considerations of family or health, remained at home. Several eminent professors of the University of Budapest, e.g., the historian Henry Marczali, the mathematician Emanuel Beke, the astronomer Radó Kövesligethy, the criminologist Rustem Vámbéry, have lost their chairs. By constant persecution and chicanery various worthy men have been driven to an early death, among them the pioneer philologist, Sigismund Simonyi.

Perhaps even more crushing than the loss of livelihood and health is the leaden burden of the spiritual atmosphere upon culture within the country. The atmosphere of terrorism and of alehouse demagogy and violence is making all scientific research or artistic creation impossible.

And if in spite of all this anyone dared to fulfil his duty as a publicist, proceedings were taken against him, and he was kept for months in gaol. Ladislaus Fényes, one of the most ideal figures among Hungarian public men, who was actually accused of the murder of Tisza, and Zoltán Szász, the brave and noble writer who alone dared to oppose the Press abuses of the Communist dictatorship, suffered this fate.

The campaign was not restricted to the exile or extermination of the intelligentsia; in order to provide a lasting basis for the new feudal absolutism, the few liberties which even the Tisza period had allowed to Hungary were abolished. The granting of permits to sell newspapers in the streets and the right of suspension of newspapers are entirely in the hands of the government. If, despite this, the Press dared to move, open force was applied. Thus, when the editor of the " Miskolczi Reggeli Hirek " (Miskolcz Morning News) ventured to describe the brutal activities of the officers of the flying corps, the officers forced their way into the offices of the paper and compelled the editor at the pistol's point to publish an apology. In Budapest, the articles in " Az Est," the " Pesti Napló" and "Magyarország," despite their mild and subdued tone, greatly upset the terrorists. On October 28, 1921, the members of the Union of Awakening Magyars forced their way into the Athenæum printing rooms, where these papers are printed, drove out the staff at the pistol's point, and then blew up the rotary machines with hand grenades and smashed the whole of the plant. The police identified the perpetrators, but no proceedings whatever were taken against them. A characteristic judgment was pronounced by the Budapest criminal court in the case against those who two years earlier had similarly broken up the editorial offices of the " Népszava," and were then caught in the act. The court found them guilty of the offence of violence against private persons and the misdemeanour of rioting in public places, and as a punishment—reprimanded them.

The conditions are similar in regard to the right of public meeting and of association. Unwelcome trade unions and associations have been arbitrarily dissolved, their property confiscated, and "yellow" unions established in their place.[1]

Not only labour or political unions and parties, for example the Republican Agricultural Party, but also unimpeachable middle-class organisations with benevolent and cultural objects, have suffered the same fate. The Budapest Habitation of the Symbolical Grand Lodge of Hungarian freemasons, and also the provincial lodges, were occupied by officer detachments, and their property, libraries and documents confiscated. A similar fate befell the Sociological Society, which was for several decades one of the most active centres of Hungarian scientific life, and in whose lectures and discussions many of the first scholars in Europe have taken part.

There was only one institution which the Horthyists did not at first venture to touch : the universal, equal, and secret franchise, which had been codified by the October Revolution. We shall see that in the second period of the Horthy system this constitutional guarantee also was destroyed. The first elections for the National Assembly were, however, conducted amid such terrorism that not a single Labour representative was able to get into Parliament, the Labour candidates having been either arrested or compelled to retire by brute force.

---

[1] On this subject see the report of the International Labour Office, "La Liberté Syndicale en Hongrie, Documents rapportés par la Mission d'Informations du Bureau International du Travail" (Geneva, 1921) Edo Fimmen, the Secretary of the International Federation of Trade Unions at Amsterdam, has also published several articles on the sombre conditions in Hungary.

# Chapter XII

# METHODS AND INSTITUTIONS OF THE HORTHY SYSTEM

But the new régime was not content with the complete suppression of popular liberties. It entered the field of positive legislation and created institutions such as are unknown in the history of modern nations. Its laws and regulations are thoroughly characteristic, and lay bare the whole mentality of the present rulers. Let me describe the main features of the Horthy institutions, in order that foreign opinion may judge the true nature of the present "Christian and National Hungary" from its own acts and aims. The following survey is limited to a few specific measures initiated by the new régime.

I. "*Land for Heroes.*" The purpose of Ministerial Decree No. 6650 of 1920 is none other than the revival of the mediæval land grants for military service. Paragraph I clearly defines the purpose of this institution :

"Patriots of unblemished record, who have deserved well of the Hungarian State by serving in its defence, may be granted real estate in token of the undying gratitude of their country ; the grant of land being made subject to the liability of the recipient to render certain defined public services. Such properties are to be designated ' heroes' estates.' "

It was proposed to give these heroes' estates the legal quality of entailed property, in other words to add to the already excessive fetters on Hungarian land distribution. Their supervision is entrusted to a special government department, whose duties are defined as follows by paragraph 10 of the decree :

"The supervision of the heroes' estates and of their possessors, the guidance and control of their due public service, and the cultivation of discipline, of patriotic feeling and of solidarity among them, require the creation of appropriate organs ; the head of the organisation will be the president of the ' heroes' association,' who will be elected by the members."

The decree proceeds to define the persons who can be members of the heroes' association, and provides certain privileges " for the possessors of such heroes' estates as exceed a medium-sized estate in area." The possessor of a hero's estate and his next heir are authorised to place the title " Vitéz " (" hero ") before their names, and an oath of loyal and scrupulous observance of the obligation of public service is required to be taken on entering into possession. Other provisions in the decree show the intention of reviving the mediæval fiefs and feudal nobility. This purpose, naturally, is not openly stated, but there is no possibility of doubt that the obligations attached to the heroes' estates have the character of military service. The whole official Press greeted the decree with enthusiasm and devoted weeks to popularising it, as creating an effective armed organisation capable of maintaining the established order and " nipping in the bud every effort of the enemies of the country."

It is characteristic of the spirit of the Horthy régime that within this organisation of Janissaries for the protection of the big estate system, class differences were given statutory recognition, certain special privileges being granted, as already mentioned, to those members of the heroes' association who possessed estates of medium size. At first it was anticipated that the great nobles and prelates would respond to the appeals of the government on behalf of this patriotic plan, with its second purpose of protecting the big estates, and would place large parcels of land at the disposal of the government, so providing, in conjunction with the mercenaries of the small heroes' estates, the means of assisting the reduced gentry to regain their old position. But Hungarian feudalism is not in the habit of showing magnanimity even in favour of its own class, and so the whole institution was condemned by the general indifference to remain little more than a farce, qualified by the inevitable Panamist scandals. Medium heroes' estates were received

by men who had had very little to do with the defence of
their country.

Despite this complete fiasco, the institution is interesting
as a sample of the reactionary atmosphere in present-day
Hungary.

II. *The reintroduction of corporal punishment* is primarily
interesting from the same point of view. One of the most
highly prized institutions of the old caste life in Hungary
for keeping in subjection its bond slaves was the whipping-
bench. Law 26 of 1920 reintroduces this as a Christian-
National institution. The law is entitled : " Concerning
the most effectual means of protecting through the penal
code property, persons, and public morality." It authorises
the imposition of twenty-five strokes for indecency, murder,
manslaughter, robbery, theft, blackmail, receiving, fraud,
arson, fraudulent bankruptcy, usury and profiteering.
Decree No. 36300, 1920, of the Ministry of Justice provides
as follows for the execution of the sentence :

" The sentence shall be carried out upon the delinquent
laid on the whipping-bench in a suitable room of the prison
building, which shall be as isolated as possible. The delinquent
shall be clad in shirt and drawers, and the strokes shall be
delivered only upon the sitting portion of his body."

It is obvious that the source of the reintroduction of
whipping is the same longing for the good old times which
inspired the institution of heroes' estates and the heroes'
association ; the victims primarily envisaged for legal
whippings were the Jewish profiteers. It is characteristic
that whipping is not being resorted to in cases of offences
against the person ; the obvious explanation is that the
present ruling class in Hungary is very frequently guilty of
just such offences in its prisons, internment camps and
barracks.

The Horthy government is trying to excuse itself for this
mediæval practice before its foreign critics by pretending
that the law is only a paper disposition and is never put
into operation, serving only as a means of deterrence. To
this it must be replied that whipping and other corporal
punishments are the very gold reserve of the present-day

" Christian National " Hungary.   One single fact will suffice to prove this.   In the sitting of the National Assembly of December 23, 1921, the Deputy Victor Drozdy called the attention of Ministers to the action of the gendarmerie in Békés :

" The Royal Hungarian Gendarmerie Command," he said, " in the County of Békés, has issued a circular, no. 1248/fgt. 1921, requesting its subordinates ' to abstain from all ill-treatment, as complaints with regard to this are coming in every day.'   At the end of the order the paper is perforated, and the lower section contains the following warning : ' At the last conference at the district command the order prohibiting ill-treatment was discussed.   It was unanimously declared that public security cannot be maintained without corporal punishment.   Both the district commander and I myself are in agreement that the punishment is almost without exception occasioned by the civilian concerned, who has brought it on himself in most cases by his impertinent and provocative behaviour.   This fact and the fact of the past revolutions make it impossible for individuals who disturb the public security to be treated with kid gloves by the gendarmes.   The above order is issued in consequence of an interpellation in the National Assembly. . . .   Consequently it need not be taken seriously. . . .   I draw the attention of my subordinates to the necessity, when they are driven to take action against an individual who behaves impudently to the patrols, of ensuring that they leave no basis for a medical certificate, that is, no visible bodily injury, and of acting not before ten witnesses but before none.   If a gendarme is unable to inflict punishment in such a way as to leave no evidence behind him, he deserves disciplinary treatment.   I repeat, serious ill-usage must be avoided, but there is no harm in a couple of boxes on the ears, and there is no other way than this of restoring the former authority of the gendarmes. . . .   This warning is strictly confidential, and is to be torn off and destroyed.   The gendarmes are, however, to be confidentially acquainted with it.   Soldiers attached to the gendarmerie and unreliable gendarmes are under no circumstances to be informed."

This order, in which the medium of the maintenance of law and order himself invites, in an official document, flagrant breaches of law and order, throws a stronger light than any sociological analysis on the moral character of the Horthy system.

III. *Internment and police supervision.*   In addition to handing over men's lives and bodily health to the tender mercies of the Terror, the Horthy system has removed all guarantees of personal liberty through its institutions of internments and police supervision. These render quite superfluous the work of the courts. Under Decree No. 4352 (1920) of the Minister of the Interior, all those persons are to be placed under police supervision or put in custody or interned, " who are dangerous, objectionable or suspicious from the point of view of the State, of the peace and order of society, or of public order and security ; also all those persons whose activity is injurious in economic life." Nothing more would be needed to prove that this decree would amount to the entire abolition of personal freedom, even if the determination of " dangerous," " objectionable," " suspicious " or " economic injury " were entrusted to an " independent " court. But the decree places the right of decision as to internments and police supervision in the hands of the police authorities and the Minister of the Interior. By it anyone who is politically inconvenient to the government can be put out of the way at any time without further ado. He can also be ruined, for § 12 of the ukase lays down that no compensation is allowed for the economic loss which may result to any person from official actions connected with police supervision, arrest, expulsion or internment. This provision sets not only the liberty but the property of the victim at the mercy of the arbitrary organs of the government.

The horrors of the internment camps form a special chapter in the history of the White Terror. The camps are hermetically sealed from the outer world, but there is reliable evidence of a large number of the actrocities practised in them. A few instances must suffice.

In the internment camp at Zalaegerszeg, a girl of 18, Manci Várkövi, hanged herself on account of the ill-treatment she was receiving. She was noticed, the cord was cut, and for a punishment she was left twenty-four hours with hands and feet tied together. Another woman, Anna Hegyi, was placed for thirty days in solitary confinement. The soldiers went freely in and out of her cell, and when she returned to the camp she was pregnant. A Slovak girl, Piroska

Paranycsura, who was standing near the fencing watching persons passing by outside, was shot dead by the guards. Anna Szentesi was also shot at, but missed.

There were other shocking atrocities at the Hajmáskér camp. Fritz Eibenschütz, formerly a lieutenant in the regular army, who had served also in the Red army, was interned in this camp. Before his liberation he was ordered to place his thumb on the table, ostensibly for a finger print to be taken. Half his thumb was then cut off. The officers laughingly told him that that was his credential. Another prisoner, Béla Királyi, had his ear cut off. Eibenschütz succeeded in escaping across the Austrian frontier, and personally reported his case in the editorial office of the " Jövö."[1]

Despite the terrorist handling of the Press, the evidence of the horrors of the internment camps spread throughout the country. In the sitting of the National Assembly on December 31, 1921, the Deputy Victor Drozdy painted these camps in the darkest colours, and demanded their breaking-up. In the course of his courageous speech Drozdy said :

" How many innocent persons there are who owe their internment to private revenge. I have received a letter from one of the interned prisoners, and he tells me that the revision committees deal arbitrarily with the cases. The interned persons have declared that they will refuse next time to go before such a commission. Sons have been interned by mistake for their fathers, and brothers for brothers ; there are actually sixty-five schoolchildren in internment. Anyone who attempts to escape is shot down, or beaten till he is half-dead.

" Corruption is rampant in connexion with release from the camps. Interned women are exposed to violation. Officers and non-commissioned officers are equally merciless. Binding is a frequent punishment. A girl of sixteen from Sátoraljaujhely, has become a mother in camp. At least she should be left no longer in this verminous barracks, but taken to hospital. Dare we allow ourselves the luxury of artificially forcing the growth of Communists in this way ? "

The Deputy Rudolf Rupert brought up these Siberian conditions again in the sitting of the National Assembly on

[1] A Magyar newspaper then published at Vienna by the Right wing of the *émigrés*.—Trans.

January 29, 1922. He read a letter addressed to him by internees, according to which conditions in the camps had grown not better but worse. Such liberations as were effected were the work of foreign missions. There had been many internments of prisoners of war returning from Russia, on the strength of innuendos or denunciations.

"I may point out to the Peasant Farmers' Party that the internees are not recruited exclusively from the scum of the towns, but include respectable rural workers. Among the returning prisoners it is mostly rural workers who are interned. The prisoners of war are greeted in every country through which they pass on their way home with flowers and music and fêtes. When they arrive home, in the camp at Csót, the underhand work begins. The most striking example is that of Cadet Michael Csiga, who fought sixteen months on end at the front and was accorded the gold medal for bravery and both the silver medals before he was taken prisoner. During the greater part of his period of captivity he was with Denikin's army. On his journey homewards he was caught by the Reds and kept several months under arrest. Finally he succeeded in getting back home. Here one of his comrades denounced him as an ex-Red soldier, and alleged that in a Tartar village he had taken part in the execution of three Tartars. The court at Székesfehérvár acquitted him, the charge having been proved to be unfounded, but Csiga was nevertheless sent back to the camp at Csót. In vain did he call twenty witnesses, mostly officers, in evidence of his innocence."

Mr. Rupert went on to describe in detail the horrors of the Zalaegerszeg camp. A convict prison would be a veritable paradise in comparison. Consumption demands endless victims. In no prison are the prisoners so mercilessly treated as in Zalaegerszeg. For small offences the internees are condemned to twenty days' solitary confinement and thrown into chains. So the State manufactures Communists. The camp has cost the country many millions of kronen.

But these and similar exposures have been of no avail whatever. Hundreds continue to languish in the internment camps.

IV. "*The more effectual protection of the State and the social order.*" Under this imposing title a law has been introduced which not only threatens "violent revolutionaries" with imprisonment or even death, but introduces a whole new category of offences into the penal code. These are described by the law as " Offences and misdemeanours against the respect due to the Hungarian State and nation." The persons for whose benefit this wonderful new class of crime has been defined are clearly stated in §7 of the law :

" Any person who makes or spreads a false statement calculated to reduce the respect for the Hungarian State and nation, or to detract from its good name, is guilty of an offence and liable to imprisonment for a period not exceeding five years.

" The period may be extended to ten years, if the offence was committed with the purpose of moving a foreign State or organisation to take unfriendly action against the Hungarian State or nation ; and if a foreign State or organisation is moved to take unfriendly action, the penalty is imprisonment for life."

Behind the solemnity of these legal phrases there lurks the intention of frightening journalists from laying bare the sins of the Horthy system before foreign readers. And in fact Zoltán Szász, Victor Gergely and others have been condemned by the courts to several years' imprisonment, for no other reason than that they dared to write in severe but just criticism of the Horthy policy. The law is intended to play the part of a Chinese wall, to conceal the Hungary of the White Terror from the public gaze.

V. *The militarisation of the coal mines.* The Horthy system has also revived serfdom ; this is the effect of its militarisation of the coal mines. Decree No. 6407 (1920) of the Premier's Office removes all matters connected with the production and supply of coal from the Government Commissary for Coal Production and Supply, and entrusts them to the military inspector for coal questions. This military organ has unlimited authority over the workers in the coal mines. Point 5 in §3 of the decree says :

" If the military inspector for coal questions is satisfied that the management of any coal mine is unable to maintain discipline with the aid of the means of enforcement provided under the regulations for service and labour, and also if the results of the production in any mine, in consequence of deliberate or neglectful action on the part of the workpeople or other employees, are unsatisfactory or fall off without sufficient reason, the military inspector shall take the necessary steps, in agreement with the Government Commissary for Coal Production, to place the employees responsible for the falling off in production in the mining works in question, together with the other employees in the works, under military discipline."

The military dictator is also empowered to have " seditious elements " interned without formality, and to set the interned workers back at their work at any subsequent time at his discretion.

This military dictatorship is in a particularly strong position, since the Hungarian miners are unable to change their occupation and are bound to the mines. Bearing all this in mind, we may maintain without exaggeration that in Hungary to-day there are nearly 90,000 men living in serfdom. The commission of enquiry sent into Hungary in August-September, 1920, by the International Labour Office, established that the military administrators had not only entirely rescinded the miners' rights of meeting and association, but had repeatedly subjected workers to brutal tortures. These workers have become pariahs, *glebae adscripti* in the most literal sense, chained to their mines. Even if a relation dies they are not allowed to leave the mining area. The military dictatorship is actually placing obstacles in the way of the managers of the mining concerns in regard to discharging workers.

With regard to this last point General Riedel, military inspector for coal questions, said to the delegates of the International Labour Office, " the management can only discharge a worker if he commits an offence against discipline or a crime—if, for instance, he has threatened his manager with a knife or has stolen. You would not believe that in Tatabánya there are workers who steal simply in order to be discharged and so enabled to go to work in Slovakia."

A more damaging admission with regard to the Horthy system can hardly have been heard than this slip of the tongue.

VI. *Numerus clausus.* The wild anti-semitism of the " Christian Course " is, of course, not directed against the great Jewish capitalists and business men : with these the " Christian " business politicians and Panamists are on the best of terms. Every Jewish bank has its own influential

Christian-National protectors and directors, even its own armed force in the persons of various pensioned officers of high rank.  Anti-semitism is directed only against the poor, hard working, genuinely cultured Jewish intelligentsia, whose greater industry and keener judgment have made them formidable competitors of the privileged gentry class. The new policy aims at getting rid of these Jewish intellectuals at all costs, although the great bulk of them have held aloof even from the moderately progressive movements, and many of them have taken a place among the most faithful supporters of feudal class domination. One of the first measures of the Horthy government was to purge the public services and the school and university staffs of all Jews, by the arbitrary application of criminal and disciplinary procedure, on the pretext that they had taken part in the revolution.  But this was not enough.  It was desired to make such provision as should ensure complete freedom in the future from the competition of Jewish intellectuals.  This was the purpose of Law XXV. of 1920, " Concerning the regulation of entry into the universities, the polytechnic, the economic faculty of the University of Budapest and the Academies of Law."  Sincerity would have given the law the following title : " Law concerning the exclusion of Jews from the higher educational institutions," for that is its whole content.

Article 1 of this law lays down that the number of students to be admitted into each faculty shall be determined on the basis of the proposals of the faculties concerned by the Minister for Public Worship and Education.  Under §3 written application must be made for admission, which is at the discretion of the faculty concerned.

" In granting admission attention must be paid not only to the requirements of loyalty and moral character and to the intellectual capacity of the applicant, but care must also be taken that the comparative numbers of the entrants correspond as nearly as possible to the relative population of the various races or nationalities, or at least to nine-tenths of them."

This provision degrades the administrative bodies at the universities to the level of police departments, and the disgraceful function is not even carried out in actual fact by the university administration ; a committee of officers of the national army and members of the Christian-National terrorist " Union of the Awakening Magyars," reports on the applications for admittance, so that in the end the professors only formally approve the decisions made by these terrorist committees.

Since the Treaty of Trianon,—as a result of the century-old follies of the racial policy of Hungarian feudalism—cut off virtually every district of Hungary which had been settled by any of the minority nationalities, it is obvious that the one and only intention of the law is to shut the Jews out of the universities, and for this purpose the Hungarian Jews, most of whom are completely assimilated, were declared a separate race and nationality. Apparently the oppression of nationalities is so much a passion of the Christian Nationalists, that now that virtually all national minorities had been lost, they hastened to make a fresh one out of the very Jews who, in the period of the forcible Magyarisation of the nationalities of the periphery, had always figured as the most faithful supporters of the idea of the Hungarian State.

The spirit of the *numerus clausus* spread also in the army. In many places the Jewish volunteers were not given arms but sent to work in labour battalions.

This wild anti-semitism is characteristic as the only serious and deep moral reaction of the Horthy system. Yet even this is a fraudulent and insincere anti-semitism, for it does not aim at shutting out the great faults and failings of the Jews, but the Western culture and freedom which these illiterates identify with the Jews.

But the Jews themselves, and even Liberalism in general, are also to blame for this extravagant anti-semitism. During the last twenty-five years the Jewish question became taboo in Hungary. In the Hungarian Liberal Press it was forbidden to offer either criticism or warning to the Jews. Anyone who pointed out the excessive preponderance of the Hungarian Jews in the leading positions in the intellectual world, corresponding neither to their relative numbers in the country nor to their relative intellectual and moral worth ; who noted that this preponderance was due largely not to higher intelligence, but to more ruthless elbowing; who ventured to analyse the anti-social qualities with which centuries of Ghetto life had endowed the Jews ; who ventured to point to the danger of the streams of foreign usurers which were crowding in amongst the simple village folk of the eastern counties, or to criticise the many faults of taste of Jewish intellectuals in Budapest,—was at once regarded as a danger to the community, a coarse and ignorant anti-semite to be shouted down by the whole Press and effectually put out of action.

In his unequal but sincere book published during the war, Peter Agoston, later a People's Commissary, referred to the menacing Jewish question. The whole of the " Liberal " Press pounced on him, and the official Jewish Press howled with rage. Realising the unexampled urgency of the question, I circulated a questionnaire to a number of prominent persons for the journal of the Sociological Society ; but such terrorism was exercised by Jewish public opinion that leading politicians, Conservative and Socialist alike, were unwilling to state their views. When the issue dealing with this question appeared, the Jewish denominational Press opened a truculent campaign against me, and the rabbis preached against me in the synagogues and roused their congregations against the journal and the Radical party.

There is for all this a Jewish question in Hungary, and it has to be solved. The essence of it is the failure of the Hungarian people, through its great cultural backwardness and lack of economic and political organisation, to make its influence felt in any sphere in proportion to its great latent moral and intellectual powers. The reserve of moral power which in other peoples proceeds from their natural endowments, the eternally renewed bodily and mental energy, is dissipated and destroyed among us by the hateful trinity of landlordism, usury and religious obscurantism. The mass of the people are cut off from the higher spiritual values. The Hungarian people has shown less and less intellectual fertility, and culture has been represented more and more by foreign elements, predominantly Jewish, and especially by those Jews who best succeeded in making their peace with that organised system of exploitation which is called the Hungarian State.  Thus the most unscrupulously reactionary Jews came to the top, and a section through the intellectual aristocracy of Budapest would have shown the most vicious combination in the world :  a mixture of the arrogance and self-indulgence, the laziness and superficiality of the county family type, with the cynicism and hedonism and amoralism of high finance.  Both economically and morally it was a very unhealthy situation, and this spiritual plague ate into Hungarian society as seriously as the material evils of tuberculosis and emigration or the cancer of illiteracy.

But when all this is said and admitted, there can be no doubt that there is only one rational solution of the Jewish question for men of honour and goodwill :  the raising and strengthening of the people and the repression of Jewish parasitism, combined, however, with an increased respect for Jewish intellectual workers.  Here, obviously, we meet with one of the crucial wrongnesses of the Horthy system : it desires to maintain unaltered the system of feudalism and capitalism, force and usury which is the prime cause of the impoverishment of our people and of the rank growth of Jewish parasitism.

The Horthyist anti-semitism is directed not to the elimination of the harmful functions of a section of Jewry but to the expulsion of individual Jews in order that their parasitic functions may be taken over by Christian idlers and adventurers.  Much more serious and sincere than its pursuit of illicit dealers and profiteers and company promoters is its vicious hounding out of those Jews, the sincerest and best of their race, who have done true pioneer work in Hungary, and without whose collaboration Hungarian culture would sink to an Asiatic level, as it is actually doing under the White Terror.

VII. *The attempt to introduce universal compulsory labour.*  In the last weeks of the National Assembly the Minister of the Interior introduced a bill for compulsory labour. It only failed to become law for lack of time to carry it through. Under this bill every man between 18 and 45 years of age was to be called upon to perform work of public utility for a period of two years. What " work of public utility " was to be taken to mean was defined as follows in §1 of the bill :

" For the purpose of this law all work is to be regarded as work of public utility which is necessary to the activities of any authority or department or public institution, the functioning, maintenance or protection of a public undertaking, and finally to the warding off of any threat to the existence of a part or the whole of the country, or any other internal danger."

It is obvious that this deliberately loose definition would put the whole of the working population at the mercy of every caprice of the government. The government would be provided with a fresh means of terrorising elements inconvenient to it, of suppressing every labour agitation by enrolling State strikebreakers, and, if it chose, of completing its secret and irregular military formations.

VIII. *The suppression of the land reform.* The true nature of the White régime is revealed even more clearly by its unconcealed hostility to land reform. For two generations past it has been plain to all that Hungary's renascence is dependent on a solution of the land question. There is no country in Europe with so unhealthy a land system. Hungary is, so to speak, a clinical case of *morbus latifundii*. Hand in hand with this evil go servile conditions and illiteracy, tuberculosis and emigration on an enormous scale.

During the war it became a matter of general agreement that a solution of the land question had got to be found. Without it no healthy economic and social life in Hungary is conceivable. Every political party had promised to assist the landless class to the possession of land. I have already described how the October Revolution hastened to bring in a bill for the expropriation of large estates. This law set the maximum ownership at 500 yokes. Preparations were made everywhere for commencing the distribution of land. Michael Károlyi set the example and made the first sacrifice in sharing out his own estate.

In the hour of victory the counter-revolution had itself promised a just solution of the land question : it claimed to stand primarily for an agrarian democracy on a Christian, national and racial basis.   For months its agitators had been inveighing specially against the great Jewish landowners, and everywhere the landless had been promised land.   The leading government party, the so-called Peasant Farmers' party, placed land distribution as the foremost plank in its political platform.   The land question has been rendered still more acute by the Treaty of Trianon, partly because it cut out of Hungary the territory in which small-ownership was comparatively common, partly because with the bulk of the industrial, mining and forest areas lost to the country, the popular feeling was stronger than ever that there remained only one path towards Hungarian reconstruction—through the creation of an agrarian democracy, provided with the means of existence by the transition from the extensive culture of the *latifundia* to methods producing a larger and better yield.

Even apart from these considerations, the social pressure towards land reform had been continually increasing. Nearly three-quarters of the agricultural population (4,200,000 souls) of the mutilated torso of Hungary consist either of landless proletarians of agriculture, or cultivators with tiny holdings who also belong virtually to the same category.   On the other hand, 68.33 per cent. of the properties exceeding 1,000 cadastral yokes[1] have been left to the new Hungary !   In the new Hungary, according to semi-official statistics, there are roughly 1,500 properties of more than 1,000 yokes, with a total area of about 6,500,000 yokes.   The total area of the country is now about 15,800,000 cadastral yokes.   Thus the large properties exceeding 1,000 yokes take up nearly 40 per cent. of the total area.   The situation is made worse by the fact that more than two-thirds of the great estates are entailed.   The church and entailed properties exceed 2,000,000 cadastral yokes.   It may be imagined how explosive is the situation, in a country in which the political parties have been

[1] 1,428 acres.

solemnly promising land reform for decades, and in which it was actually begun by the October Revolution.

The new régime had, therefore, no way of escape from dealing with this question. It could only secure the support of the country districts by promising an early and a just land reform. This obligation was all the more incumbent on it towards a " racially pure, Christian " Hungarian people, since in the preceding decades the Jewish landowners had increased without bounds, and even the bulk of the Church and State *latifundia* had passed into the hands of Jewish lessees.

But there is no possible solution of the land question save through the abolition of the system of great feudal estates, through a broad plan of land distribution, through the abolition of entail and the secularisation of church lands.

This, however, was the very policy to which the " Christian-National " régime was most averse ; it had come into existence for no other purpose than to save the great feudal estates and the church lands. Nevertheless, at least an ostensible solution of the question had to be found. The National Assembly resolved upon a reform which is essentially nothing but an elaborate formula for *preventing* the use of the large estates for the purposes of land reform, a formula which does no more than give the government the opportunity of rewarding its propagandists or distributing alms.

It is impossible to go here into details of this rabulistic legislation by means of which the legislators have taken away with one hand what they gave with the other, or to explore the labyrinth of regulations issued under it : this would require a small volume to itself. It must suffice to mention a few of the most fundamental provisions, and their practical results. The Horthy régime promised the landless or virtually landless majority sites for houses and workable small leaseholds or properties. The grants have remained mostly on paper, for the following reasons :[1]

---

[1] The two pertinent laws are No. XXIX. of 1920, " Concerning the allocation of sites for houses," and No. XXXVI. of 1920, " Concerning the conditions for regulating a juster distribution of landed property."

1. All elements regarded as unreliable by the Horthy government are shut out from the benefits of the reforms.

2. For the agricultural proletariat the law proposes to grant three yokes per head. This in itself makes the reform valueless ; the aim is apparently to provide further cheap labour for the great estates. On the other hand it allows wide scope for the establishment of counter-revolutionary medium-sized estates, even of large estates, and for the rewarding of bureaucrats and officers.

3. A maximum area for estates, with a right of State expropriation of the excess, is not fixed ; the division of properties is only authorised " in so far as it does not hinder the efficient and rational management of those portions of the great estates which are not alienated."

4. This provision effectually sabotages the whole reform, especially as the execution of the laws and regulations is entrusted to official organs which are perfectly well known to be the most willing of tools of the feudal ruling class.

5. A period of five years is laid down within which alienation may be effected. After this period it is to cease. But the whole of the administrative apparatus is deliberately working at a snail's pace, so as to prevent anything being done. The underlying idea of the government is that in the course of these five years it will succeed in creating a thoroughly reliable administrative and military organisation, with which it will be able if necessary to wage open war against the agricultural proletariat.

6. The whole of the long and costly process of claiming and securing the allocation of land is paid for out of the pockets of the recipients. This shuts out from the benefits of the reform the very persons most in need of them.

7. Purchase is proceeding at exorbitant and usurious prices, amounting to a further exploitation of the poverty-stricken rural population. Under §44 of the law, " Such a purchase price is to be fixed as will provide the existing owners with compensation fully equivalent to the value of the property at the date of alienation."

8. The Hungarian government has recently been again deceiving the rural population by the announcement that

owners of property exceeding 1,000 yokes will be required to make payment in real estate under the levy on capital, and that in this way 400,000 yokes will be released for the purpose of the land reform. It may safely be assumed that the administrative authorities will sabotage the reform once more in this connexion; but even if the capital levy should actually yield 400,000 yokes, this quantity would not meet the needs of the landless persons, even putting their number at no more than 1,200,000 ; and apart from this the soaring prices would be beyond their means.

9. While the Hungarian people continues to be without land, a land sale bureau has been opened in America, to enable the landed aristocracy to sell for dollars to rich buyers.

10. The law has instituted monopolies in the sale of parcels of land in favour of a few financial institutes under the protection of the government.

11. The law also takes care to provide that if here and there feeling is so bitter that an estate has to be parcelled out, the owner shall receive compensation in another part of the country.

12. The law also provides an opportunity of sacrificing the middling and small landowners to save the great land-owners.

13. The fraudulent nature of the whole reform is best proved by the fact that no financial provision is made for carrying through any serious division of properties, or for enabling the State to exert any serious influence upon the land market. The provision made exists only on paper, and if it were put into effect it would not suffice to attain the purposes set forth.

14. Nothing could illustrate more vividly or more fully the way the land reform laws have been carried out than the speech of Victor Drozdy, the courageous Liberal Deputy, in the sitting of the National Assembly on December 2, 1921. Drozdy is one of the few white ravens who are really in touch with the Hungarian tillers of the soil. Among other things he said :

" According to the latest official report 4,000 yokes were distributed in the past year for building sites. Assuming that

4,000 yokes will provide 10,000 sites for dwellings, it will take us 100 years to carry out the law and supply the million applicants. As regards the land reform law, virtually nothing has been done. The first step is to be taken, perhaps, in connexion with the capital levy, when the owners of over 1,000 yokes have been induced to pay the levy in kind. This, according to official calculations, will release 400,000 yokes. But if we glance through the statistics supplied by the Minister, we find that there are 1,200,000 approved applicants who desire to take advantage of the law to increase their small farms. It is easy to see that with one-third of a yoke apiece available from the capital levy for these 1,200,000 applicants, it will take another hundred years at the present pace to supply their needs."[1]

M. Drozdy went on to produce a mass of concrete data showing up the swindling practised in connexion with the land reform, culminating in cases in which the poor people not only failed to obtain any land, but failed to get back the money they had paid as a deposit. " If we look for the cause of the fiasco," he added, " we find it in a systematic obstruction of the law : the authorities are themselves refusing to put it into operation. A number of interested persons are working under the surface and moving Heaven and earth to prevent the law from being a reality."

Drozdy advanced further concrete instances in proof of his contention. In many places the authorities sent gendarmerie to seize the peasants' applications for land distribution. There were even cases in which the magistrate (szolgabiró)[2] himself terrorised the applicants. There were cases in which poor villagers, assembled to discuss the dwelling sites question, were forcibly dispersed by the gendarmerie.

Similar cases were reported by the Deputy Michael Kerekes—since prematurely dead—who was one of the few who dared to stand out in opposition to the White Terror. Speaking in the National Assembly, he showed that "the land reform can only be carried into effect by also reforming

---

[1] This calculation is clearly over-optimistic, since the law and regulations for the capital levy provide ample opportunities for sabotage ; and the calculation also leaves out of account a very substantial sectio  of the agricultural proletariat.

[2] An all-important administrative official for whom there is no exact equivalent in English. (German, Stuhlrichter.)—Trans.

the administrative body—by giving Hungary an entirely different administration." He stated that the village notaries were not even posting up the regulations concerning the land reform. " This is running the risk," he said, " of revolution. It is our duty, therefore, to call attention to it." He added that the notaries were acting under direct inspiration from their superiors. " Quite recently at an official enquiry the representative of the Ministry of Finance made a speech totally irreconcilable with the law, and calculated to create disturbances. He said that as the land reform is a revolutionary innovation it must not be furthered but hindered."

15. A still more lurid light is thrown on the " land reform" of the Horthyists by the decree issued by the Minister of the Interior on April 28, at the time of the election campaign, " Concerning the prohibition of the subversive agitation which is being carried on in connexion with the land reform." This typical Horthyist decree enacts that anyone who ventures to cavil at the land reform shall be liable to 15 days' imprisonment and a fine of 2,000 crowns. §1 says expressly, " The encouragement of any persons, whether publicly or by house to house visits, whether collectively or individually, to any effort or attitude or proceeding at variance with the law XXXVI of 1920 for the just distribution of land, is prohibited." The decree is characteristic not only of the so-called land reform but of the election farce which was in progress at the time.

This sabotage of the reform of land ownership is the clearest proof of the insincerity of the continual professions of the Whites of attachment to a Magyar racial and national policy. For a Radical land reform would not only mean the economic and ethical renascence of Hungary, but is bound up with the future of the Magyar race, as in the absence of such a reform, the race is either being proletarianised, dying off, or emigrating. Rather than allow any reform, the White régime has concluded agreements with various shipping companies with regard to the transport of the Hungarian emigrants who are compelled to seek refuge across the ocean, mainly on the free soil of Canada.

In this depopulating Hungary it is becoming more and more impossible to maintain the great estate system. Sooner or later the great landowners will be compelled, whether they like it or not, to subdivide their estates. But among their crippled agricultural proletariat they will be unable to find purchasers with sufficient capital, and the way will thus be clear for the influx of the more prosperous peasant farmers of the neighbouring States.

Thus the age-long policy of Magyar feudalism is repeating itself, the policy which exterminated the Magyar serfs and replaced them by immigrant serfs, more submissive and obedient, of alien race.

From this very incomplete sketch of the Horthy régime the reader will be able to see the terrible abyss into which this country and its people, worthy of a better fate, have been plunged. A veritable mediæval system has been spread over the country, degrading the countryman to the status of serfdom, subjecting the town workman to militarism, and rendering impossible any sort of free intellectual development. It is fairly symbolic of this rebirth of the middle ages that in some districts the corvée has been reintroduced, as Deputy Négyesy proved in Parliament from concrete instances.

# CHAPTER XIII

## THE HORTHY SYSTEM (*continued*)

THE events and institutions, the ideas and tendencies sketched in the foregoing chapters may perhaps tempt the foreign observer to give up Hungary in disgust as the final refuge of Balkan barbarism and demented nationalism. Such a judgment would be very superficial ; the situation cannot be properly understood without an analysis of the moral condition into which the unfortunate nation has fallen. Until the recent times of crisis, the pick of the intellectual and moral forces in Hungary could safely have stood comparison with those of any other of the Succession States. A comparison of Hungarian literature, art, science and journalism before the Horthy period with the corresponding achievements of the Succession States, would not be unfavourable to Hungarian culture.[1] How comes it, then, that such shocking acts of brutality are being committed in the country ?

The explanation lies mainly in the fact that, while the average quality of Hungary's best intellectual and moral leaders is very high, the standard of the average citizen is much lower than in the neighbouring countries, and the broad foundation of the social pyramid is still ill-organised and ignorant, as the result of centuries of feudalism, usury and extortion. Moreover, opportunity for real talent has been scarce in consequence of unashamed favouritism and family cliques. This was a country of amateurs indiscriminately pitchforked into office. A further explanation is to be found in the nature of the leading minds of Hungary.

[1] Cf. in this connexion Louis Hatvany's book " Das Verwundete Land " (" The Wounded Country." Vienna and Leipzig, 1921), which gives a fairly true picture of the literary work of Hungary before the collapse. The political and historical portion of the book is, on the other hand, in many places narrow and biassed.

Since these consisted largely of Jewish and foreign elements, they lived in a sort of ex-territorial relationship to the backward population and its aspirations. Then came the dictatorship of the proletariat, the brutality and extravagant demagogy of which stirred up the converse type of demagogy. Thus arose a kind of biological reversion from the extremity of revolution to the extremity of reaction.

The brain of the unhappy country has been destroyed. The four or five thousand men who represented European ideals and culture among us, are either languishing in the prisons, or interned, or starving in exile, or if they are still in their homes they never know when they will be insulted in the street or even dragged out of bed by some gang of " Awakening Magyars." Even the better public opinion in Hungary was always indescribably flabby and backbone-less. Even in normal circumstances it was a very rare event for anyone to take a stand for his convictions. Neither economic, nor moral, nor religious conditions favoured real spiritual independence. How much less now under the White Terror ! Now it needs courage not to howl with the wolves but merely to keep silent and wait. Almost all serious thought is now silenced in unhappy Hungary, and the Horthy régime has wiped out the achievements of the last quarter of a century.

Counter-revolutionary tendencies now develop un-restrained. The Regent exercises the rights of a King and holds his court with an ostentation rivalling that of the old monarchy. The most notorious of the terrorist officers form his bodyguard. Admiral Horthy, whom the more serious generals of the old army looked down upon as a mere obsequious court lackey, has had neither the conscience nor the energy to discountenance the gross malpractices of his " best officers." On the contrary, he has been the devoted servant of this criminal clique, feeling that he owed to them his rise to power, and that without their support his position would be untenable. Coming from the ranks of the Calvinist lower nobility, he had never been regarded as their equal by the magnates and higher clergy in the counter-revolutionary camp. They desired to get rid of him, for despite all his professions they doubted the sincerity of his legitimist sentiments. Consequently, as the tension between Horthy and the aristocracy and between his officers and those of the regular army increased, he surrounded himself more and more with his own bands, on whom he could depend. Thus a powerful Horthy camarilla grew up, controlling economic and political life and the public administration. The personal adherents of Horthy worked themselves into all the influential positions. Swindling business organisations were formed on an enormous scale (e.g., the " Ergon " and the " Futura "), out of which the staff of the camarilla enriched themselves by taking bribes and fees for jobbery and official favours. With the aid of unlimited terrorism and demagogy the most vocal of Horthy's creatures were foisted into the National Assembly, while his royal right of nomination enabled him to put his friends into the most important government posts.

At the same time the arming of the counter-revolution began. The same Entente diplomacy which carried out so mercilessly the disarming of Germany and Austria, made not a word of protest, even gave every possible assistance, while the Hungarian counter-revolution equipped a considerable army—contrary to the Treaty of Trianon. Careful and reliable estimates which have been made assess this army at one cavalry and seven infantry divisions, nearly 70,000 men. A whole series of disguised military formations have also been created in addition to the regular troops. The customs guards, the finance police, the gendarmes are simply so many component parts of the armed forces of the counter-revolution. In addition to these, all the officials belonging to the ruling class and all the young reactionaries at the Universities have been armed. The numbers in this irregular army are hardly less than those of the regulars, and the expenditure on them is estimated at from thirty to forty milliard crowns. Under the title of " river guard " a regular Danube flotilla, to consist among other units of eight full-fledged monitors, is established by Law XIV. of 1922. These military formations are led mainly by officers from the old imperial-royal army.

The prophetic vision of Alexander Petöfi has been fulfilled : Hungary has really become the last refuge of the expelled Habsburg dynasty.  Zoltán Szász has well named the " Christian National " system the " black and yellow restoration."   All the Habsburg officers and the hangers-on of the old Vienna court poured into Budapest ; and the whole of the Central European reaction, and the Russian too, are now weaving their dreams of restoration there.   The Horthy army is predominantly an army of officers, since the men are unreliable.   The system of a mercenary army ended in complete fiasco, and the troops are only kept in the ranks by violence, intimidation and fraud.   News of the brutal treatment of the men by their feudal officers often leaks out from the barracks.

This hidden infection by the old imperial-royal army is completing the ruin which war, revolution and territorial mutilation had already begun.   A considerable portion of the labour of the famished people goes, not to cultural activities, social welfare and the increase of production, but to the support of the unproductive army.   Reliable calculations show that more than one third of the national budget is applied to the maintenance of the so-called " police institutions," which aim solely at the protection of the counter-revolutionary oligarchy.

Even the National Assembly affords no defence of liberty, no constitutional guarantee against this officers' army and the ruling camarilla, since the present Parliament came into being when the White Terror was at its height, and three-quarters of it consists of reactionary elements.   Not a single representative of the Socialists or of the genuinely democratic parties was elected.   The so-called " Peasant Farmers' Party " is, as regards its overwhelming majority, totally unrepresentative of the country population ; the big land-owners and the clergy have packed the National Assembly with so-called " monocle-peasants "—large landowners camouflaged as " peasant farmers."

Such a body was naturally incapable of any sort of serious democratic reform.   The whole of its wisdom exhausted itself in the " national " devices mentioned in the last chapter. It could not even bring into port the often promised revised constitution. That, however, is a piece of good fortune ; for this constitution was to know nothing of universal suffrage, proportional representation, or the referendum, and its main pillar was to be the revival of the old feudal House of Magnates in some form or other. For the rest, the proceedings of the National Assembly were more and more taken up by scandals. For in spite of the unbounded terrorism and beer-house electioneering, some eight or ten earnest, courageous and irreproachable men succeeded in entering this Parliament. They made steady progress in their opposition to the government system, solidly backed by the democratic and liberal elements in the country as these came to their senses. Though frequently threatened with death, they have fulfilled their duty with noble self-sacrifice, and have acted as the conscience of Hungary in these terrible times. Rarely has a group of men displayed such courage as Rupert, Kerekes, Rassay, Giesswein, Drozdy. These bold fighters have been a real force in the National Assembly, and their campaign for decent government has stirred up public opinion throughout the country.

In consequence of their unsparing criticism, the sittings of the National Assembly have proved more and more dangerous to the Government. But the discredit into which the whole régime has fallen is not only due to the Opposition campaign, but still more to the logic of facts, which has exposed the lies of the White counter-revolution before the uncritical masses.

The White party possessed two war cries, warranted to rouse the fanaticism of large sections of the population. One was the restoration of the territorial integrity of the country, the other the reconstruction of economic life through the elimination of the Jewish financiers. To attain the first object, a great irredentist and *revanche* agitation was commenced. All the leading government politicians and the whole of the press declared without intermission that " they would not renounce a single acacia tree," and that the Horthy army, " the only reliable army of heroes in Europe," would soon reconquer the lost territories. The atmosphere was

heavy with *putsch* plots.  Every " band " had its own plan
of campaign for the realisation of the irredentist dreams.
The public awaited events in a veritable fever, for the White
heroes had promised the recapture of Pozsony, Kassa,
Nagyvárad, etc., by a fixed date.

There was equally feverish activity for the attainment
of the other object, " the ending of Jewish domination."
There was constant abuse of the Jews, brutal attacks on
defenceless individuals, posters inciting to violence, and much
demagogic oratory.  Not only the great guns of the Horthy
party, but such prominent statesmen of the old régime as
Count Julius Andrássy and the eloquent Bishop Prohászka
took part in this odious campaign.  The whole government
press played a thousand variations on the theme that from
now onwards the golden age of Christian Hungary was
beginning, that an end was soon to be made of Jewish usury
and spoliation.

But months, even years, have passed, and the very
opposite of these promises has materialised.  The national
heroes signed the Treaty of Trianon without a word, they
went even further and delivered over the whole country to
be exploited by foreign capitalists.  As for territorial
integrity, they failed to recover a single acacia tree from the
victors ; only from Austria, their comrade in defeat, did they
recover one or two towns, with the support of the Italian
reactionaries.  Public opinion saw more and more clearly
that Horthy and his staff were insincere in their shouts for
territorial integrity, and were merely exciting the patriotic
sentiments of the masses in order to divert attention from the
misdeeds of the " detachments."

In the matter of anti-semitism the public had similar
cruel lessons.  The economic life of the country had fallen
into the hands of corrupt and ignorant adventurers.  No
day passed without disgusting financial scandals.  A number
of the reputable business men fled abroad.  Many of the
most eminent technical experts emigrated to the Succession
States.  Under the Horthy camarilla the position of the poor
in the towns became more and more unbearable.  The
judiciary and the administration openly supported agrarian

profiteering.   The scarcity of fuel and foodstuffs in the towns became steadily worse.   Hunger, high prices and increasing unemployment, the shocking house famine and the extravagance of the Horthy camarilla, at last opened the eyes of the most backward sections of the public.   It was seen that the cleansing of Hungarian public life from the Jews was the same sort of lying promise as the restoration of territorial integrity :   " Jewish " usury, speculation, profiteering, and exploitation had become an even greater burden than in the past.   At most it was the poorer Jews who were ruined ; the plunder gained by the big sharks of the banks and of the Bourse was greater than ever.

After this object lesson the White party lost its adherents among the masses.   This would not have meant the collapse of the system if the staff of the counter-revolution had remained united.   But their solidarity soon disappeared. Feudal and clerical Hungary more and more openly set itself in opposition to the Horthy régime.   I have already referred to one of the reasons for this antagonism.   But the discord was accentuated by new and more weighty factors. The *ancien régime*, which at first was the humble servant of the Horthy party, acquired a growing fear of the evil spirits which it had been harbouring.   The nobles and the higher clergy began to long for peace and order as soon as Horthy had crushed the two revolutions.   The hangman had done his duty, the hangman could go.   They would have been glad to restore the more discreet and elegant class domination of the past ; it had at least worn European clothes.   There was too much of the peasant for them in the Horthy system, however tame and submissive these peasants might be.   Nor did the campaign against the Jews please the aristocracy, which had always been ready enough to share the dividends and monopolies of Hungarian high finance.   The flirtation with land reform was also most unwelcome to the owners of the large estates, for all that the government used every means of sabotaging reform.

Consequently the attitude of Hungarian feudalism towards the Horthy camarilla became steadily more unfriendly.   For the time being matters did not come to an open collision, especially as Horthy began to make a stand and tried to give a legal basis to his system and to mask the Terror as much as possible. He gradually got rid of the loudest shouters, and did his best to replace them with nobles and representatives of the Tisza period. A milder tone was also adopted towards the Jews. Father Bangha, the notorious Jesuit demagogue, the real organiser of anti-semitism, discovered a blood relationship between the Magyars and a portion of Hungarian Jewry, through the medium of the Semitic Khazar tribe, which is said to have taken part in the founding of the country.

But all Horthy's complaisance towards aristocratic Hungary was in vain ; there came a complication in foreign policy which brought the united front of the Whites to an end. It arose out of the Habsburg question.

Horthy's policy was originally legitimist ; at all events its most influential supporters formed a united front around the person of ex-King Charles. This attitude was due to the pressure of the feudal lords of Hungary, who looked upon their big estates, their House of Magnates and their privileges as insecure, unless not only the monarchical form of State but also the Habsburgs were restored. The view of the government was that Hungary was still a kingdom, and its government a royal government ; the Regent was simply the deputy for Charles of Habsburg so long as international pressure prevented his return to the country. Horthy, the government, the ministers, repeatedly affirmed their loyalty to the " crowned " king, and had kept up constant diplomatic intercourse with the exile of Prangins.

When, however, it was seen that the iron ring forged by the Little Entente made Habsburg restoration impossible, various parties and groups formed among the Whites. The shibboleth of all these movements was Elective Monarchy ; they were monarchists, but did not recognise the claim of Charles of Habsburg to the throne of Hungary ; they contended that the nation had recovered its old right of election. This catchword covered two entirely contrary tendencies. One was represented by the members of the

Peasant Farmers' Party, and sprang from the traditional hatred of the Habsburgs. They wanted a " National King " ; but who, in the existing situation, was best fitted for this dignity, they themselves did not know. For many of them, particularly among the Magyars of the great plain, this catchword covered a more or less tentative return towards the republican idea, which, under the pressure of the White Terror, no-one dared to advocate openly.

The other camp of the " elective monarchists," which was much better organised and more influential, was divided into groups which favoured either some other Habsburg pretender, or a member of the Bavarian or Roumanian royal families. But the most serious of these groups was the staff of the Archduke Frederick, the former victorious commander-in-chief, who supported with solid millions the claims of his son Albert to the throne. To this group belonged, and still belongs, Julius Gömbös, an intimate of Horthy and president of the most influential of the terrorist organisations.

This growing activity of the elective monarchists filled the legitimist nobles and prelates with quite intelligible fear. Ex-King Charles' supporters saw with dismay that they were between the upper and the nether millstone ; on the one hand they were threatened by the democratic-republican movement, the spirit of the October Revolution, on the other by the Albert group. And there were even increasing indications that Horthy himself would not refuse to exchange his position as " Regent" for that of " National King."

This nervousness reached an intolerable pitch after Charles' first unsuccessful Putsch. The legitimists learned with a shock that in consequence of the determined opposition of the Little Entente their position was becoming untenable, and their supporters were deserting in crowds to join the opposition movement. Charles and his supporters felt absolutely that they could only save their position by producing a *fait accompli*. Charles must again return unexpectedly and put himself at the head of the loyal army. It was hoped that the determined behaviour of the ex-King would paralyse all opposition in Hungary, and that it would embarass the Little Entente, who, under the *douce violence* of reactionary circles in the Big Entente, would surely not treat Charles' return as a *casus belli*.

These were the antecedents of Charles' second attempt. No doubt its main lines were known to Horthy himself and his astute Prime Minister, Count Bethlen, who incarnates all the slimness of the feudal Transylvanian politicians; at most they were surprised by the bold rapidity of the movement. But it was soon evident how ill-prepared this coup had been by Charles and his loyal magnates. Instead of pocketing the affront, the Little Entente at once mobilised against Budapest, and informed the Horthy-Bethlen government that if they were not able to remove the ex-King within forty-eight hours the Little Entente would do so by force of arms.

This ultimatum dismayed not only Horthy and Bethlen, but also the whole of the Hungarian counter-revolutionaries. It was evident that if the Little Entente marched on Budapest (and it was clear that the Horthy army could not for a single day resist its concentrated attack), not only would the Government fall, but there would inevitably be a popular revolution. The camarilla of the White Terror went through two anxious days. For Horthy there was no hesitation ; he could only save his domination, and even his life, by accepting the task of arresting and removing the " crowned King " to whom he had so often sworn allegiance. But it almost looked as though the Regent would not be capable of giving effect to his wishes. The regular officers were not prepared to march against their "King." Hours of desperate panic followed ; Horthy and Bethlen rushed about wildly ; the ex-king was but a few hours' journey from Budapest. At this critical moment the situation was saved by the energy of Julius Gömbös, a staff officer, already mentioned as the confidant of Archduke Frederick. He mobilised a portion of his terrorist bands, and organised an " ad hoc " army from the ranks of the poorer students of the University. This " army " of a few thousand men, scraped together from all sides, and not even armed, put to flight the " loyal " army with a few rounds of artillery, and one of its detachments arrested the king.

By this bold feat of arms, Gömbös, an interesting survival of the type of mediæval *condottiere*, became the real master of the situation, controlling the actions of the Regent and of the Government. But Gömbös saved the Horthy régime only by digging its grave. For by firing on the King, arresting and dethroning him at the command of the Little Entente, the Horthy régime has irrevocably incurred the bitter enmity of the Hungarian feudal nobility, which, with its fine historic sense, realises that the *ancien régime* can only be preserved on a legitimist basis. When the Horthy camarilla arrested Andrássy, Rákovszky and other legitimist leaders for fear of a fresh royalist coup, and kept them in custody for some weeks, the resentment of the aristocracy against the perjured Horthy knew no bounds. From now onwards the legitimists were for war to the knife against Horthy and his system ; and many who had helped to set up the government, and had supported or at least tolerated it, suddenly discovered their social and moral conscience, and made passionate attacks upon the White Terror, upon the murderers of Orgovány and their highly placed protector. Horthy and his camarilla, who had previously been more or less respectable through their association with legitimism and the *ancien régime*, lost their halo once and for all, and were exposed to public contempt as a mere terrorist graft association.

This general trend of opinion convinced Count Bethlen that the National Assembly could no longer be kept together, and that nothing could save the government unless it could secure a reliable, reactionary, docile majority through a general election. It was, however, clear that new elections on the basis of universal, secret and equal suffrage would simply end the existing régime at once, and open the way to a republic and to the ideas of the October Revolution, beginning with land reform. Bye-elections had yielded huge majorities for the candidates of the Liberal opposition, and everything indicated that a fresh general election would spell disaster for the government.

The Horthy-Bethlen camarilla took the only path open to them. The word was given : Back to the pre-revolutionary franchise of Tisza and Wekerle and to the old electoral system. Even, however, in that National Assembly, devoted to the Whites, there was no majority for the confiscation of the popular franchise, the one remaining achievement of the October Revolution; particularly since at one time the Entente had itself, by the mouth of Sir George Clerk, demanded the introduction of universal suffrage. But the government did not shrink from extreme measures. They dissolved the National Assembly, and imposed upon the nation by arbitrary decree a new franchise and electoral system. This decree robs of the suffrage about a million and a half Hungarian citizens (including eight to nine tenths of the women electors), and introduces in five-sixths of the electoral districts the system of open voting, which in pre-war days was the disgrace of Hungary in foreign eyes. The situation so created was much worse than under the Tisza-Wekerle Law of 1918, although even that Law was repudiated at the time by Hungarian progressive opinion.

But the camarilla felt instinctively that even this could not make the country safe for their autocracy. The Hungarian nation is much too intelligent and independent to be forced by any deprivation of rights to provide a subservient majority. The ruling clique could not stop at half measures in illegality, and found it necessary to revive one after another the worst election practices of the Tisza era.

They nominated their creatures as Lord Lieutenants, to canvass the provinces. The electoral districts were gerrymandered to suit the interests of government candidates. The whole of the minor officials were kept docile by the hope of fat jobs and the fear of punishment. Through the government connexion with the banks, pressure was exercised on everyone dependent on industry. The actual voting was complicated by a whole network of chicanery. Open bribery was the order of the day.

But even these pre-war practices[1] proved insufficient to secure the suppression of public opinion. The Hungarian

[1] See *Corruption and Reform in Hungary*, by R. W. Seton-Watson (1911), and the much enlarged German edition *Ungarische Wahlen* (1913).

people were strong enough even in the Tisza era to withstand corruption and intimidation. The Parliamentary majorities of the " 1867 " government in Hungary were always obtained from among the national minorities, which, through the sins of Hungarian class domination, had remained completely unenlightened politically and educationally. Now that we have lost the national minorities of the frontier territories, and that Hungary contains a uniform and racially pure population, it is less easy to keep the country in political servitude by the old methods; and still less since the revolutions have raised the self-respect of the people and the high prices of agricultural produce have assured economic independence to large numbers of the peasant farmer class.

In such circumstances the government added to the old electoral abuses newer and more drastic ones.

In many places permission to hold opposition meetings was simply refused, or if it was granted the meetings were broken up by armed terrorist troops.

The opposition parties were forbidden to disseminate their programmes. An order was issued prohibiting any discussion of the most burning question, that of land reform.

If all this failed to produce the desired result, the opposition candidates were simply arrested, thrown into prison, and proceedings commenced for their internment. At the same time their nomination lists were confiscated by the police. Armed terrorist troops were concentrated wherever the hated government candidates could not get a hearing.

In order to intimidate the public, the White Terror broke out with renewed virulence. The air was full of threats, and in the Budapest newspapers there again appeared the sinister stereotyped police notices about unknown bodies found in the Danube. The Hungarian elections of 1922 were not real elections, but incidents in a civil war. But civil war presupposes an armed conflict between classes struggling for supremacy ; and there is nothing of this in Hungary to-day, but only an attempt by Horthy and his armed force—a few thousand armed reactionaries, officers, officials and students—to compel the overwhelming peaceful majority of the Hungarian people by every kind of violence to bear in silence the yoke of the Whites.

Meanwhile, the Entente, which through its League of Nations is hypocritically taking under its protection even the freedom of conscience of the inhabitants of Pacific islands, looks on without protest while some of those who are responsible for the world-war and for a system of extreme national repression, subjugate anew one of the most industrious and upright of the peoples in the Danube basin, a people whose recovery is essential to any attempt at reconstructing Central Europe.

Thus the joint policy of the Entente and of Hungarian feudalism condemns our unfortunate people to fresh trials and convulsions, which can only end in international complications or in revolution.

CHAPTER XIV

## THE HORTHYIST NATIONAL ASSEMBLY: ITS
## ANTECEDENTS AND PROSPECTS

THE first edition of this book was printed at the beginning of the electoral campaign of the Bethlen government.  It is desirable briefly to summarise the subsequent developments in Hungary, in order that the foreign observer may be enabled correctly to estimate the present position of the White régime.  A short sketch of this " electoral campaign " has been given in Chapter XIII.  The methods there described have since become still more sharply defined, and have developed into a system probably unique in Europe.

It has already been mentioned that the Bethlen government was only able to lay down the lines of the new franchise law by an open breach of legality.  The first National Assembly was to have been a Constituent Assembly, and its principal task was to have been the settlement of the constitution, and, in connexion therewith, of the franchise law.  The government, however, had not even worked out the draft constitution, and it only brought in the franchise bill in the last weeks of the first National Assembly, much too late for it to be debated.  The National Assembly was dissolved without passing the franchise bill, and a new franchise was promulgated by decree and is now the basis of Hungarian Parliamentarism.

This electoral statute completely destroyed the universal and secret suffrage of the October Revolution.  The franchise is granted to men of over 24 years of age, conditionally upon a two years' residential qualification and the attainment of the fourth standard in the elementary schools.  For women the residential qualification is the same, the age minimum 30 years, and the educational qualification the attainment of the sixth standard. In consequence of the movements of the population since the war the effect of the two years' residential qualification is to disfranchise large sections of the population. The educational qualification bars out a large section of the farm servants and day labourers, and of the owners of dwarf estates, who are themselves a part of the rural proletariat ; it has also to be proved by producing school certificates, which are obtainable only with difficulty and often not at all.

But all these restrictions were not enough for Count Bethlen. The statute names fifteen categories of persons who are absolutely excluded from the franchise. Thus, in open violation of Article 76 of the Treaty of Trianon, all persons are excluded who are under detention for political offences. No State official, professor, teacher, cleric or lawyer who has been removed from his post as a disciplinary measure (not necessarily by the courts) on account of his " unpatriotic conduct," may be elected. Moreover, the statute enacts that no one who had been living abroad for more than a year before its promulgation could even be nominated for election. Thus election was made impossible for every émigré.

Even these measures were not enough to satisfy the government. In every electoral district except Budapest and eleven other municipalities, public voting was established. The Minister of the Interior, Count Klebelsberg, explained that this was necessary in the villages in order to keep popular passions within bounds.

The election campaign was, of course, put entirely at the mercy of the government. The statute enacted that no party meeting might be held without a police permit. The provisions concerning the nomination of candidates aimed at hampering the opposition election organisation. In districts with 10,000 voters or under, nominations had to be signed by at least 10 per cent. of the voters, and in larger districts by at least 1,000 voters. The demand for this large number of signatures amounted to a circumvention of the secret polling in Budapest and the eleven other municipalities where it existed. It was often impossible to procure so many signatures without holding meetings of electors, and as party meetings required police permits, candidatures were reduced to dependence upon the good-will of the government; for if it chose it could disperse any meeting of electors for signing nominations, as an illegal assembly. Opposition supporters tried to get out of the difficulty by passing nomination sheets from hand to hand. But in many cases the gendarmerie confiscated the sheets, beat the signatories, put them under police supervision and even made arrests.

A great difficulty in the way of opposition candidatures was that official forms had to be used, and these were only issued by the Minister of the Interior, in return for payment, and in the provinces by the local courts. In many places these official proposal forms were bought up by the government electoral agents, so that there were none remaining for the opposition candidates. But the Bethlen government was not content with these paper guarantees for extorting a docile majority for it out of the electorate. It placed the elections under the control of Julius Gömbös, of whom mention has before been made, and who organised a veritable terrorist force, to intimidate opposition electors and to break up opposition meetings. Election atrocities were the order of the day. A record of the serious and minor election abuses would fill a volume. I have only space to mention a few typical cases, in chronological order.

March 10. The " M.O.V.E." officers' organisation announced that it covered the whole country and intended to take an active part in the elections. On the motion of Gömbös, its president, it resolved to divide the country into strategic areas and to send out armed bands of terrorists to break up opposition party meetings.

March 11. The government split up the electoral districts on a system subtly calculated to improve its own chances.

March 14. In the Szekszárd electoral district, gendarmes and police prevented Dr. Eugene Sebestyén, the Rassay party candidate, and the ex-Deputy Drozdy, who was taking part in his meeting, from speaking. The commandant of the gendarmerie declared that if these two gentlemen did not at once leave the district, he could not be answerable for their lives. One of the gendarmerie officers added that Drozdy would not get out of the district alive.

March 16. The government had false electoral registers exhibited, thus again delaying the compilation of the lists of voters.

March 21. In the Budapest Inner City Club the Awakening Magyars broke up an election meeting of the former prime minister, Ladislaus Lukács.

March 21. In Regulation Z604/922 the Minister of the Interior laid down that in order to prevent demagogy, those individuals who from a national standpoint were dangerous and politically objectionable must be watched with the greatest care, and that a report was at once to be sent to the Minister from any district in which they appeared.

March 28. Bloodshed and disorder in Debreczen. Gangs of Awakening Magyars, armed with iron shod sticks, broke up an opposition party meeting.

March 28. Emmerich Biró, a Rassay party candidate, was kidnapped by the gendarmerie at Tápiószele.

March 28. The government prohibited a meeting of the Andrássy party at Pécs. Albert Bartha, ex-Minister of War, proved that the gangs who were breaking up meetings were in receipt of pay from the government.

April 4. In view of the death of King Charles the government prohibited all public meetings from April 4 to April 18 ; the prohibition was subsequently extended to May 1.

April 4. At a banquet in the Elisabeth Casino in Budapest in honour of the opposition leaders a bomb exploded. Fortunately the opposition leaders were late in arriving, but nine citizens lost their lives, and more than fifty of those present were seriously injured. Everyone knew who the perpetrators were, but no proceedings were instituted against them, and a government organ, " A Nép," wrote that the opposition had better disarm, and then there would be no more bomb explosions.

April 8.   The Government ordered a police search in the offices of the Awakening Magyars, but only permitted search to be made in certain parts of the building.   Even so the police discovered a number of bombs in the house.   The editor of the Horthyist paper, " Hazánk," admitted to the police that he had in fact distributed bombs.

April 19.   The League for the Defence of Public Rights, which had been occupied in collecting the complaints of the opposition, proved that opposition voters, especially Jews, were being omitted wholesale from the lists of voters, and that the nomination forms were being bought up in advance by agents of the government party.

April 24.   In Jánosháza the peasant farmer Ladislaus Pozsónyi was stabbed by gendarmes in the presence of three Ministers, because the crowds refused to listen to the Ministers.

April 27.   The government ordered that the elections should be held in two sections as the whole of the Hungarian armed forces were not sufficient to maintain order !

April 27.   The government prohibited the printing of the party programmes of the opposition, and placed every possible difficulty in the way of their distribution.

April 28.   The government issued a regulation prohibiting, on pain of arrest and fine, the very mention before the electorate of the various questions connected with the land reform, that is of the most burning questions facing the country.

April 29.   The government forbade the celebration of May day.

May 1.   In Szentes the chief of police forbade the well known publicist Emmerich Veér to make his programme speech, on the ground that he was a member of the Republican party.

May 7.   Ladislaus Fényes, candidate for the Pétervásár district, one of the most distinguished and most popular publicists in the country, was expelled by gendarmerie.

May 9.   Count Bethlen declared that if the government failed to obtain an absolute majority at the elections he would dissolve Parliament.   Barnabas Buza, former

Minister of Agriculture, who had carried through a law for radical land reform, was ordered out of his district.

May 12. The government prohibited every sort of political gathering and public meeting for the period from May 21 to June 3.

May 13. The government placed M. Belicska, the Honvéd Minister (Minister for Defence), in supreme charge of the troops to be sent to the polling booths.

May 13. The candidate Louis Szilágyi was placed under police supervision in Berrettyóujfalu. Ladislaus Fényes, candidate for Pétervásár, was arrested and interned in the town hall. Stephen Friedrich was forbidden to make his programme speech. The candidate for the district of Rétság, Elemér Huszár, was arrested by the authorities.

May 18. The Minister of the Interior had his opponent at Sopron, the Socialist Dr. Edward Hébelt, placed under police supervision, and refused to allow him to make his programme speech.

May 23. Barnabas Buza was driven out of his electoral district, and his nomination papers were destroyed by the authorities. Ladislaus Fényes had the same experience in his district. Ernest Nagy, a Rassay party candidate, was arrested in his district and interned at Nyiregyháza.

May 27. Gendarmes arrested the opposition candidate, Géza Babotay, in his district.

Under such auspices were the elections carried through. As can be seen, not only were the worst electoral practices of pre-war times revived, practices which formerly were adopted against the non-Magyar nationalities on alleged grounds of patriotic anxiety, but they were raised to a fantastic pitch against purely Magyar voters. Everywhere votes were bought and sold, officials terrorised, and the economically dependent classes intimidated. In open sittings of Parliament the government was charged with expending more than 2,000,000,000 crowns on corrupting the electorate, and this grave charge was given no serious reply. And where all these infamies failed through the sturdy uprightness of the population, the armed bands of government terrorists stepped in and made it often impossible for the voters to go to the polling booths. Hundreds of opposition committee men were brutally beaten or driven from their district or thrown into prison. Max Fenyö, the well-known liberal opposition candidate, a brilliant writer and director of the Hungarian Industrialists' Union, abandoned his candidature, saying that he could not look on idly while his supporters were harassed and persecuted and their lives in danger. Here is another case, typical of the government's methods : In the district of Pétervásár, from which, as already mentioned, the Liberal candidate, Ladislaus Fényes, was driven out by the soldiery, no details of the poll were issued, despite Fényes' repeated public challenge. Amid the unexampled terrorism this brave rural electorate had abstained altogether from voting, so that out of several thousand electors only a few hundred votes, and those bought, were received by the government candidate. Equally stubborn courage was displayed by the peasantry in the Tarpa district, whom no terrorism could induce to leave their popular candidate, Ernest Nagy, in the lurch. In the end the government simply stopped the polling.

Thus the new majority of Horthy, Bethlen and Gömbös was obtained not by the methods of Western parliamentarism, but of the backwoods. And even so the final result was a great moral defeat for the government, since not all its terrorism prevented the opposition from securing 80 out of the 245 seats in Parliament. The Social Democrats had surprising success, returning 25 members, some from purely agricultural districts. Of the 30 members for the capital, elected by secret suffrage on the proportional system, 24 belong to the opposition. In the eleven towns in which the voting was secret, the government obtained only 10 of the 20 seats, despite mass arrests everywhere of the opposition electors. *Thus the government owes its majority entirely to the open voting, which gave free field to the system of armed terrorism.* In the 195 districts with open voting the government obtained 149 seats. The true feeling in the country is unanswerably demonstrated by the fact that *in the districts in which voting was secret the government obtained only 18 per cent. of the votes, and 67.2 per cent. in the districts with open voting.*

The legitimist (pro-Habsburg) opposition is represented disproportionately beyond its true strength in the new National Assembly, with 24 members. The reason is that the open vote favoured the legitimists as well as the government, for in the great estates they are all-powerful lords, with ample means of influencing their " vassals." The Liberals, on the other hand, came off poorly, partly through the backward state of the Hungarian bourgeoisie and partly because a large section of the lower middle-class voted for the Social Democrats, finding the tactics of the Liberal opposition too timid and vacillating.

But the true meaning of the recent elections is conveyed by the composition of the majority, the so-called Unity party. The dictatorship established over the polling by Bethlen and Gömbös attained its special purpose : *it succeeded in almost annihilating the former powerful government party, the Peasant Farmers' party*, through the treachery of its leader, Stephen Szabó of Nagyatád. The real peasant farmers are no longer a danger to the feudalism of the White régime. The "Unity" which has replaced them is, however, split up into two sharply opposed groups. The larger group consists of the personal adherents of Count Bethlen and is nothing but a reconstruction of Tisza's old National Party of Work ; it is composed of feudal and plutocratic elements which desire simply to restore the pre-war political and economic system : the rule of the gentry and the prelates and the Jewish usurers. These elements are hostile to the wild terrorism and the anti-Semitism of the Horthyists, and aim at recovering their old dominance by legal methods—that is by the use of a State army and the regular gendarmerie— restoring the old county "self-government" under aristocratic control, and dissolving the illegal " bands " and terrorist organisations. About two-thirds of the Unity party now in power consist of adherents of the old Tisza party, and nine out of the twelve Ministers in the Bethlen cabinet in the summer of 1923 were former confidants of Count Tisza.

This group is opposed by one much less numerous, but politically very influential, comprising those elements which recognise M. Gömbös at their personal leader. Gömbös is the real leader of the Awakening Magyars, and of all the other terrorist organisations and concealed military formations. His group has intimate personal connexions with the Regent Horthy, and it is the rallying point of all the adventurers and profiteers who were the soul of the counter-revolution, and who will have nothing to do with any consolidation of the country which would endanger their position as idle aristocrats. It is just as reactionary as the Bethlen group. Its main characteristics are extreme anti-Semitism and a noisy advocacy of *revanche*. It is in favour of an elective monarchy, as offering the best prospect of rewards for its services as *condottieri*. Bethlen himself and his followers, on the contrary, are masked legitimists, waiting only for the moment when the Little Entente is weak and disunited enough for them to be able to bring back into the country the " legal heir to the throne."

These two groups soon fell into hot rivalry. Bethlen opened a campaign against anti-Semitism, without, of course, touching the *numerus clausus ;* his ostensible purpose was the stabilisation of the Hungarian currency. He ordered the arrest of Ivan Héjjas, who was preparing a coup against the Burgenland. But both these moves failed. The Awakening Magyars pursued their Jew-baiting more vigorously than before, and Ivan Héjjas had to be released after two days owing to the threatening attitude of the terrorist formations. This organiser of massacre had a triumphal procession through the streets of Budapest. The famous old Kossuth song, which in the past had proclaimed the gospel of the new freedom to many thousands of liberated serfs, was resung in the name of a robber chieftain.

Thus the old Tisza system and the new terrorist system stand in sharp opposition to one another. Bethlen's aim was to restore the old House of Magnates, in a rather milder shape, to provide a reliable army for the *ancien régime*, and to disarm the terrorist organisations. But he was unable to take any serious steps against these bands, to whom he owes his " electoral victory," and who are connected by many close ties with His Highness the Regent. The resuscitated Tisza party is thus the prisoner of these evil spirits which it helped to conjure up and has supported and shielded.

Thus Count Bethlen, despite all his Transylvanian acumen, is unable, even with his huge government majority, to solve the difficult problem of the Hungarian counter-revolution. If he moves to the left, Gömbös terrorist bands will crush him ; if he moves to the right, he will be ruined by the wild demagogy of the anti-Semites and the irredentists, for he will lose the support of the Entente powers, who tolerate him at present as the victor over the Habsburgs.

He has no third choice. *The only other course is one which he can never take—namely, a return to the democratic and republican order instituted by the October Revolution*, and still supported by the overwhelming majority of all Hungarian workers (peasants, workmen and intellectuals), which would make short work both of the old Tisza system and of the new Gömbös system, both of the feudal régime and of that of the comitadjis.

*       *       *       *

Over a year has passed since the above lines were written, and the subsequent political evolution of Hungary confirms in almost every particular the thesis of this book. The " White Régime " has shown itself increasingly incapable of solving any of the urgent problems that confront it. It is not merely economically but morally bankrupt.

The new Parliament, born of an illegal restriction of the franchise and of open terrorism, has, after eighteen months of existence, no constructive work to show. The promised Bill for the revision of the constitution was not even introduced ; no attempt was made to introduce a new franchise law to replace the *curtailments* of the franchise and of secret voting contained in Count Bethlen's decree ; the long planned Second Chamber remained a reactionary dream of Count Bethlen's, with his other favourite scheme for the extirpation of the last remnants of county and municipal self-government, supplanting it by a rigid system of centralisation.  The constant suppressive discontent of the landless proletariat was not even relieved by the solemnly promised amendment of the disingenuous agrarian laws described in Chapter XII ; the repressive legislation of the first days of the Horthy period remained unaltered in spite of the agitation of the Liberal and Socialist minority ;  no legislation was attempted to solve the vexed question of the form of the State (monarchy or republic) ;  no serious step was undertaken to improve economic and political relations with the neighbouring States.

Count Bethlen saw clearly that the new Parliament was organically incapable of doing any useful work, and he constantly prorogued it as soon as it had provided for the most urgent administrative and financial needs of the State. The short sessions which were permitted expired as a rule amid a stormy atmosphere of personal wrangling and of ever growing scandals, which even compromised the honour of some members of the government and of the leaders of the Horthy system.   The last of these scandals was the most vehement and ignominious.   Stephen Friedrich, the former Premier and notorious founder of the " White " régime, read in Parliament a secret report of the Minister of Justice, M. Emil Nagy, in which he denounced an immense graft affair (August, 1923).   Some of the leading banks of Budapest (naturally mostly in Jewish hands) had issued gratis shares in certain newly organised joint stock companies, the profit-earning capacity of which was generally believed to be considerable ; notably the rubber company of Dorog.   A busy traffic began between the Jewish bankers and the anti-Semitic leaders of the régime in the giving and receiving of these gratuitous shares. Some scores of Deputies wrote personally to the banks, asking in the most abject terms for these corrupt presents. It is said that more than a thousand names were on the distributing lists of these banks.   It is widely asserted that the wife of Premier Bethlen, the Minister of the Interior, the Chief of Police, the Chief of the Detective Department, the Deputy Solicitor General and sixty-five Members of Parliament obtained these share allotments as bribes from the " Jewish usurers," each receiving a sum proportioned to his political merits. This report of the Minister of Justice caused a sensation in the National Assembly, and the scandal grew even greater when it became manifest that certain elements of the opposition parties (namely some adherents of M. Vázsonyi) were equally compromised. It was no mere demagogic exaggeration when the newly elected Deputy for Czegléd (the former electoral district of Francis Kossuth and of Michael Károlyi), M. Lendvay, one of the noisiest and most ferocious of the " Awakening Magyars," called this National Assembly a " den of criminals," and denounced the whole régime as a shameless betrayal of the " Christian National " spirit. This agitation was only stopped by the prorogation of Parliament once more.

This terrible condition of the National Assembly is due mainly to the corruption and falsification of the franchise which makes the manifestation of honest public opinion impossible ; to the almost intolerable economic crisis, which renders life among the working classes (both intellectual and manual) so precarious ; and to the utter insincerity of the present governmental system. The present Parliament is unable to do any serious work, because its admitted programme is manifestly opposed to the real needs of the present day in Central Europe. The official programme would mean the restoration of ancient Hungary by means of a war of revenge; but Count Bethlen is being driven towards a reconciliation with the neighbouring States, in order to obtain a loan without which the position of the present régime is untenable. The official programme seeks to purify economic life from Jewish influence, but the necessities of the situation are enabling the Jewish capitalists in Hungary (the only existing capitalists) to play a more and more preponderant part.

Count Bethlen sees clearly the impossibility of this situation. He is endeavouring to re-establish a middle line in Hungarian politics, the so-called Liberalism of the Tisza era, which would mean the domination of the great land-owners in alliance with Jewish *haute finance*. But this line has become manifestly impossible ; not only because of the moral and economic changes suffered by the mass of the people through the war and the two revolutions, but because the Magyar aristocracy is itself no longer the compact camp of pre-war years. Count Bethlen is certainly not less a legitimist than Count Apponyi and Count Andrássy and the Roman Catholic hierarchy, but as head of the government he is obliged to try to steer an opposite course. He would be inclined to a policy of rapprochement towards the newly founded states, he would even be ready to re-establish the Republic for the sake of a loan.[1] This means that Count Bethlen would be willing to adopt the main planks of the October Revolution, for their part in which he is keeping many thousands of his fellow countrymen in exile and many hundreds in gaol, while his judges have confiscated the entire fortune of Count Károlyi and even of his innocent little children.

But in spite of his opportunism it is impossible for Count Bethlen to solve the difficulties of the situation by becoming an Octobrist. If he were to make a serious effort in this direction he would fall a victim, perhaps even in the physical sense of the phrase, to the great Habsburgist aristocracy and the terrorist bands. That such an eventuality is not altogether impossible, is clearly demonstrated by the fact that a few months ago the most turbulent elements of the terrorist wing and many adherents of the legitimist camp, several of them intimately connected with Count Andrássy, formed a " United front for protecting the Magyar race." That is to say, the admirers of the late King and those who fired at him are now in the same fraternal camp. But everyone knows that the motive of this political combination between M. Gömbös and other Fascists and the supporters of the Habsburgist Magnates, is not so much to protect the Magyar race as to threaten Count Bethlen, should he attempt any serious measures against the

---

[1] This highly interesting statement was made by Mr. R. G. Caldwell at a dinner given to him on September 20th, 1923, at the Century Club in New York, on the occasion of his return from Europe ; Dr. Samuel M. Lindsay of Columbia University presiding. Mr. Caldwell described to his friends his personal interviews with the leading statesmen of Central Europe. His remarkable address was issued verbatim to the Press.

Habsburgist-Fascist coalition. And Count Bethlen will certainly not take this risk, because it could only be taken by a statesman who is solidly backed by the democratic forces in the country, by the masses of the small peasantry, the workers and the creative intelligentsia, that is to say, by the forces of the October Revolution, in the overthrow of which by illegal military formations, by the destruction of the franchise, by imprisonments and the muzzling of the Press and a long list of exceptional laws, Count Bethlen himself assisted.

Under these circumstances the way is blocked for every serious constructive effort in Hungarian politics. There are no programmes ; public life abounds only in intrigue and conspiracy. There are many secret flirtations (even the staunchest defenders of the race and their leader, M. Gömbös, are not foreign to them) with one or other of the countries of the Little Entente, with the republican idea, with radical agrarian reform ; but these have no other aim than to overthrow Bethlen and seize power for the extreme nationalists and the Habsburg group. Even the Liberal and Socialist opposition is partly intimidated, partly corrupted, and the few honest and capable men in Parliament are entirely powerless against the general current. Amid the continued terrorism it is impossible for them to adopt a sincere programme of reforms, which must include the re-establishment of the Republic, peace with the neighbouring States and the serious handling of the land question.

The extreme weakness of the present Liberal and Socialist opposition is mainly due to the fact that the majority of its leaders are now dispersed all over the world as exiles or émigrés. But the fear of the émigrés is still acute among the present rulers. The calumnies against these leaders continue, and a fresh prosecution has been instituted against them—based on the emergency law already quoted—for " debasing the good name of Hungary in foreign countries." In spite of this the prestige of the émigrés among the masses of the Hungarian people is constantly growing. The name of Count Károlyi especially, as has repeatedly been stated in Parliament, is surrounded by a legendary halo among the workers and the landless peasants, who regard him as the heir to the traditions of Rákóczy and Kossuth.

The logical outcome of such a political atmosphere is the total lack of security in jurisdiction and administration. The faith in justice is being undermined in Hungarian public life. The most brutal and murderous of the private feuds of the former period have ceased, but bloodshed and petty pogroms are still no rarity. From time to time the provincial newspapers contain articles headed " A bloody night again," describing the latest exploits of the " Awakening Magyars." Apart from such excesses on the part of armed bands, private crimes are committed under a political disguise. For instance, a jeweller of Buda named Louis Otto was recently killed by a member of a terrorist group recently founded, under the name of " The Camp of the Active Magyars," by men who regarded the " Awakening Magyars " as insufficiently effective. Military intrusion is also continuing into civilian jurisdiction, though there is now much less of this. For instance, a provincial merchant named Ellenbogen was arrested and kept in prison for months by the military authorities, in a case in which he had been definitely set at liberty by the civil courts.

But these and other similar instances of physical terrorism are perhaps less oppressive than the general moral atmosphere of public life : the continual threats and incitements in the press and in public speeches, the class spirit displayed in the courts and throughout the administration. This spirit was especially marked in the case of Count Károlyi, when without a single piece of legal evidence and after rejecting all the evidence and witnesses for the defence, the court confiscated his estates and declared him a traitor to the country, at the secret instigation of the government, which desired a rapid judgment to forestall any further intervention from the French " Ligue des Droits de l' Homme." No less dishonest was the recent judgment of the Court of Appeal which raised the sentence upon Zoltán Szász (one of the noblest figures of Hungarian Liberalism, who has been outspoken in his denunciation abroad of the crimes of the Horthy régime) from two-and-a-half to four-and-a-half years' imprisonment for " an offence against the honour of the Hungarian State and nation." At the same time this court discharged two anti-semitic propagandists who had been sentenced by a lower court for inciting to race-hatred.

In the situation thus briefly surveyed it is not surprising that economic collapse should be threatened, and that a sense of insecurity should hamper all really productive work. It is sometimes argued that the financial bankruptcy of Hungary is a phenomenon analogous to that of Austria and is therefore to be healed only by an analogous method : by an international loan and the suspension of the reparation claims of the Succession States. But this view, though supported by the high financial authority of Sir William Goode, is a quite mistaken one. There is no analogy between the economic situation of Austria and Hungary. The economic collapse of Austria was inevitable because the new republic was too poor to recover by its own forces. But Hungary, in spite of her losses of territory, remains a rich country, which by a sane economic policy and strict parsimony could regain her strength. The opposite path, however, was followed by the government. The feudal land system makes it impossible to develop the very considerable economic resources of the country. The preparation of the war of revenge and the constant irredentist conspiracies against the new States, make friendly intercourse with them almost impossible, so that the administrative, economic and intellectual activity of the country are heavily shackled. Stephen Szabó of Nagyatád, the renegade peasant leader, himself uttered last August in a moment of candour these remarkable words : " Hungary is engaged in economic war with the Succession States, and this war is harder and more harmful than that which we fought during the world war with arms." But such saner announcements of the Cabinet Ministers are constantly counter-balanced by the jingo utterances of other leaders. For instance, the Regent Horthy, last August, made a speech in Karczag, when knighting his latest batch of feudal " heroes,"[1] in which he

[1] See p. 177.

proclaimed that the war for the restoration of the old frontiers is approaching, and that he has signed advantageous treaties with foreign powers. This speech, though officially suppressed by the government, is authentic, and is a fresh aggravation of the international situation. No wonder if under such conditions race hatred and international mistrust are growing from day to day in the Danube basin. During a long journey this summer in Slovakia and Transylvania I had the unhappy experience of noting how the antagonism between Czechoslovaks, Roumanians and the Magyar minority was becoming even more envenomed, mainly through this spirit of *revanche*.

But the chief handicap to Hungary's economic recovery is the political and administrative dictatorship of the feudal leisured class, amounting to a political and administrative enslavement of the working classes and the landless peasantry. The economic result of this is that the great landowner class is virtually exempt from all serious taxation, while the common people are compelled by armed force to support the idle " gentry " and a host of sinecurist officials and former Habsburg officers. The " Christian Course " favours the unscrupulous exploitation of the landless proletariat and the working classes, pressing wages down to the lowest level in Central Europe.

The resulting situation is nearly desperate. The immense majority of the Hungarian people, not only in the cities but even in the most fertile country districts, is living now at a famine level. M. Drozdy, one of the Liberal opposition leaders, stated in an address delivered recently before the Hungarian colony of New York that the average earnings of a labourer in Hungary are 30,000 crowns a week. Making allowances for the relatively greater buying power of Hungarian money within the country, M. Drozdy came to the conclusion that the Hungarian worker receives three dollars a week. Under such circumstances it is not surprising that infant mortality shows an alarming increase, and that the general moral atmosphere of the working people is deplorable. One of the most respected of the Hungarian Deputies, Rudolf Ruppert, urged in Parliament that the " country is menaced by a famine revolution," and this belief is general in the ranks of the intelligentsia. M. Szabó of Nagyatád himself announced in a public speech that we are hurrying towards a catastrophe. The government has already begun to take relief measures, in view of the danger of famine during the winter months in the villages of this rich agricultural country. The correspondent of a very moderate, even timidly Liberal daily, the " Pesti Napló," reported in a lengthy article (August 25) the indescribable misery of the landless peasantry in one of the most fertile districts. The writer of the article, who had supposed that destitution and famine were confined to the working and the middle-classes of the cities, was startled to find great masses of the peasants, who are uncritically envied by the inhabitants of the towns, also leading a most wretched existence, with milk or meat as unknown to them as to the cellar-dwellers of Budapest. In such conditions it is not to be wondered at that vehement strikes have been occurring in recent months, only to be suppressed by the armed forces of the government.

There is consequently a very strong current of emigration, which the government finds it difficult to check. Last August three thousand iron workers (this is the best organised trade union in Hungary) announced their intention of emigrating. During September and October, 1923, about 3,200 workers left the country quite openly, according to the report of the Hungarian Trade Union Federation. But the administrative chicaneries with which legal emigration is impeded promote a much greater illegal and secret emigration. It is said that the Turkish visa is an object of traffic, and anyone can get one for 400,000 crowns. But some hundreds of unfortunate emigrants who arrived recently at Adrianople were driven back by the military. It is certain that every month many hundreds of workers flee in secret from this "Christian and National" country, to escape from their starvation wages and the humiliations to which they are subjected.

This being the general economic, social and moral atmosphere of Hungary, it is doubtful whether the well known scheme of Sir William Goode, of saving Hungary by the panacea of an international loan and the suspension of her liabilities, could really be helpful to our unfortunate people. To promote this plan, Sir William advises the Hungarian people to abandon all political controversies and form a united front in order to obtain the loan. The eminent financial expert evidently sees only an economic question in the Hungarian problem, and therefore he indicates a plan which resembles very much the fable of the wolf and the lamb. But the economic side is only one side of the Hungarian problem. The political and moral side is of no less importance.

Certainly in the distress into which nationalist megalomania, race hatred and usury have plunged our unfortunate country, an international loan is absolutely necessary. But no such loan, nor any other financial alleviation, can help Hungary, so long as the present political and moral course is being continued. Only radical political and moral reform can make a loan effectual. Without freedom for the democratic forces in the country, without a new policy in its international relations, a pacific policy inspired by the principles of free trade and cultural rapprochement, without a thorough reform in the land system and in social policy, no financial assistance can help us. On the contrary, it would only make the situation worse, by making it easier to prepare for a war of revenge and by entertaining more opulently the two or three hundred thousand drones of the Horthy régime.

The real friends of Hungary therefore must not only procure a loan for us, but in the meantime must guarantee the minimum of political freedom and moral self-determination which can alone make this loan really productive and reconstructive.

Permanent peace is impossible in the Danube basin until the Hungary of feudal landowners and Judaeo-" Christian " finance has been converted into a Hungary of labour and democracy.

CHAPTER XV

# THE FUTURE OF HUNGARY

THE main purpose of Admiral Horthy and his whole system is to rescind the principal achievements of the October Revolution—the republican State, the land reform, and the rule of the workers—and to restore the pre-war Hungary. Thus they are not merely incapable of bringing peace and consolidation to the country : day by day the wounds of the war and the two revolutions become more inflamed.

Having thus neither the ability nor the desire to apply effective remedies, they are driven to the use of brutal stimulants to maintain the failing pulse of the moribund social order. As we have already seen, they have two such stimulants at their disposal : anti-Semitism and the idea of *revanche*. I have already shown that this policy offers no solution to the Jewish problem, and only makes it more acute by encouraging the growth of the parasitic functions of the Jews. Still more dangerous is their irresponsible and vicious playing with a policy of *revanche ;* this not only undermines the future of Hungary but of the whole of Central Europe. Any sort of consolidation of Central Europe, and hence of Europe as a whole, is completely out of the question until the freedom of peaceful intercourse and trade has been restored in the Danube basin and the Balkans. At present the frontiers are barred by military cordons and armed troops stand ready to pounce ; and an economic area whose parts are naturally closely interdependent has been prostrated by an artificial comminution, with its consequences of chronic unemployment and food crises. The various governments maintain paid agents in one another's territories to produce unrest there by their chauvinist demagogy. The irredentist minority groups which are thus being formed in the new

States, and artificially worked up to a passion by the propaganda of nationalist illusions, are letting go every opportunity of productive work, refusing co-operation in the affairs of the State, and awaiting the arrival of the day of reckoning. So long as all this continues, the work of regeneration for this suffering area cannot even begin ; the spirits of war and anarchy and their close companion, destitution, march over it in triumph.

And what is the policy of the Horthy system ? It has coolly signed the peace treaty without the slightest intention of fulfilling it. It is steadily militarising the country. It is sending out chauvinist agitators, disguised as Bolshevists, into the Succession States. It is completely exhausting the exchequer by maintaining a legion of idle officers and espionage bureaux and by giving rewards to unproductive officials for making opinion in its favour. In its nationalist megalomania it is continually hatching international intrigues, and to further them it is delivering the economic life of the country into the hands of rapacious rastaquouères. Sooner or later this policy will push Hungary into a final disaster. It is an insane policy, if for no other reason than that it is altogether out of the question, after the terrible losses of Hungarian lives and property, to instigate her suffering people with the slightest prospects of success to enter upon fresh warlike adventures. A war would simply be the prelude to a fresh civil war. In very truth this is no policy for the Hungarian people, the Hungarian hand and brain workers. It can be no more than the policy of those 80,000 to 100,000 persons who have shared among themselves the loot of the counter-revolution, and are only concerned as to the means of retaining it.

So cynical a system tends to add daily to the numbers of those who desire a return to Russian methods. The grave errors, disappointments, and suffering of the Red dictatorship are forgotten ; and there is a widespread feeling that, in comparison with the White Terror, the Red Terror was for the masses a time of freedom and dignity. Meanwhile the capitalist policy of the Entente is making general the conviction that the West is the chief protector of the Horthy system and that salvation can only come from the East. Above all, the murders and cruelties of the armed bands and of the Awakening Magyars, the continual provocation offered by the Horthy system to every instinct of humanity, have kindled in the tens of thousands who have been driven from work and home and tortured in body and soul a spirit which is no longer open to reason, but solely to motives of hate and revenge.

There can be no question that the Whites have made propaganda for the Red dictatorship more effectively than Béla Kun and his followers could ever have done.

Only methods of democracy, self-government and Socialism can lead us out of the " Christian National " inferno. In home politics an effort must be made to effect the final conversion of Hungary into a workers' State. Any tolerable order of society can only be built up on a just accord between industrial and agricultural interests, directed and organised by really productive brain workers. These three main branches of creative work must fight side by side for the removal of every sort of political or social oppression, and of income drawn in idleness. All that is of potential value in the inheritance from past years can be fitted into the framework of one or other of these branches of activity. Every sort of abuse and parasitism must disappear from the society of the future.

In foreign politics also, only this spirit can produce any good result. There must be an end of chauvinism and of agitation for *revanche*. The war and the imperialistic peace treaties which have been drawn up in its spirit have shown that national problems are not to be solved by armed force : for this settles nothing, but merely creates fresh irredentisms in place of the old ones. Take, for instance, the case of Hungary. In order that some 1,700,000 Slovaks might be freed, 1,000,000 Magyars and 260,000 Germans are now exiled from their homeland ; in order that 3,000,000 Roumanians might be incorporated in Greater Roumania, about 1,700,000 Magyars and 600,000 Germans have been separated from Hungary ; in order that 500,000 Serbs might build up a new State with their racial kindred, about 400,000

Magyars and 300,000 Germans have been forced into a new allegiance ; in order that 250,000 Germans might return to their racial home, about 50,000 Magyars and a like number of Croats have had to share their fate.  In round numbers, 5,500,000 souls were liberated from the old irredenta, at the price of plunging 4,500,000 into a new one.  [These figures are approximations :  I have not exact data.]

Thus the method of force and conquest does not touch the essence of the problem.  If we were to reconquer our old territory in a fresh war the *irredente* would only shift their position, and the fundamental difficulty would remain.  The question is incapable of a territorial solution.  The problem is one of racial autonomy in language and culture, and the racial organisation of populations within the common territory.  Hence this question, in common with every social question, depends for its solution essentially upon democracy and self-government and Socialism.  The policy of *revanche* cannot be the policy of civilised Hungary ; not only because this policy would merely maintain the counter-revolution in power, but because no decent human being can desire that his nation's development should be at the expense of the suffering of others.

Thus in the world of to-day there can be only one genuinely national Hungarian policy, to do everything possible to secure democratisation and social progress in Hungary and the Succession States, and to work in unison with them to secure on the one hand such international arrangements as will enable ethnic needs to be met and complete freedom of trade to be introduced between Hungary and her former territories, and on the other complete equality of rights in the political and the economic sphere, and full racial and cultural autonomy for each national minority or diaspora.

The idea of *revanche* must be dismissed both in Hungary's own interest and in that of Europe.  Similarly, in the interest both of Hungary and of all Europe, the demand must be resolutely made, and relaxed for no consideration of opportunism, for the earliest possible economic union of Central Europe and of the whole of Europe, for respect for the Magyar minorities in the neighbour countries, for equal citizenship for every Magyar who is finally transferred to another State, and for his right to remain Magyar in speech and culture and to live in unimpeded contact with the Magyars who have remained in their mother country.

If we could attain all this, it would be of much more value than if the old feudal Hungary had remained in existence, with a governing class of a few thousands using their power to set the various populations at one another's throats and to block the cultural development of all of them. In an economically integrated Europe, with national autonomy introduced everywhere, the national frontiers would have no more meaning than have to-day those of counties or departments or urban or rural areas within the State.

And this goal is no mere Utopia; the courageous determination and enthusiasm of a single generation could attain it. The one condition is true democracy, honest self-government, and an energetic advance along the path of sane Socialism. In an international order of this type Hungary, freed from her feudal and capitalistic gangs, would become one of the most productive, enterprising and important of the Danube countries. Her ten millions of people would be of incomparably greater significance to European civilisation than ever were the twenty millions of pre-war Hungary. One need only turn one's attention to Denmark, Norway, Sweden or Switzerland, in order to realise what can be achieved by small nations, if they are free and progressive.

Our Central European policy must be based primarily on these three conditions of democracy, self-government and Socialism. An orientation either towards West or East would mean nothing better than servitude to one or other imperialistic policy. The peoples of Central Europe are indissolubly bound together by geographical, economic and cultural ties; they must depend primarily upon their own resources in building up their future. And the German genius, when once set free from the fetters of militarism and imperialism, will naturally assume a leading part.

But this democratic and pacifist Central Europe could not exist under the violence and chicanery of the *ancien régime*. Only when Labour asserts its power in England, and when in Russia, after the convulsions of Bolshevism, a workers' and peasants' democracy comes into being; only under the protection of these Eastern and Western bastions, can there grow up that New Europe which may rise out of war and bloodshed to a higher and purer stage of development.*

* It should be pointed out that this was written many months before the elections of December, 1923, removed speculation as to Labour's fitness to govern from the realm of pure theory.—Trans.

# INDEX